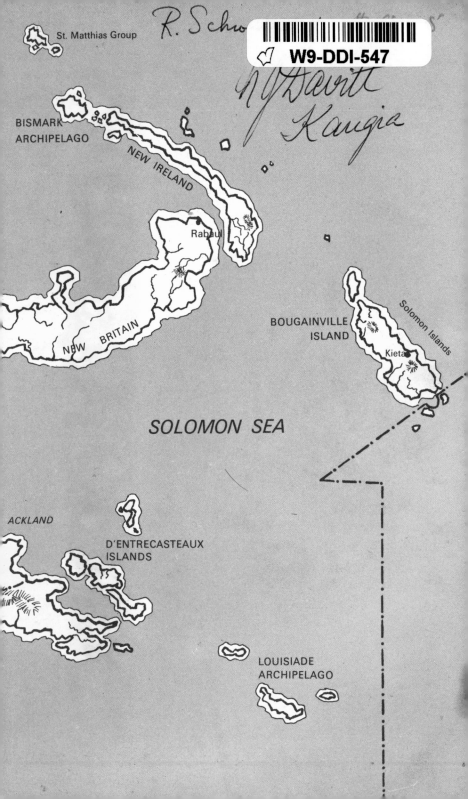

St. Matthias Group

BISMARK
ARCHIPELAGO

NEW IRELAND

Rabaul

NEW BRITAIN

BOUGAINVILLE
ISLAND

Solomon Islands

Kieta

SOLOMON SEA

ACKLAND

D'ENTRECASTEAUX
ISLANDS

LOUISIADE
ARCHIPELAGO

NEW GUINEA
JOURNEYS

NEW GUINEA JOURNEYS

Jack McCarthy

[signature]

RIGBY

RIGBY LIMITED • ADELAIDE • SYDNEY
MELBOURNE • BRISBANE • PERTH

First published 1970
Copyright © 1970 J. McCarthy
Library of Congress Catalog Card Number 73-104093
National Library of Australia Card
Number & ISBN 0 85179 117 4

Wholly designed and set up in Australia
Printed by Lee Fung Printing Co. Ltd

author's note

I wish to make grateful acknowledgment of the assistance given to me by the management of the *South Pacific Post*, of Port Moresby, in permitting me to make use of some material and photographs which appeared in the pages of that journal.

contents

		Page
Journey 1	Journey into Decay	1
Journey 2	Journey into Hope	68
Journey 3	Journey into Genesis	87
Journey 4	Journey into Fear	125
Journey 5	Journey into Depression	162
Journey 6	Journey into Fantasy	174
Journey 7	Journey into Contradiction	190
Journey 8	Journey into the Future	222

illustrations

	Facing page
Yali Singina of Yabalol, a native leader	36
Yali with two of his wives	36
Sacred flutes made from bamboo pipes	37
Instruments made from gourds	37
Cult House at Yabalol	52
Some of Yali's people bringing provisions	52
Freedom flag in West Irianese refugee camp	53
West Papuan refugee	84
West Irian Refugee Camp	85
Yako Camp at Vanimo	85
Preparation of "underground" literature	100
Children at Yako Camp	100
Aerial view of Vanimo	101
Goldore Timber Lease at Vanimo	101
Father Leo of Pes Mission, Aitape	132
Cane furniture made at Pes Mission	132
Weaving cane blinds at Pes Mission	133
Local Politicians, Bougainville	148
Meeting to discuss land dispute	148
Road from Kieta to Paguna, Bougainville	149
Typical Local Government Council House	180
Dopima No. 3 Village	181
Patrol Officer at Dopima No. 3 Village	181
Coconut plantation, Aramia Village	181
Bush grave in Aramia country	181

Canoe and paddlers, Balimo   196
Old houses at Dopima No. 3 Village   196
Two Kieta lads with ceremonial head-dress   196
People of Aramia Village   196
Baubaguina Village   197
People of Baubaguina   197
Women enjoying a chat   197
Father and son   197

introduction

As the title implies, this book is the story of periods. It has no chronological sequence or direction, but was written with the purpose of recording people and places as I have seen them during thirty-four years of life in the Territory of Papua and New Guinea.

They are, in the main, the personal impressions of one who has wandered over many parts of the Territory, and who has returned to see some of those places and to speak to some of those people again.

There is so much to see, and there are so many to talk to, that it would be impossible to confine all of my impressions within a single volume. A great deal has been omitted from these pages.

I have tried to reflect the feelings of some of those who have been most affected by the onrush of civilization and modern administration. The old people, to whom the benefits of our way of life have not always brought happiness. Those who are imbued with a sense of freedom, but who have been frustrated, and have become pariahs of society. And those who, in some ways, have tried to readjust their old, traditional ideas to fit the pattern of modern progress, but still remain confused.

There is tragedy in tradition, because it dies hard. In dying, it leaves discards which modern society cannot fit into any scheme of progress.

Just as tragic as this waste of human life and talent is the waste of land and opportunity. Through neglect and depression, far too much is lost. Sometimes it seems that most of the country is a huge drain, down which the people and potential are being sucked relentlessly into oblivion.

You may ask the reason for this. The answer is: "Money." Yet the remarkable fact is that, before they had ever heard of money, a primitive people were able to live, multiply, and contentedly use this land which modern civilization, despite all its scientific and industrial techniques, seems only too anxious to forget.

Jack McCarthy

1 | journey into decay

THE BOW WAVE of the *Kuru* pushed lazily down the channel with the ship's wake spreading fanwise, rocking the flotsam of timber, leaves and scum, and splashing with a faint hiss among the jumble of mangrove roots a few feet to port. It was mid-afternoon and the water was flat and oily with bright patches of reflected sunlight and black shadows of crowded trees mirrored in sharp etchings.

We swung to starboard, striking a steady course midstream to slide between the brown patches of mudbanks less than three feet below the surface, then back to port and once again hugged the low, slimy bank beneath the limbs of overhanging timber.

It had been like this all day. In fact, ever since we had offloaded at Baimuru sawmill and left the main channel and the barely perceptible swell of an incoming tide, to turn into this maze of ten thousand waterways that led through the Kikori delta.

There was nothing here but Nature. Raw, unruly and relentless Nature, and the calm, glass-like surface of the water as passages opened and closed, twisting in an inextricable pattern that defied all handbooks of navigation and all mariners who lacked the knowledge of our Hanuabadan captain, which had been acquired over the many years he had been sailing these waters.

With the engine chugging quietly we kept a steady pace, tacking with a touch of the helm to port or starboard as we traced an invisible passage through sandbanks and shallows, through mud and detritus, at times almost heading from bank to bank but always forward without faltering.

I had first sampled these delta channels thirty years before on the old *Papuan Chief*, under Skipper Andersen, a tough Scandinavian seaman and a veteran of the Gulf of Papua and its south-east monsoons.

1

I still remembered that we had taken the main channel, past Cape Blackwood and into the full flow of the big river with our speed gradually being reduced until we were slow ahead. Mudbanks were changing, breaking almost from day to day as stormwaters from the far distant mountain ranges swept down to the ocean, bearing the remains of forest and swamp grass to form small islands of their own until they were carried farther by the swirling rips of muddy currents.

We had nosed into some of them, stopped engines and reversed and then, slowly under way again, with two crewmen in the dinghy ahead swinging a lead line, had crawled slowly forward until clear again in the mainstream. The procedure never varied, for the *Chief* had a fair draught and she was then the largest vessel serving Kikori government station.

This time the trip had been pleasant and uneventful all the way from Port Moresby, with a calm sea, clear skies, and only the faintest signs of rolling when we approached the Purari delta.

Now I noticed that the swells began far out to sea when the flat, monotonous silhouette of the delta country barely showed through the heat haze. Once these huge, wide mudflats of the open gulf had been much closer to shore. They were nasty things to cross when the wind was up and the long, rolling swells broke in continuous crests of foam a mile or more in length.

Now there were underwater signs of mud before there were any signs of land. This showed that in three decades the land surface of the delta had crept a long way farther out into the gulf. I recollected a contention of G. A. V. Stanley, old-timer and geologist, that when the earliest explorer sailed this coastline, his route took him close up against the Aird Hills and that the delta fringe we were about to enter did not then exist.

Possibly in another hundred years or so, these mud-stained seas we were then sailing will become another section of land, forest and jungle, with its own mudbanks and winding channels.

Evidence of this growth is everywhere in the delta, with clumps of vegetation and mud becoming small, isolated islands linking up in chains. Passages through which coastal vessels previously sailed are closed and the water is forced into narrower channels which, in turn, cut through other mud islands to form new patterns.

The delta is a panorama of the elemental processes of living and dying; of a continuous timeless battle between the powers of earth and the forces of water with a third contender, the primitive vegetable kingdom, seizing every possible square inch of thick, clay mud to implant its seeds and multiply.

It is a war of the elements that never ceases, with first one and then

2

the other making slight gains, sometimes consolidating its hold, sometimes being destroyed or suppressed, and revealing to the returning traveller, over a wide span of years, a very noticeable process of change.

The same type of scenery can become very monotonous when one is sitting on a well-found ship travelling at five knots—there seems to be no change in the high, almost forbidding walls of plant life.

There is variety in forests of nipa palms, tangled jungle growth, tall stands of shady timber and long stretches of high swamp grass and there is an elemental fascination in it as you watch, hour after hour, trying to catch the lights and shadows or peer into dark, silent creeks, or wonder what the country behind the curtain of high grass may be like.

Sometimes there are flats and terraces with closely woven creeping grass and sheltered by almost symmetrically placed trees . . . almost as if they had been planted by human hands.

But this apparent orderliness is a quirk of Nature, for search as you may, there is never a sign of human habitation, and you realize that it is only a freak picture that the flood waters have left, and that the next flood may sweep it away.

Rawness on such a vast scale has its attractions, for here is a section of the world fighting for survival. Always there is the unanswered question: Why, with all our knowledge of scientific agriculture, can we not feed ourselves on these thousands of square miles of newly emerging soil where Nature runs riot with a harvest of any vegetable matter that will take root.

Primitive man has become adapted to these conditions and can find sustenance in grains, fibres, shoots, and leaves, where we civilized people would starve.

The soil is dank and sour, being clay of a heavy consistency and leached by a high rainfall, close to 300 inches a year. The life that springs from it is tough and coarse as it must be if it is to adapt itself to such hostile surroundings. But there is still a wide gap in what the jungle will produce in spite of its adversities and what Man can produce with all his accomplishments.

There are lone areas with patches of tall coconut palms standing like monuments, which indeed they are, for they mark the places where once communities of men, women, and children lived in their traditional way, with their dances and ceremonies and their allotted tasks, ordained by a social system of tribal rule that was severe, but just, and based upon the community's needs.

Sometimes one can glimpse the decayed remains of beams and posts lying at crazy angles in the rubble of a vanished population.

3

Mostly there is nothing but the coconut palms to mark the spot and a thick carpet of secondary growth hiding its relics.

It is so easy to say, "I remember," and this was the phrase that occurred repeatedly in my mind as we travelled this silent land, and was to occur more and more frequently in the weeks that followed as I travelled old-time tracks and waterways that I had journeyed on before.

The shadows of the past were emphasized by the desolation of the present and they carried a host of regrets.

Kikori, in the 1930s, was the headquarters of the Delta Division, a district in its own right with a population of many thousands and administered by three government officers, a Resident Magistrate, an Assistant Resident Magistrate, and a Patrol Officer.

In these 10,000 square miles of rawness, authority was where the flag flew, and this was often only in a transient camp that covered a few square miles, with the tenuous threads of law and order stretching back to the long, thatch-roofed office that sat on the slope of the main station.

Beyond its radius, tribal rule was very powerful and, at times, quite presumptuous, and there were many dark corners where the people knew no other authority than that of their chief and the fear of the puri-puri man with his sticks, dried lizard skins, stones, and potions.

If they had heard of the white man's law they were seldom affected by it, for what could one lone officer do, patrolling in a dug-out canoe, in such a vast, inhospitable area?

For those in the main waterways, government was a visible entity at infrequent periods, with perhaps a village policeman, chosen by themselves and appointed by the Resident Magistrate, as the sole symbol of that power.

Away in the interior, among the swamps and the reeds, the jungle and the mud, life remained almost undisturbed and the people obeyed their traditional leaders.

They had their own dubus and dances, ceremonies of initiation and marriage, their own leaders and exponents of witchcraft and sorcery with tight circles of wabus, or widows, and gentlemen whose skills in the practices of headhunting and cannibalism were widely acknowledged.

Down at Goaribari Island, two white missionaries with a dozen of their native catechists had been murdered and eaten just three decades before and there were still many men who were walking around who could boast of their part in the event.

4

Envious ones who had missed out on that particular highlight of local endeavour were taking a quiet tally of heads for themselves by more devious ways so that they could wear the black feathers of a killer which ranked like the campaign ribbons of a general.

Skulls for the next Hawa'a dance were still in demand as I well knew from the gory accounts given me by an ancient employee who had a remarkable aptitude for knowing when and where the next bloodbath, a Hawa'a or a Buguru ceremony, would take place, and was constantly reminding me that he would be pleased to guide me to one as a spectator.

Once, on a moonlight night, I fell in with his wishes, and we paddled down in his ramshackle canoe to a side stream that plunged into the black abyss of a mangrove forest and through a small passage leading towards a clearing some fifty feet ahead of where we stopped.

This, my companion advised me, was the nearest a stranger could approach in decency and safety, the latter an essential ingredient, for one never knew what the wild and woolly gentlemen might do if a stranger were found at the height of their ceremonies.

There were about two hundred men and women cavorting in the moonlight and between the glow and smoke of fires, dolefully chanting a dirge as they stamped, one behind the other, in large circles. Somewhere in a darkened hut a drum beat out the time.

This preliminary canter was obviously only a warming up process, for soon their voices rose to screams and yells, and there began a frenzied display of perverted eroticism and sexual indulgence, with men and women scrambling around on the damp soil like animals, with the drum still beating as the circles broke and reformed into snaky lines of men and women, still one behind the other, stamping and screaming in orgiastic desire.

This was the Buguru, and there are few white men who have seen it in its entirety as it may go on for days and nights in a continuous, unbridled round of sexual orgy until exhaustion sets in and the dancers lie where they drop, sleeping until they recover sufficient strength to drag themselves back to the village.

There was no place there for a stranger, black or white. On occasions there have been some who did intrude and had their bleached and decorated skulls set on posts as the main attraction for a future Hawa'a dance, to the gratification of its exponents, who were always looking for new heads to produce fresh fun.

The old man touched my arm, pursed his lips and nodded as a sign that we should leave. We clambered back through the mangrove roots to our dug-out canoe, pushed quietly into the channel and drifted back to the main creek, pursued by hordes of voracious mosquitoes, and thankful that they weren't the lust-maddened, feathered, and painted men whose screams and yells we could still hear.

In those days the paramount leaders had full powers of authority and they were obeyed without question, each within his own territory, and although the institution of village constables had been well established and was spreading to outlying villages, they never overshadowed the powers of the chiefs, either in personality or authority, for they exercised the powers of their appointment mainly when a crime had been committed that called for district office intervention.

A recommendation as to the person who would become the village constable was usually left to the people. They made their recommendation to the Resident Magistrate, and he invariably approved, issuing the lucky chap with a secondhand uniform from the station store, one pair of handcuffs, and putting him on the pay sheet at thirty shillings a year, plus the prestige of being a servant of the government.

It was commonly said that either the village idiot or the village smart man took the job, the former because he was forced into it by common opinion or the latter because he thought there might be a chance of personal gain.

In general, the V.C. was a middle-aged man with a family, level-headed and conscious of his limited responsibilities, with a real interest in his people and which he genuinely tried to retain.

Once I was sitting in the main office at Kikori talking to Syd Chance, the Resident Magistrate, when the sounds of angry voices brought us both out of our seats.

Outside there was a crowd of about thirty villagers surrounding a very dejected looking V.C. whose hands were pinioned behind his back with his own handcuffs. The people thrust him forward and told their tale.

Three weeks before they had brought this particular gentleman in to be appointed their V.C., and when this had been approved had escorted him back home full of good cheer.

However, pomp, power, or the people's adulation had quickly gone to the man's head, and one of his first orders had been most definite. Every family should provide one single girl as a member of his household. He backed up this decree by announcing that failure to comply would be regarded as a slight upon his government position and that parents would be put to work making roads.

Mothers and fathers naturally saw no attraction in handing over

6

their darling daughters to such an individual, and when he began waving handcuffs as a threat to back up his orders, they jumped him, locked him in his own irons and frogmarched him back to the station.

He was last seen wrapped in a loin cloth bearing a big broad arrow and apparently wrapped in thought also, possibly trying to work out where he had gone wrong, or plotting some other cute scheme.

The angry citizenry were told that their next recommendation for the position should be of a different calibre.

Being bushmen they were not overburdened with an intelligent appreciation of the white man's ways, and while they were very obliging, there were times when our particular type of thinking just didn't register.

One of my jobs was to service a seaplane making regular trips to the station, and the pilot decided that a reserve fuel dump should be set up.

He off-loaded a few drums of high octane fuel next trip. These were ferried across to a high mudbank on the river's edge, the pilot and the magistrate coming along for the trip.

The V.C. and his cohorts were there to receive and stack them and listened very intently to a lucid and simple explanation that no fire or smoking would be permitted near the dump. Aviation gas didn't like that sort of thing and was liable to blow up and take the station with it, they were told.

With that off our minds we clambered back into the canoe and glanced back.

The policeman and two of his friends had perched themselves on top of the drums and were busily striking matches to light their trade twist cigarettes, with the V.C. still loudly enjoining his companions on the need for extreme care.

Aided by a strong arm and a few well-chosen words, the policeman disappeared into the river and the station was saved, but for long afterwards I had a haunting suspicion that at any time there might be a big bang and a flash from the mudbank.

Puri-puri artists who practised sorcery were always characters to be reckoned with for they invariably bore themselves with an air of mystery and noble detachment from common mortals, safe in the knowledge that if they became upset they could make trouble.

With his little bag of tricks, his power over highly superstitious people was tremendous and heaven help anybody who trod on his toes.

Like all good professionals, there were degrees of standing.

7

Some were specialists in tribal lore and tradition, keepers of the masks and paraphernalia of the dubu house, masters of ceremony at initiations and marriages, and all-powerful on dark habits of dark minds.

They were the ones who ran society, the backroom boys who pulled the strings and were profound in esoteric mysteries and prophecies with psychological abilities that were pretty high.

Fear was their main weapon and the mere whisper of a puri-puri man hanging around was sufficient to make people still their tongues and roll their eyes. It was a repelling sight to see one sitting in his hut or in the dubu, charcoaled, befeathered, his lips red with lime and betel nut, with steadily masticating jaws, and the look of complete disdain he gave everybody, engendering a snaky feeling of disgust and doubt.

One could never imagine any woman settling down to domestic life with such a man and indeed I cannot recollect hearing of any one of them having a wife and family. Possibly they were anachronisms of life, just asexual monstrosities.

There were female counterparts to these nasty-minded gents in the form of wabus, women without men, ancient old crones whose husbands had died and whose usefulness in consistent labour had come to an end.

Shrewdly they banded together like a haggle of witches and, with their secret knowledge of jungle plants, weeds, and grasses, could brew love potions that brought young couples together, and concoct other mixtures that would relieve the unfortunate consequences of too much lovemaking.

They were right on the doorstep when medicaments were needed for abortions, sterility, fevers, ills, aches, or pains and, for a consideration, would preside over childbirth or mutter incantations over the sick.

They always had a finger in the pie when marriages were being arranged, making an unholy partnership with the puri-puri man to ensure that there was a suitable rake-off from both families involved.

I have known them to be able to prevent a young woman from child-bearing for a long, long time, in order that she could become a prostitute, and then, when the novelty had worn off, or age and decay had set in, the wabus would fix another mixture, arrange marriage, and let the woman become a respectable wife and bear children.

Remarkably, these primitives had a more intensive knowledge of bush drugs and contraceptives than our own laboratory scientists, and they were not only surer but more positive in obtaining results.

Many people have tried to find those plants and have tried to bribe the secrets from the old women but without success. The men know nothing, and if you ask the wabus they look at you and chuckle. It is their hold on life, the only economic possession they have, and society is always seeking their aid.

"This is it," one old hag said to me once as she reached into her dilly bag and held out a handful of dried grass and laughed in my face. There are so many grasses—which one was this?

At one period I was consistently afflicted with a low fever, with head pains, dizziness, and vomiting which quinine and aspirin would not shift.

There came a whisper one day of an old woman in a nearby village who could get rid of my trouble so I nodded my head and they brought her along.

For half an hour she stood over me, massaging my skull and muttering to herself, and then she left.

In twenty-four hours I was up and working and felt fine for the next eighteen months. Then I went down with a sudden attack of malaria that left me sweating and calling for the old dame.

"She is not here any more," they told me. "She died two months ago, from fever," and they left me to battle it out, for they knew of nobody else who could do as the old woman had done.

Apart from the dark and seamy side, the delta in those far-off days was a populous place filled with people who were happy and active, housed in large villages with the rivers ringing with the sounds of canoe paddles, the thump of sago sticks, the shouts of men and women, and the laughter of children at play.

Each village was a place of vibrant life; children yelled and sang at their games, young women worked in the gardens, the older ones made fishing nets and baskets from cane, large, conical shaped affairs which they took to the creeks, where they plodded, knee-deep in mud, catching a type of yabbi, called "Pai," which had one extraordinary long claw and was usually minus the other.

The older men made canoes and fishing nets and the younger ones waded into the swamps to fell sago palms and float them out to the handling areas, which were usually at the end of each village.

Evenings and early mornings were the time for mud crabs, large and luscious and as big as dinner plates. You could buy ten of them for one stick of twist tobacco, the general medium of exchange, with a rate of four sticks as the equivalent of one shilling, set by the Resident Magistrate.

One stick bought taro, plantains, crabs, or a thirty-pound

bundle of wet sago, and there was always a market wherever one travelled, for tobacco was often more useful than money and it would pay for canoes and paddlers from village to village.

Money was mainly the medium which came from returning labourers who had been paid off from plantations in other parts, and this, with the small, steady income from government employees, chiefly the station police, was the only source of actual money. Later, the incoming oil exploration companies gave a stimulus to local income, and while these companies were operating, the economic standards of a large segment of the population improved considerably.

The effects of the infusion of this extra money were felt over a very wide area for the companies operated in some of the remotest parts of the district and, for the first time, many of the bush people were introduced to western standards of living and to western amenities in food, clothing, shelter, and modern tools and equipment. In addition, a lot of their compatriots, employed by the companies, were being absorbed into different circumstances and conditions, and the ideas of an improved way of living soon spread to the backblocks.

The old-time traditional way of bartering food and tobacco, which in many places still survived, soon gave place to a money economy as wages circulated and people went out in search of canned foods and western clothing.

The transition was not an easy one, for the introduction of pounds, shillings and pence among an illiterate people still beyond the spheres of western culture and thinking brought much confusion and aroused new fears.

One lad I remember offered himself for work under the old indenture system where the recruit stood before the magistrate, had the details of employment explained to him and touched the pen as a sign of his assent, with the magistrate endorsing "X" as his mark on the agreement.

"You will receive twelve shillings and sixpence a month," the magistrate told him and was surprised when the young man shook his head and said he didn't want it.

"My father told me that when I went out to work I must receive ten shillings a month," he explained and insisted that he would only work for ten shillings a month, for what his father had said was true and he must obey him.

The magistrate, the interpreter, and others around tried hard to explain that the agreed wage was higher than ten shillings a month. They spread two lines of coins on the desk to illustrate the difference but the lad still refused. Finally, the agreement was endorsed at ten shillings with a rider saying that the man had no conception of money and therefore was not to receive twelve and sixpence as previously stated.

Another man I saw had paddled for days to reach a trade store and buy himself something with the first "money" he had received.

He rummaged around an old rusty tin and produced a bonus coupon taken from a tin of cocoa which some smart, unscrupulous person had passed over to him in payment for food.

Money, so far as he knew, came in bits of paper, and he could hardly believe it when the storekeeper told him that it was valueless. Fortunately the owner took pity on his ignorance, gave him a quantity of food as a present and took him aside to give him his first sight of real money and to explain its values.

Three weeks later the same man came paddling back with a canoe load of garden foods and crabs which he handed to the storekeeper as his way of saying thanks, and the word went round that this man was good, and five minutes of kindness produced quite a lot of dividends in terms of confidence.

Strangely, despite their lurid background, their filthy practices, and their excesses of passion, the Goaribaries were always pleasant and sociable to outsiders in normal human relationships. They worked willingly for a just return; they dealt honestly; they were always prepared to help the sick; they spoilt their children, and had an open approach to strangers, with none of the initial surliness that is a feature of many other native people.

Furthermore they seemed to thoroughly enjoy life and would tackle any job no matter how difficult or dirty.

"Give a Goaribari plenty of food and women and he's your pal for life," was a saying I'd heard many times and fundamentally this was true. He lived so completely within the framework of his own society that he had no time for vain ambitions or regrets, a situation that, unfortunately, is seldom found today.

Village life was complete, an entity within itself, touched very infrequently by government, and there was not the fear of government that has become one of the features of its consolidated power. There was, in some instances, resentment of government when it tried to enforce its laws, and one patrol officer, who is now a District Commissioner, had a very narrow escape when, entering a village to arrest a murderer, he became the target of a spear thrown by a man who loudly maintained that tribal killing was no concern of the government.

I met the officer returning through the bush with two prisoners instead of one, followed by a crowd of expostulating friends demanding the two men's release.

Latent hostility of the people against a superior authority imposing itself upon the powers of their own leaders was common but seldom rose above the surface. It is hard for old men, empowered by generations of traditional autocracy, to give way to clean-shaven youths sponsored by an authority which cannot be fought, and this applies generally, for I know of many people today who, after listening to instructions from a councillor with a silver badge and a nice clean shirt, turn to the old men to ask what should be done.

In some areas it has become a form of surreptitious indirect control, with the councillors in the front rank shaking hands with visiting officials and the wise old men standing back until the singing and flag-waving dies down so that they can give their sanction to future actions.

There has been some talk of reviving the old village constable system and this would be a wise move, particularly in the more remote and less developed areas, for the standards of appointment would be far higher than in the past, and the personal ties between the village official and the people would be renewed and maintained. These do not always exist under the councillor system. Despite educational programmes and publicity to the contrary, the greater percentage of village people still consider the local government councillor purely as an Administration instrument and not one of their own true tribal representatives.

In the very early days the government was often openly challenged.

This occurred at Kikori when the station was first established. Once, when the officer in charge was eating his lunch, a police orderly appeared, saluted smartly, and reported that a fleet of war canoes were on the river below the station and had come along to fight the government. Would it oblige?

The government was most upset and it certainly would not oblige. "Tell them to go home. I am having my lunch," the officer is reported to have said, and the orderly, with another smart salute, turned about and toddled back down the hill to pass on the word.

This was a bit of strategy the warriors hadn't even considered, and after they had talked things over, and concluded that this was quite a satisfactory reason for refusal, they took their paddles and went home.

If such diplomacy existed today we would not have so many brush-fire wars, which of course wouldn't do because we're civilized.

The substance of the community centred in the dubu houses which were exclusively male preserves. Ornately decorated and

12

designed, they were the depositories of traditional artifacts, masks and symbols of tribal law which were brought out publicly only on ceremonial occasions. Having the attributes of esoteric-religious properties, only selected men could handle them, while women and the uninitiated were despotically proscribed from looking at them.

The sacrosanct nature of some of these articles was very real, as I once found to my discomfort at a later date and in another place, and for those who broke the bonds of secrecy, by sight, speech, or some other manner, retribution was swift and sometimes permanent through the aid of poison or a spear thrust through the ribs.

There were other houses of restriction used by boys and youths, and serving as initiation retreats in which the entrant, often a mere child, would be taken by his uncle into a secluded, individual cubicle to be taught the rudiments of tribal law, of knowledge and culture under a system of progressive initiation which would finalize, in the years to come, with his ultimate acknowledged status as a man.

Teaching was severe and intense, lasting for periods of months when the child would associate with no other person than his mentor and was forbidden to be either seen or heard by his mother and female relatives, or any other woman.

They would be taken out to exercise at night, their heads covered in a large, wickerwork basket, and a warning sounded for all women and girls to get out of sight. Their meals, provided and cooked by their families, would be served through small windows let into the walls of the dubu from where the uncle would collect them and serve them to the child.

The youngsters were also taught the disciplines of silence, respect, and obedience so that, in the years to come, fortified by age and experience, they could teach others the same qualities.

I have gone into their houses and seen these youngsters squatting demurely on mats, each lad painted in white ochre, sitting quietly like novitiates at prayer. The cubicles were clean, the mats were new, and around the sago-matted walls hung the skeleton heads of crocodiles, trophies of their hunting skill in the nearby swamps.

This must have been a period of trial for youngsters who would normally have been outside in the sunshine screaming their heads off in play and happily bathing in muddy creeks. It was rigorous and exacting but it was the essence of tribal consolidation and human endurance, for when the time came to burn into the flesh the symbolic cicatrices and weals, these kids could take it without a murmur.

This, too, is fast disappearing, for there are no crocodiles to hunt, nor is there spartan seclusion from the other sex at primary and secondary schools. Nor are there legends and tales and beliefs that have survived from centuries past, nor the hard, physical pains of qualifying as men.

Today's youngsters go to school with suitcases, not spears, and they paint their hair with pomades instead of mud and ochre, while flying, high, dry and comfortable, has taken the place of paddling in a crude dug-out canoe.

Apart from the big dubus there were other, smaller buildings, used by the men as clubhouses and "dogboxes" when the women played up. Many times I have heard the married men commiserating with one another over their domestic troubles and it seemed most ludicrous for a warrior of local renown, painted and feathered, to be clutching his spears and cowering in a corner of the dubu because his wife was on the warpath, but that happens in the best of circles and I wonder how many of our much-medalled generals of renown have suffered the same indignities.

Some villages had widows' dubus—not the high, crocodile-mouthed and decorated type of the men, but long, low buildings that could hold a hundred or more souls, and were usually built on the outskirts of the village.

To these the women were relegated for their periods of mourning, dressed in long, ankle-length grass skirts, their bodies painted black with charcoal and vegetable dyes, their hair plastered in mud and ashes, and their whole appearance as unprepossessing as possible to signify their lowly estate and their devotion to the memory of their deceased mate.

Unwashed, unhonoured, and segregated for months to lead lives restricted by public custom: disdained, repulsive in appearance and attitudes, they were a menace to strangers who wandered too close to their stamping grounds. Many of them were young, healthy, and sexually frustrated females, and God help any man who came within reach of their claws.

With their narrowed eyes and crooked smiles, the sibilant whistles from bared, blackened teeth and an atmospheric miasma of sweat and filth, the sexually hungry females required no psychologist to expound what was going on in their minds.

It was a social system that had its indulgences and restrictions, kept the community secure, and permitted aberrations of conduct which, by our standards, would be condemned as animalism.

To these people it was a means of keeping them in a state of homogeneity and in many ways prevented the introduction of disruptive tribal and family forces.

14

No society which permits the use of its womenfolk as prostituted commodities can regard adultery as an offence, and whenever trouble did arise it was invariably based upon default of payment or suitable recompense. A by-product of this attitude, and their lack of moral values according to our conceptions, was an almost complete absence of sexual crimes such as rape and assault, and children were never molested.

No child was an orphan in the sense that it had no protectors, for any couple without children would be given one by others who had large families, or a child was adopted when its parents died.

The old and ancient had a place in the community and they were looked after. Some were people with traditional knowledge, respected and honoured; some had the arts of sorcery and were obeyed and feared; others had genealogical aptitude and could recite everybody's family tree, understand the blood relationships, and were in demand on ceremonial occasions.

There were the keepers of the ravi and dubu houses, masters of ceremony, comptrollers of the insignia, masks and decorations, the long droning horns and the ululating bullroarers, and who co-operated with the teachers of lads under initiation by telling them the secrets of each object, its purpose and its place in the community's traditions.

Ritual and sorcery controlled a lot of their lives, blending together in the fundamental aim of consolidating, preserving, and controlling the people as one huge unit, so that in trouble there would be help, in war there would be unity, and in the good times, sharing.

There were discards in this society though most were more easily dispatched by poison or spear thrust.

I saw one old woman dragged from an attic where she had been hidden by her family against inquiring official eyes. She was blind and half-eaten away with acute venereal disease. Nobody wanted her; nobody would take her into the station for medical attention, and it is quite likely that the old girl had refused to go because hospitals were regarded as places where people went to die.

Pushed up into the attic, she had been fed whenever they thought about her, but a stray whisper to a visiting police patrol had resulted in her being dragged out and taken to hospital, and a summons for those who had failed to report her condition.

She was beyond care, lingered a while, and died, adding one more confirmation that hospitals were places where people died.

But life, generally, was good, for there was traffic on the rivers and waterways, with lone paddlers speeding like taxis in small, one-man, dug-out canoes barely six feet long, turning and twisting

15

to the currents with perfect balance and harmony of movement, and there were large village and family groups with twenty or more paddlers, all in rhythm and timed by the hollow boom as the blades struck the sides of the canoe in unison.

Women were by far the best paddlers and one could distinguish a female crew from afar by the distinctive, sharp, jerking movements of their buttocks as they stood and dipped the blades of the paddles. This was accentuated by the bustle of grass which each woman wore between her legs, standard female fashion for the whole region and their only article of clothing.

The up-to-date miss of those days was always most particular about the perfect fit of her bustle and, with so much more space to fill up, decorated herself in plaited arm ganas, or bands, beads, necklaces and sometimes a wide-mouthed, half-moon shaped mairi of pearl shell, indicative of her standing in the community.

Crocodiles were not then a commercial commodity and if you saw one you shot it and left it at that. Only the youthful initiates killed them as part of their training and the skulls were hung on the walls of the cubicles to show how the lads were getting along in their studies.

There were other skulls in the dubu, human skulls, those of their own people who had died and those of their enemies killed in battle or by stealth, mementoes of conquest.

No respectable dubu existed without its skulls, while at Kerewa, the main home village of the Goaribaries, there was a house of skulls with rows of eye sockets and jawbones, stacked one above the other, staring blankly out across the muddy waters and over the flat tablecloth of jungle as mute reminders that violence and death were constant companions of every man, woman, and child.

Women have quite a distinctive position in Goaribari society, although like their sisters elsewhere, they have the hard work and menial tasks to do and are subject to the uncertain caprices of their menfolk.

They are, however, or rather were—for social changes are creating differences between the old and modern generations— chattels in the true sense of the word, movable objects that could be used as commodities, as part of a business arrangement, or as a social gesture.

This situation they acknowledged without a murmur and, in fact, stoutly upheld as correct behaviour whenever doubts were expressed.

The community's attitude towards sex was one of indulgence, provided it was kept within the limits of traditionally accepted codes, and a man could, according to his own choice, have one wife

16

or a dozen, and as he was lord and master of his household, he could dispose of them as he wished.

Moral attitudes of such a people must be judged according to their own circumstances for only they have the right to set their own standards while they live entirely within their own free society.

Today, all this has changed and their attitudes would certainly not be acceptable in civilized society. There are few primitive societies now that have not come under the influence of western culture and law.

But the old-time Goaribari, living as he did within his own tribal framework, could not be classed as immoral by our standards. Rather he was unmoral for he regarded certain forms of sexual licence as perfectly justifiable and would probably have been shocked to learn that in other societies, of which he knew little or nothing, his own convictions on sexual freedom would have brought severe criticism, his actions, punishment.

He was justified in acquiring as many wives as he could support, and the community endorsed his motives when he used them as commodities in dealings with other men, or in wife exchange as a gesture of friendship.

Some sections would have regarded him as being rather odd if he had not done so; if he had prevented his women from participating in a Buguru ceremony, where sex was free, and engaged in openly, he would have been frowned upon in no uncertain manner and told to mend his ways.

The entrenchment of missionary and government influences were changing a lot of these old ideas but they were still being practised when I arrived in the delta and were accepted without dispute by the older people.

One court hearing which I attended centred around the killing of a man's pig, and appeared at first to be very routine, until the evidence came out in detail.

An old man had wanted the young man's pig and had made an agreement that the young man could use the old man's wife—who happened to be quite young—in payment for a certain number of times, a normal village transaction which raised no eyebrows.

Each day the young man came to the old man's house and went into an inner room with his wife, and the old man put a little bamboo stick aside as a mark that the payments were being made.

The transaction being completed, the old man went for the pig but the owner refused to hand it over. Very upset by this show of bad faith he killed the pig, claiming that it was his by right of purchase.

17

The young man foolishly complained to the magistrate, omitting the lurid details but claiming punishment for the old man.

Much to their surprise, there was a sudden shift of roles, from claimant to defendant, resulting in a gaol sentence for adultery.

Outside the court there was the usual crowd of villagers and hangers-on awaiting the verdict, and when the full account reached them, loud objections were voiced by all the women present. The gist of their argument was: Why should the government bring in a law preventing a man from trading his wife? It really shook the little community that such justice, or injustice to them, should be permitted. There were even suggestions of appealing to the Governor, Sir Hubert Murray, on his next inspection visit.

I doubt very much whether it affected any future transactions of a similar nature, although the villagers probably dealt with double-crossers without invoking the assistance of the court.

Noticeable also was the fact that at the weekend dances—and there was always one on somewhere—the men went alone, leaving their wives at home.

I made discreet inquiries from some of my employees who said that taking their wives to a dance somewhere else was a pure waste of time. The hosts had wives and they shared them. The compliment would be returned at some other dance, and if the women wanted to dance they could do that too.

Such behaviour naturally had its inherent dangers, the greatest of which was venereal disease. In those days it was rampant, the official figures showing that about eighty per cent of the population was infected and, for a government whose annual income was gauged in thousands and not the millions of today, the impossibility of full medical control of this menace was obvious.

Kikori then had only one native medical assistant who was little better than a hospital orderly and was nowhere near as well trained as today's graduates from medical schools. The hospital was a native-material building, erected by the station staff and labour, as were all buildings at the time, including the R.M.'s house and office. Patients came in for treatment and then wandered out, using the hospital as sleeping quarters. The fact that a man and his wife might both be patients under treatment did not deter them from carrying on the trade of prostitution after they had presented themselves for regular treatment. Some just got weary of hanging around the station and went back home.

There was little hope of controlling this with a bare minimum of official staff, a few police, no medical patrols, and a population that didn't care a hang anyway.

18

During this last trip I questioned a medical assistant in one of the villages on the present incidence of venereal disease, and rather surprisingly, he told me that there was none. He said that the patients in the hospital were sick mainly with respiratory ailments and stomach infections.

This sudden switch from one extreme to another within a few years is a bit hard to believe but it is noticeable that the health standards among those people I saw were much better, and measures taken by Department of Health officials have certainly greatly improved the people.

The pendulum appears to have swung again in favour of mission activities, for although there is a modern hospital now at Kikori, the mission bodies have multiplied and gained strength in social work.

There are still only three officers at the station, although they were all away at the time of my visit, but there are now a number of trained native public servants in health and education, and the formation of a local government council has added to tighter control over the area.

The ordeal of a girl on her wedding day has probably vanished, but in the past it was customary to segregate the bride in one of the houses under the care of an old woman while the dancing and feasting went on and she was made physically available to all male guests at the ceremony.

Today, if you speak to the younger people and mention the Hawa'a and Buguru, they stare blankly at you, admitting that they know nothing about them except from what they have heard from old men's tales.

There may still be pockets where these ceremonies prevail. One old man told me that in the far hinterland of the Turama River country the Buguru dance is still held. If so, then it must be in a distant and remote place, for these districts have seen a steady influx of government, mission, and oil company people and one must travel a long way into the interior to find the standards of primitiveness that were common in pre-war days.

During the boom in crocodile shooting there was big money to be earned. One hunter is credited with having secured 1,000 hides within a week, but this industry has lapsed, and the trapping, shooting, and skinning are now done mainly by bush people, some of whom travel for weeks to distant parts, as far as the swamps of the Upper Strickland and the little-populated country between the Wawoi and the headwaters of the Aramia, all with the urge for money and the food and clothing to be gained from traders.

19

In some respects the changes over thirty years have been depressing. Civilization has made its impression on what were once some of the most backward of people. It has brought health and education, more dependable means of communication, and a better awareness of white man's ways. It has given the younger generations an opportunity for a better and fuller life and for a chance to rise above the muck and filth of village existence and the life-long struggle for existence under some of the harshest conditions imaginable, with death and disease always around the corner and accepted as inevitable.

It has done a lot to break down the people's superstitious fears, their prejudices, their bloodthirsty ways, and their indulgence in moral laxity.

"We have got rid of their evil practices," a missionary told me towards the end of my trip, and I refrained from asking the obvious question, "What have you put in their place?" I had journeyed far and had seen a lot of the sadness that civilization brings, for there is a complete and irrevocable desolation in the lives of most of these people and a lot of it could have been avoided.

The spirit of a united people that was once happy and strong has been torn apart and the remnants that remain are weary with age and sickness. Deep down in their hearts they know that the world has gone past them and though their children may build a better nation, they, themselves will never have any part of it. Decimation and desolation are the two big burdens that hang over the delta today.

We pulled into the main reaches of the Kikori River as the afternoon sun dipped westwards behind the low ridge on its farthest bank, and we edged gently against the current and over the river.

There were changes since I had seen it last. The river looked much wider and its banks seemed free of the ragged edges of mud islands and pandanus palms that I had remembered. But this was only to be expected, for in a country which is watered heavily by cyclonic storms building up in the Great Papuan Plateau and the Leonard Murray mountains almost nightly, the flood areas of the delta are some of the most affected parts of the Territory.

Up above us, on the ridge, were a new hospital and a school and, as we put our engines down to slow ahead, the heavy staccato roar of a bulldozer came down-wind from the area where Public Works men were putting the finishing touches to Kikori's first airstrip.

Away ahead, the red roofs and glinting walls of the station buildings shone out in the evening light. Still farther ahead, white

20

blotches against the dark olive green of timber pinpointed Keith Tetley's place, store, tavern and guest-house and my rendezvous.

The western bank, that I had once known as a deserted stretch of river marked only by a few thatch-roofed government buildings, had come to life. In the clear evening air they presented quite an attractive picture, but I noticed that the opposite bank was deserted as it always had been except for one small, native built kombadi, a rest house for transients.

Now even this had disappeared, and there were no signs of habitation as far as the eye could see. Settlement had begun on the west bank, and it was as if a line had been drawn down the centre of the river separating the civilized from the uncivilized.

The high throb of an outboard engine was heard as a small boat came speeding downriver, wheeled in a wide circle, pulled in and tied up alongside. A tall, lean man climbed aboard.

"I'm John Senior," he said.

I was pleased to see him for I had heard a lot about him at different times although we had never met, and I had always had a desire to meet and talk with him for I knew that John now owned and operated the trading site and house where I once lived and that he, like myself, was a man with a deep interest in this country and its people.

Within a few minutes we were on our way (in his boat) back to the house, climbing the familiar front steps and sitting on the same old verandah, talking about the past.

To John Senior I owe many thanks. My visit had been entirely unplanned and, at the best, I had only expected to travel within easy reach of the government station, see and talk to some of the people, perhaps meet some old acquaintances and try to familiarize myself with present-day conditions. Limited time was my biggest handicap.

I knew what I was up against, travelling in this region, for I had experienced the difficulties before. You just cannot plan in advance. Walking for any long distance is almost a physical impossibility, unless you're prepared for an expensive and tedious patrol of several months. There are few mission and private craft, and the best that you can expect is a sturdy dug-out canoe with a willing crew and an overload of optimism that the weather will remain fine enough to permit a reasonably comfortable journey that fits into your schedule. Travelling for long distances in an open, unprotected canoe is far from pleasant.

Within a few minutes of our meeting, John had offered me a ten-day trip on his own vessel, *John Mac*, due to sail for the Turama, the Bamu, and Aramia Rivers and to Balimo, the farthest point of his business ventures at the place of the Western District government sub-headquarters.

Because of this offer and his aid, I was able to extend my visit to six weeks. I gained insight into many places and people I could never have reached otherwise, and I was also provided with a wealth of information about the background of his sixteen years spent in the area. All this helped bring my knowledge of the area up to date; after all, I had been away for thirty years.

The main purpose of my journey was attained and recorded as a summary of impressions, correlated by facts, of a population existing under the burdens of unfulfilled hopes, despair and decay, and of a country that once possessed vivacity and desire but is now as torpid as the muddy waters that fester in its swamps.

It was from the deck of the *John Mac* that I was also able to see the antithesis of this dejection, to view at their own level other people who are multiplying and consolidating their efforts towards a better and fuller life. But that was in another place, with other people.

For a few days I stayed at Keith Tetley's house, a mile upriver from the station. Tetley was then the House of Assembly member for the area, and in the evenings, among the company of a few local residents, I learnt about local happenings, the promises, the expectations, the potential, and a few substantive accounts of retrogression that were not healthy to hear.

During those days I sent out feelers among a few of the native people I met, about others whom I had known in the past. Where were they now? Alive or dead? These conversations produced a pleasant and unexpected result. One morning an old employee of mine, named Momi, appeared. I remembered him as a young and active man in spite of a foot deformity caused through an accident as a child.

He and his wife, both grey-haired and showing the rigours of age, had brought his canoe and an invitation to go along with them to their village at Baubaguina, a few hours' paddling down the river.

I could only promise an overnight stay, for John Senior had indicated that he was almost ready to sail. The arrangement was that Momi would drop me off at one of the villages on the coast on the return trip.

By traditional standards, Baubaguina is not a Goaribari village although it contains elements of that people. Once it was the site of a large community, for it has an excellent position on top of a ridge, a clear view of a lot of country and high enough to be free from the miasma of the low-lying swamps. Now it is a new village, an experimental settlement.

It appears to have started as a project, launched by a district administration official. The idea—to group sections of a number of delta communities into one locality where better ideas of village settlement could be demonstrated within easy range of the main station.

As far as I can gather, as an experiment it is a success in that it is an improvement on the old-fashioned method of building crowded, dank, and unhealthy bush material houses one against the other.

Each house is in a small separate plot; there are footpaths and individual gardens of shrubs and flowers; and the land is high and dry though somewhat steep as it dips down to the river bank. Some of the land behind the village is being used for food gardens but this is limited.

In fact it is a splendid example of what can be done. But apparently it has not been followed consistently by other people, for I heard of no other project of this nature.

The man in charge is a village policeman, a smart young man, pleasantly active and with modern ideas. But even he had his problems.

"We are a village of different people," he told me. "We come from five or six different villages and we own no land here. Our family lands are still where we came from, and to keep up a supply of food we have to go back regularly to our own gardens and to our own areas of coconuts to make copra.

"There are no people left in my village," he continued. "Some of them are here and the remainder shifted to other places and now our place is dead."

I was to see his own village later, a collection of timbers eaten by white ants, collapsed houses, scrub and pockets of coconut palms.

"This means," he said, "that we are away for several weeks at a time, gathering food and making copra, and when the bad season comes we just cannot get back there. We also have the job of bringing our copra back here in our canoes and that is a heavy task, and a long one, too. Before, one of the local vessels would call and pick it up, but that doesn't happen any more and we must bring everything in to the station."

He admitted that conditions were better in this village than in his own, that it was cleaner, healthier and better for the children who were close to a school, but that he was continually worried by the pressures of existence and the lack of facilities to get food and to handle the produce.

"There are some old people here. They cannot paddle these long distances, and they cannot work so hard," he said. He indicated

23

that his people had increased responsibilities to look after the older folk and that the move had put an extra strain on them.

What he said was very true. The migration of the people had been viewed from a social angle only—but the subsistence economy of their village life did not fit into this pattern. Practicalities seemed overwhelmed in achieving the ideals of more space and cleaner air.

It would seem that population migration cannot be substantiated unless it is accompanied by some type of economic opportunity, however lowly. In this example, the lack of conveniently available land for food-raising was its weak point, while the small cash benefits previously obtained from their produce were offset by the obstacles of time, distance and labour, and there was no form of small, local industry which could serve as a sheet-anchor.

The fact that other communities had not followed this lead is another point to consider, for they are a people of discernment and very practically minded. The food bowl is more important than fresh air.

Some two weeks later I started my real trip on the delta when John Senior eased the ship's engine and set me ashore at the village of Dopima, on Goaribari Island, one of the far-out places right on the coast of the Gulf of Papua. From here I was on my own.

Dopima is the third village bearing that name. The first earned notoriety as the scene of the massacre of Chalmers and Tompkins and ten mission workers on Easter Monday, 1901. The second was built inland on a rise of country which, according to the local story, was later evacuated on official orders in preference for the present site on a strip of black coastal sand between the ocean and a backwater creek near Cape Risk.

The story the villagers told me was rather peculiar. "The government told us to move out of the bush and down here to the beach," they said, "and we were told that we were to watch for ships in trouble during bad weather so that we could go out and help them."

This story seems highly improbable, because the village faces the wide, open Gulf with Cape Blackwood a long green finger in the distance and the intervening stretch of water notorious as one of the roughest of all passages during heavy south-east weather.

I have sailed these waters in bad seasons and know how terrifying the seas can become as they sweep from seawards across many miles of submarine mudbanks, churning into huge, angry swells and tearing the land away in their fury. Mariners caught out at sea during these times are in real danger of swamping and foundering, or of being caught out of control and swept on to the beaches to be smashed to matchwood.

24

Risk Point is a living example of what can happen, for it bears the scars of past storms in a whole forest of dead timber standing like skeletons along the beach frontage. And the sea is encroaching every year. No village dug-out canoe could survive such weather even if it were able to get off the beach.

The probable reason appears to be that at the new location government patrols will have direct access to the village and so will avoid a hot, difficult scramble to an inland bush site.

The village has a population of about seventy with the sexes about equally divided, but the number of older folk is higher than that of the younger generation, and many of the women are widows.

The buildings have their fashions, some old and others new, with the traditional type built one against the other in a jumble of rooms and passages, and the modern houses, set individually, each having its own garden plot, reveal quite roomy dimensions, substantial and open to light and fresh air—a far cry from the maze of dilapidated passages, small doorways, and low dark recesses of the older quarter.

The black beaches are firm, hard and wide, heavy with a mixture of titanium oxide and other minerals, and as you walk the foreshore, you can feel the sand clinging to your feet like a soft, warm blanket. I picked up a handful and was surprised at its weight. In the sunlight it shone with a rich, cobalt blue tint and as it dribbled through my fingers, a myriad of tiny, bright lights were reflected.

These are the black sands of commerce, containing rutile and they originated from the volcanic deposits of Mount Bosavi, 9,500 feet high and 130 miles away in a direct line. They seep through the country in wide, tenuous pipes to be washed out as alluvial on the beachheads.

A geologist friend of mine to whom I showed a sample shrugged it off as, "not being worth two bob." But he did explain that if one could extract the precious metal from the dross by a simple process at reasonable cost, the find would be worth millions.

From what I could understand there are complications in the extraction process and these beachheads would create an exorbitant cost that would not be justified. So the wealth of Midas lies mixed with the delta mud and is there for the taking, for any who wish to try. But first, have that formula for cheap extraction.

These beachhead deposits have been known for many, many years, and mining authorities have at various times been given grants to work them. I have yet to hear of anybody making a success of it.

Thirty miles out to sea is the rig of a petroleum exploration company, testing the seabed for black gold. At night, sitting on the beach in the bright moonlight, you can gaze at the reflection of lights from the rig hung in the sky like a halo.

There is wealth in this country but it will take millions of dollars to discover it. The Australasian Petroleum Company has spent $63 million in oil search work since 1937, and still has to tap a gusher, and there have been other companies and prospectors searching these western lands for the last hundred years or more. There have been gas finds, and indications of oil and signs of other minerals. But that is all. And there are many abandoned mining camp-sites in the jungle that give testimony to futile quests.

The beach at Dopima was wide and spacious, and gently sloped to the warm soft ocean. It was right on the doorstep of the rest house in which I camped and with the perfect weather—it was a bit too early for the tempestuous south-easterlies—became a secluded haven for resting, bathing, writing, sunbaking and talking with my neighbours. Each evening we would gather to watch the lamps of the fishermen as they waded in the shallows with upraised spears, and to take advantage of the night breezes to relax and talk over the incidents, the problems, the pleasures, and the hopes of the day.

Half a mile away, up at the point, there was desolation and disaster, for the sea was eating the land away in great gulps, tearing into village gardens and plots of coconut palms, denuding the soil and leaving the tall trunks lying at incongruous angles on bare clumps of roots that would be washed away seaward next stormy season. Already many of these trunks were standing like dead fingers with the tide lapping around them. Surely it cannot be many years before the whole of this south-eastern end of the island vanishes into the ocean.

It was during one of these moonlight get-togethers that coincidence struck.

Sitting next to me, the village policeman turned and asked, "Do you know who I am?" I had to admit that I didn't.

"I was with you before the war on the Strickland River," he said, "and I was the one who carried you from the camp on to the raft when we took you down to Lake Murray. You were very sick then and knew nothing about it."

What do you say to a man who had helped to save your life thirty years before?

I had certainly been very sick, and so close to death that it had not even been frightening. I have a misty semi-conscious remembrance of those days when blackwater fever struck and I was alone,

600 miles inland, with carriers and police who had no realization of the seriousness of my condition. I would still be there had it not been for a ration party, delayed for a week because of bad weather. The European leader had come into camp and found me, and the man sitting next to me was the one who had organized the building of a raft to carry me over three sets of rapids downriver to Lake Murray, where a boat was waiting to take me to Daru and hospital.

His memory was far better than mine for he told me of details I had forgotten, the names of those who had been with us and what had happened to them. Some were dead, one was blind, and others were still working.

He told me that he had continued working until he was too old for heavy bush duties and had returned to marry and settle down. He had been appointed the village policeman.

Both he and his son had two wives each but there was trouble in the family for one of the son's wives was a flighty lass who had found another lover and was now awaiting trial by the local magistrate.

A few days later, a visiting patrol officer arrived. He was a young native man, exceptionally smart and keen. His main purpose was to give a blackboard talk to the villagers on voting procedures and the meaning of the forthcoming House of Assembly elections.

As I sat at the back of the group gathered under the trees, and listened, a realization of the difficulties of imparting to these people some conception of parliament and their electoral rights became abundantly clear.

The patrol officer spoke clearly and easily in Motu—he was a Papuan from the south coast—as a teacher might to a class of children, but his audience showed little interest and sat silently, with blank stares of incomprehension, during his talk.

There were no questions or remarks when he had finished, and they continued sitting quite placidly until he told them to get up and go, which they did, very solemnly and still in silence.

This young man was performing part of the official political education campaign, a system of blackboard talks illustrated with drawings. Yet there was no apparent awareness or understanding among the people. In fact what was even worse, I heard later that the talk was being interpreted in many misleading ways.

Until the details of political life are related to the peoples' own economic circumstances it appears futile to lecture grandiloquently on human rights, freedom of expression, and the complications of a system which most of the people in the rural areas of the Territory still regard as only another form of government control.

I have had experience in political organizing. The pragmatic

27

approach to the basic needs of men and women is the only one which succeeds.

This is not being followed in the Territory because the political scene has too big an overlay of officialdom, and ideas which are not reconcilable with the official attitude are seldom pursued. One need only look at the confused state of political parties and groups, most of whom meet with considerable rebuff in their embryo attempts to become established.

Follow this through to the elected members of the House of Assembly, and the proceedings each session, and one need not be surprised at the continued failure to form any substantial opposition. It is not possible under the circumstances that prevail.

The excellent job that this young patrol officer did during his two hours in the village, in the inspection of water supplies, sanitary arrangements and the hearing of local complaints, apart from the manner in which he gave his talk, was impressive.

He had assurance and capability and a sympathetic approach which put him in right among the people. Many government officers on similar missions are surrounded by their police escort. This man was not. He sent his police away, moved freely around, his voice never rising above the tone of normal conversation. His visit was personal rather than official and was much more effective.

Even the flirtatious and voluble lady, with the plethora of lovers, he quietened with a few words, an achievement which obviously amazed her legitimate husband who had probably been trying to do that for years. He collected the old man and his daughter, her husband and one of the lovers and sent them aboard the boat for later treatment by the magistrate at Kikori.

We walked back to the beach together and he described some of his difficulties.

"There is always a fire hazard in these old villages," he said, "and the crowding together brings sicknesses which could wipe out the whole community. It is very hard to make them understand this although we repeat it to them every time we come."

He spoke of the overall lethargy of the people and of their apparent lack of ability to entertain new ideas. "Of course," he added rather candidly, "they have so little and there is nothing substantial in these areas to encourage them."

I wished he could have stayed longer, for he was an honestly perceptive young man. However, he had a strict routine. "I go to Gouri, and Aidio, and then round to the Turama and I have to be back at the station by the end of the week," he explained as he pushed off in the dinghy for his vessel.

28

If the people of the indigenous public service in any future independent government have as much character and personality as this one young patrol officer, then it will be a success, for it will have individuality. But that is an awful lot to expect.

I went back into the village and stood beside a group of old men, listening to their discussion of the recent political talk and the interpretations. Each was different, and I remembered the words of an old greybeard.

"Crocodiles, old age, and sickness have destroyed my people," he had told me.

Crocodiles are solid creatures and everybody knows what they do; old age is understood and accepted; but sickness unto death is a mystery governed by evil influences. I wondered how long it would be before they included "politics" among the things that split them apart.

We had been paddling for nearly two hours, travelling in a wide arc to the middle of the big channel in order to get around some shallow mudbanks, and were now rounding a headland with a patch of thick bush.

Within another half mile the mouth of a narrow creek opened on our left and we turned into it. It was like a dimly lit tunnel, crowded on its right bank by a forest of nipa palms, their roots spreading a carpet in sour, viscous mud, their fronds forming an archway over the creek and meeting with the branches of trees on the other bank. The air was heavy. There was complete silence, an atmosphere that affected the paddlers for they stopped their talking and sat almost like black statues as the canoe drifted on. Mudfish jumped out of the water in rapid, jerky movements, and clambered over the roots of the palms. Otherwise there was no movement except ours as we glided gently towards the bottom of a sloping bank that rose about eight feet above our heads.

The man in front of me, usually most loquacious, nodded his head and pursed his lips at the bordering undergrowth.

This was the site of Dopima Number One village, and where we were now resting had been the execution spot sixty-six years before, of ten Kiwai native missionary lads after their two leaders, Dr Chalmers and the Rev. Oliver Tompkins, had been massacred one hundred feet away under the coconut trees. Somewhere inside there, obliterated by jungle growth, they had all been eaten.

This act of savagery and its cannibalistic aftermath had brought world-wide anathema to the name of Dopima; had brought a gunboat to shell the place into ruins; had brought reprisals and gunfire for long afterwards and an avenging fleet of Kiwai warriors

29

who had murdered every man and woman they could find and had abducted all the young children. It had also brought about the suicide of an administrator.

Many years before I had heard feathered warriors almost boasting of their part in the mass murder. There had been moments when they talked of the feast which followed and I had seen the eyes of the young initiated men light up as they listened. But these tales were always told out of range of women's ears and in the sanctity of the dubu. How much was true and how much was false I never knew.

I climbed the slippery bank and pushed my way into the thick undergrowth. When it became too dense I stopped and looked over the top of the shrubbery towards the forest of coconut palms. There was nothing but the palms, yellow with age, and a thick billowy carpet of secondary growth. Almost against my feet a snake glided across the fallen leaves and twigs. I turned back to the canoe.

The feeling of death was everywhere. It had affected the paddlers, for they pushed off without a word and silently took the canoe back up the tunnel of fronds and out into the open water where the sun was bright and the birds were singing.

Only when we were in midstream did they commence talking again, for the curse of 1901 remained a curse in 1967, and there are few who will talk of it even if they know anything. Local history books are silent, for it is neither wise not just that the sins of the grandfathers fall on today's children.

It was not until some weeks later, on my return to the main river, that I met Ninai, a middle-aged, slightly stout man with an exuberance of good humour. I had been looking for him, for I knew that he had a tale to tell of those dark days. I had called at his small trade store at Baubaguina but he was away; I had asked at villages along the way without success and I had been told he was upriver, downriver, and had gone away to other parts. In fact I had given up hope of ever meeting him. Now, in the middle of the Kikori River, he came paddling homewards with his wife and child. We hailed him and pulled into the nearest bank.

He said that he knew me but I couldn't remember him. Possibly he was a child when I was there before as he seemed barely over forty and was a fine, well-built, healthy looking man.

Ninai had been mentioned as the last living man who had witnessed the Chalmers' killing, but I knew that he couldn't have done so and he admitted that he hadn't. However, his uncle had been there and Ninai remembered the stories his uncle had told him. These he recounted with bursts of laughter that rocked our canoes alarmingly, so we edged closer to the bank for safety.

30

"There was a Buguru ceremony at Dopima village when the mission boat arrived in the main stream," he began, "and people had gathered from many villages for the event.

"The Doctor and his friend came into the creek with ten native evangelists and went to the village landing place. They left their native helpers with the dinghy and walked up into the village, one of them going into a new women's dubu that had just been built.

"When he came out again the crowd began pressing round them and one man, named Gahi Bai, began telling the people to kill the white men.

"Gahi was a tall, thin man. He had just been married and had been initiated as a chief, and as he had never killed anybody before he wanted to show how important he was and kept on shouting out to the natives to kill the missionaries.

"A lot of the people didn't want to kill them, but Gahi had the young men with him. They all began to shout. While they were arguing a young woman stepped out of the crowd and threw off her grass skirt. Standing naked in front of everybody, she warned the people that if they killed the white men there would be big trouble.

"Gahi yelled out, 'Don't listen to this woman,' and stepped behind Chalmers and speared him in the back.

"When he fell down the men rushed in and clubbed him and then killed Tompkins. Then they all ran down to the creek and killed all the native mission men who had come with Chalmers.

"They dragged the bodies into the village and stripped the clothes off them and prepared for the feast which they had that night with the heads of Chalmers and Tompkins on poles in the village."

Ninai began laughing again and we all had to hang on. "Do you know," he continued, "they even boiled the missionaries' clothes and rubber shoes and tried to eat them, too. They had never seen rubber shoes before."

According to Ninai, his uncle must have tried chewing the rubber shoes because he was very sick the next day, and Ninai laughed again at the memory.

He said that sometime after the massacre, when the news reached the Kiwai people of the Fly River, they sent out to Goaribari Island a war party which crept up on Dopima early one morning and killed all the men and women they could find. They also killed all the older children and abducted every baby to take back to Kiwai.

"These babies were brought up as Kiwais," Ninai continued, "and they never knew that they were really Goaribaries."

He said that the dubu at Dopima was six hundred feet long, which would be certainly far bigger than any I have ever seen. This was quite probable in view of the dubu's importance in those times of fighting and cannibalism, and for a large village, as Dopima was in those days, carrying a heavy population of warriors and initiated men, there would have to be ample accommodation, not only for its inhabitants but also for the masks, insignia, weapons, sacred objects, and the hosts of traditional implements always kept under security.

Ninai told me that his uncle had been one of those who had escaped from the vengeance of the Kiwai warriors. He had been working in the bush when he had heard the noise and screaming and had joined some others who were running away.

Apparently the avenging force had never been expected and the first the sleepy people had known of them was when the clubs began to fall.

One of my old-time employees had been a Dopima man, born in this same village, and he had been present at the time of the massacre although, in conversation, he always shied off the subject when it was mentioned, and would admit only that he had seen it.

He was an old man when I knew him, a friendly creature with streaks of grey in his curly hair; his body bore the flabbiness of age and his whole attitude was one of weariness.

For one who had been a cannibal he was very gentle and he bore the aura of a gentleman of the old school, a man of experience who respected traditions. A bit slow in his mental adjustment, he never committed himself to an answer, or made any statement without first considering deeply what words he would utter. Then he would give his opinion rather ponderously and walk away.

For quite a while after I first met him, I suspected that he might be mentally retarded but this opinion had to be scrapped later when I discovered that he used this quality of hesitation with considerable advantage to himself.

He was called Tom, although his proper name was Awuga, and on the subject of the massacre he was always rather reticent but, somehow or other, remembered to the smallest detail the subsequent feast.

He was, by any standards, an epicure of human flesh and wou' become almost rapturous when describing the many processes of cooking it. It was this that made me rather suspicious about the killings because he was also an encyclopedia on fighting and killing, on the details of victims he had known, and on the joys of securing a skull to adorn the dancing post of a coming Hawa'a.

He made everything sound very gory and it was during such talks that he threw off his apparent lethargy and hesitation of manner; his eyes would light up and his face glow with enthusiasm.

He had obviously been a most meticulous cook and a fair judge of meat.

"This is the best part," he'd exclaim, patting his buttocks, and then go on to describe the qualities of other parts of the anatomy, often in rather lurid detail. His least enjoyable moments must have been when he received a portion of meat from a fat man, "because fat people always have a strip of fat across their bellies," and that was contrary to his taste.

I could imagine him sitting down to a village feast, viewing with a critical eye a heaped up mixture of meat piled on to a banana leaf, and probably cursing the cook.

His ideal meal I will always remember for he described it so enthusiastically, and so often, that no conversation was complete without it.

"You roll sago in a long leaf and bake it," he would whisper, his thoughts still on the memories of some tribal barbecue, "and when it is cooked you spear a piece of meat, hold it in the flames and let the juices drip down on to the sago stick."

Apparently the diet suited Tom for, despite his age, he was big and strong and he had never lost his yearning for human flesh. In fact, it seemed that he bitterly regretted having given up the habit for he was born in a transitory period when government and mission authorities were expanding, and neither of these institutions took kindly to cannibalism.

These influences had led his youthful ambitions astray and this sad chapter in his life he often confirmed by headshakes and deep, mournful sighs—though which of the two powers had the greatest effect of changing his menu was hard to say. The substitution of tinned corned beef was never to his liking and he always complained that it gave him indigestion.

There were occasions when I suspected that he was casting an appraising eye over my own body and once, partly in levity and partly to reassure myself, I asked, "If I were killed, Tom, would you eat me?"

He reached out and gripped my arm, pressing gently as if in a display of brotherly affection. "No," he replied, "I wouldn't because you are far too thin." His voice carried a tinge of disappointment.

I was never sure because, at times, he still got that meat hungry look in his eyes and I had no wish to be too handy if he ever changed his mind. I always kept a close check on my weight and watched my silhouette.

But we became firm friends which one naturally does with a man who is a cannibal and has told you that he won't eat you. He was

33

really a placid creature, a good husband to his young wife and their baby, which had been presented to them by another village woman, for I doubt if Tom could have made the grade as a father, and the custom of giving babies to couples with no children was common.

Sometimes he'd lapse into what appeared to be a coma, unaware of what was going on around him, retrospectively viewing the past with a mind full of thoughts medieval and ancient. Probably, in his heart, he was once more with the old gang, testing the balance of the stone clubs or analysing the menu of a prospective feast.

There were times when he would retire to his own backyard and stage a one-man dancing session of his own before his wife and a few of his cronies. There, with an upraised tomahawk and a few feathers stuck in his hair, he'd stamp around in a tight circle, chanting his favourite tune and slashing at an unoffending tree trunk.

Quite often his display would draw spectators who, from a safe distance, would pass rude remarks, insinuating that he was nothing better than a mad hatter. Fortunately for them he took no notice, and I doubt if he even knew they were there. If he had, the tomahawk might have been used for more lethal purposes.

For all his idiosyncrasies he was a good fellow and a staunch companion who always tried to do his best in an indulgent, slow, and quiet manner. He took me once to a peep-show view of a Buguru ceremony, which was a risky experience as far as he was concerned and not a very pleasant or comfortable one, thanks to mosquitoes, the slimy roots of mangrove trees and the chance of being caught. But he had been most anxious to show me this tremendous event — as it certainly was in their lives — and, after many invitations, I had agreed to go.

I never saw an Hawa'a dance and had no intention of trying to, for an experience shortly after my arrival in the delta gave me a perpetual feeling that it wasn't exactly safe entertainment.

The resident magistrate and myself, being the only two Europeans on the station at that time, were sitting talking on his verandah one night when an American couple suddenly walked in. I believe that they were wandering anthropologists but where they had been was a mystery for the magistrate told me later that he had no idea there were strangers within miles of the place.

Anyway, with four people for once, we sat down for an evening's bridge game and were thoroughly enjoying ourselves when there was a knock at the door and the police sergeant marched in. He snapped to attention, swung a salute at Syd Chance, and deposited two freshly-cleaned and highly decorated skulls right on the bridge table, thus ending our evening's game.

34

The story was that two prisoners, who had been released a week previously, had been given rations and told to walk back to their village, a couple of days away.

Everybody had forgotten about them when an old dame reached the office one morning and asked when her son, one of the prisoners, would be returning home. Being assured that he had been released she began her journey back, accompanied by the police sergeant as a kind and sympathetic guide.

According to the sergeant, they had followed the river down, cut into the bush, and reached a deserted village to find evidence of an Hawa'a dance with two skulls still on top of posts.

After a bit of scouting the sergeant unearthed one frightened man hiding in a garden hut who confessed that the skulls were those of the two ex-prisoners. They were strangers and had walked into the village one evening just as the jolly folk were preparing for the dance. With two new heads unexpectedly appearing on the scene, they welcomed the lads, fed them and put them to bed. That night they killed them and prepared the skulls for the dance, which was doubly enjoyable and a jolly good time was had by all, particularly by all those then out of favour who had expected their skulls to be used.

So the sergeant came back with the old woman carrying her son's skull in company with the other unfortunate's and the prisoner in handcuffs.

It was a most opportune moment for the anthropologists who, when I left to walk home, were busily scribbling in notebooks and drawing sketches of the table adornments among the playing-cards. Fortunately that was before playing-cards became illegal property in the Territory or the case may have been more complicated.

The skulls later took an honoured place on top of the office safe and joined the company of several others, one of which was reputed to be that of a white man.

More than once I have seen tearful relatives bringing in the skulls of their fond ones. This invariably resulted in a police patrol going out to search for gentlemen with head-hunting inclinations.

One individual who must be mentioned was Kivau, hereditary high chief of the Goaribaries who had fourteen wives. His subjects scuttled for cover and held their breath whenever he walked abroad.

He was always traditionally dressed in a wide bark belt, a large pubic shell, cane arrow guards over his wrists, a thigh bone dagger, dogs' teeth necklaces, and black killer feathers strapped round his shaven skull.

When he came around, people automatically flattened themselves

35

against walls and trees like plasticine for he seldom went visiting. If he wanted to see anybody specially he would send for them.

Once he came to my place with an invitation to go down to his village as his guest, a trip I later made for I was curious to see just what he was like at home. There he turned on a feast of pig, crabs, bananas, sago—everything—served by his retinue of wives. He acted as the perfect host and was not by any means the fearsome looking creature he was outside his home town.

I missed an opportunity to discover his background as it would have been embarrassing to question one's host on any bloodthirsty episodes he might have been engaged in, but if tape recorders had been invented and one could have got Kivau really talking, there would have been some wonderful tales.

As it was he was a taciturn man who spoke very little. In all our conversations I never heard him refer to anything but his immediate problems and general actions.

During my recent trip I met one of his sons, a fine middle-aged man with only five wives. The hereditary chieftainship had been abolished and he was an ordinary local government councillor dressed in a clean white shirt and lap-lap, and wearing a bright, shiny official badge.

I'm sure his father would have looked with disdain on these trappings and would have been shocked to think that the power of tribal chieftainship had descended to the size of a metal badge with an infinitesimal degree of authority.

But neither Tom nor Kivau lived long enough to go on the scrap-heap at the mercy of a new order. They were fortunate for they would never have fitted into delta society as it is today. It would be impossible to imagine Kivau, if he had been alive today, standing up at a meeting, in the role of councillor, and saying, "If you please, Mr Chairman." He was a leader, born and bred. He gloried in the authority of his office which was recognized and respected by his people.

The yearning of these swamp people to improve their economic circumstances is very real and perhaps, in comparison with their overwhelming limitations, their own efforts are remarkable. Only in the Highlands, and in isolated regions of the coastal belts, have I seen people working with such enthusiasm and endeavour, independent of all outside influences, including that of the government. The western districts' peoples have never been blessed with the munificence of the government as have their compatriots in the more attractive and more accessible regions.

In this age of scientific planning it pays to be within easy reach of

Yali Singina of Yabalol (Madang); a native leader for twenty-five years. Sometimes criticized for being a benevolent despot

Yali with two of his wives and several loyal supporters

the central authority, with roads and access by sea and air, so that experts, authorities, specialists, missions and advisors can travel in comfort, dispense wisdom, and return to their home base before dark.

One could call this computerized development, where everything falls into its proper place.

But beyond the ends of the roads, in waters where ships cannot travel, and in places where airstrips are considered uneconomical, social and economic development falters and often fails.

Government is costly and with the official policy of "centralization of areas of highest potential," to quote some official minutes, such areas as the delta are left right out of normal reckoning.

This policy, which I have heard described at an official meeting as "the chicken and egg policy," places undeveloped areas and people at a tremendous disadvantage and results in steady deterioration.

One side-effect is that the people who receive government benevolence in full are fast losing their initiative to do things for themselves, and if the traveller wishes to see the real heart of a people struggling to improve itself then he must go out to where life is at ground level, away from the embroidery of official projects and patronage, to where existence is still raw and hard.

Here there are few officials, perhaps only one or two, but they are men who are trying to cover tremendous areas with limited resources and they are doing excellent jobs that are plagued by shortages.

The individual field officer is invariably one who is devoted to his job and must be satisfied with small returns and little achievement from months of hard work under some of the worst conditions. Usually he is trying to implement a policy which defies implementation, attempting to make understandable objectives which are incomprehensible to the illiterate people, and encouraging self-help among communities in which hope is at its lowest ebb.

It requires far more than a book of regulations and a computerized plan to solve situations which these men face up to daily, and that is why, in the more progressive of outback regions, one finds officers with character, leadership, and personality. Central government has not yet found any means of quenching the spirit of the pioneer, a trait that persists when you get away back-of-beyond.

At Dopima, my temporary headquarters, I found this spirit of enterprise still alight, although only in a small way. The one who was encouraging it was the village policeman.

"We are going to make copra on a co-operative basis," he confided. "Up to now each family has been making its own but this hasn't been satisfactory because there are so few family trees and

The sacred flutes, made from bamboo pipes, can produce eerily beautiful sounds

Locally grown gourds provide instruments whose powerful sounds balance the lighter flutes some people won't work them. There have also been instances of stealing nuts and this makes a lot of trouble. Another of our troubles has been getting the copra to market or to the trader. Under the old ways, no family made much money for themselves and many have become disheartened."

He told how he had now organized his people to build small copra driers and smoke houses. Everybody worked under his direction, the men gathering nuts and the women bringing in timber and husks for firing.

The nuts are opened and the flesh is taken out at the smoke houses. The general processing of raw coconut meat into copra is undertaken by all, while the heavy work of bagging is done by the men.

He said that the scheme had expanded and that canoes were sent out to abandoned areas to recover coconuts. Arrangements had been made, too, with other communities to purchase their nuts.

"We still have the job of getting our copra into Kikori," he added, "and that is a long way away."

One of their ideas is to take the copra into the station, and when there is sufficient loading, to put it on one of the coastal vessels, with one of their members, bound for Port Moresby. There it would be sold direct to the Copra Marketing Board.

This is rather ambitious and complicated, for quite apart from the expense there are factors which they do not understand. Strict honesty is required in the agent travelling with the consignment, for he would receive the payment and be responsible for the purchase of needed stores to bring back. Freight charges are high and there would be fares to consider, plus supervisory care at the receiving end.

If the consignment were sold locally to a trader at a lower rate, these additional expenses would not be incurred, and there would be no business transactions beyond their present level of experience and understanding.

How they have resolved this, I do not know, but the manner in which they were tackling the job, without official aid, was a very healthy sign for there is no other enterprise in which they could engage. It was a small affair, important to themselves, and indicated a resurgence of individuality which is so badly lacking throughout the region.

The comparison between the optimism of this village and the despondency of the next village, Kerewa, when I reached there, was startling.

Kerewa was a wreck, a ghost village of ancient timbers and ancient people, sitting in a mud basin among surroundings as drab and despondent as its inhabitants. The first view of Kerewa is not very encouraging as you clamber from the mudbanks up greasy, moss-covered tree-trunks that act as steps and stand on the damp, stinking ground inside a rough pig fence.

Negotiating the pig fence is an effort in itself and requires a considerable amount of balance and aptitude as well as a firm grip to prevent yourself falling into the mire beneath. The fence is made from pointed timber posts, standing one against the other. There is a rather rickety arrangement, like a stile, as an entrance.

The main purpose of the fence is not to keep pigs out, but to keep them in—it is really a large, solid pigsty enclosing the area beneath the houses. Within it, the pigs wallow and churn up the stinking, oozy slime that never sees sunlight.

Nine or ten feet above, on lanky stilts, sit the houses which form the main section of the village, and if one wishes to see traditional, old-time Goaribari architecture, this is it.

They crowd against one another in a jumble of rooms and narrow passages, in a confused mass of timbers and sago thatch, aged and weary, and with a drab, dull look of flatness, without colour or form, as if the mud in which they rest has saturated every crack and wrinkle.

The unclean and monotonous appearance of this village is depressing with its flat expanse of struggling grass and weeds, and the background of coconut palms, their fronds hanging listless and yellow through lack of nutrient in the soil.

"Who would want to live in that place?" a young government official asked me when I returned to Port Moresby and spoke of what I had seen. "There's nothing but mud, mangroves and the mentally deficient"—a harsh, vicious judgement from one who had never stepped beyond the boundary of urbanity and its privileges.

Around each house is a boardwalk—if one can call it that—of unevenly-laid tree trunks, loose, slippery, and a horror to those not used to walking on such crude surfaces. They are also dangerous for there are wide gaps between the slack logs.

Why have they not replaced these primitive, unsafe structures by cleaner, better and safer constructions?

The answer lies mainly in the attitudes of the people themselves. They are traditionalists, though not conservatives in the accepted sense for that implies careful preservation. Traditionalism here has brought apathy and personal inertia; these have been bolstered by a complete lack of outside incentives. Why rebuild a house that has become a derelict when it is far easier to move into the crowded tenement next door? It is like the proverbial hole in the roof. When it rains it is too wet to go out and fix it, and when the sun shines there is no need for repair.

Once Kerewa was a city of houses with thousands of people spread widely over many acres under groves of coconut palms. It is the oldest village of the delta, the traditional home of the Goaribari people.

It was a main centre of primitive culture with its dubus and skull houses, with independent family units joined under a patrilineal allegiance to their own leaders and warriors.

Land and population pressures, together with personal and family idiosyncrasies, inevitably brought splits as groups moved out to become established independently in other places, although they still remained one big family and were re-united on ceremonial occasions, and they maintained constant communication with one another.

Today, it has eight houses, stained with age and the smoke from many fires, smelling of mustiness and decay, and sheltering a mere ten men, thirteen women, three girls, two boys and half-a-dozen young children.

Their leader is the village policeman, an old and withered man but still slim and sprightly and proud of his heritage. It was in this man's house, and sitting on his only chair, that I met his "people."

The room was large, with dark mahogany-brown walls of sago, and the support beams were blackened from the smoke of cooking fires. A pale blue film of smoke lazily hugged the roof, pushing its way through the thatch into the open air, and there was a rattle of enamel plates from a kitchen hidden behind a partition.

We had barely settled down when the village policeman reached up and tinkled a small, brass bell suspended from a beam. It appeared to be a relic from some old vessel. Soon there were sounds of padding feet as the villagers filed in silently, in ones and twos, and squatted on the floor or slid into dark corners. They were old, wizened and bent, with deep-set eyes and scrawny limbs, dressed in a variety of torn, dirty shirts, loin cloths and dresses, some of which I noticed had been pulled on hastily over roughly made grass skirts.

They shuffled through the doorway like ghosts, silent and hard to distinguish in the dim, diffused haze of smoke. The men sat in a semi-circle before the policeman, while the women moved off into corners as if apologizing for their presence.

Behind them came a few children, bright eyed and wondering. They squatted together behind the old men and peeped curiously at me, giggling among themselves until somebody silenced them.

"These are my people," the policeman said, by way of introduction. They sat there silently like petrified mummies.

He spoke in Motu, a language I know, and told them who I was, what work I did, and that I was a wanderer returned who had known them long ago, had worked with them and their families and had come to see and hear them.

The dull eyes turned and surveyed me, and from three of them came words of recognition as they spoke together in their own tongue.

"These people remember you from before," the policeman interpreted, but the subject wasn't pursued and it probably registered only as another incident that could be talked about round the smoky fires at night.

A woman cackled from the darkness, pointing a bony finger at me and spoke something in the sing-song tone of her own dialect. This also passed unheeded.

One girl and a couple of youths sidled in from an alcove, and the crash of a falling dish in the kitchen beyond shattered any impression that we might have gone back in time, and served to set the policeman talking again.

"The young people have left us," he declared simply. "They don't want us any more. They want dresses and dances and boyfriends and parties and they go off to Port Moresby to find them. They no longer listen to us when we tell them what we want. The schoolbooks teach them differently, and they say our old ways are no good. They want to play and make money."

We were interrupted by a young, pleasant-looking girl of about eighteen walking from the kitchen. She was smartly dressed in a cotton frock that obviously had been tailored for her. In this gathering she was shy and quiet and didn't seem to fit in.

"You see her," the policeman exclaimed. "She is my wife. She is young and strong and looks after me and does what I tell her. There are no women like her around here any more. They have all changed and gone away."

Shortly afterwards, another woman came in—a small, gentle but tired-looking woman about the same age as the policeman, with soft brown eyes and an innate sense of hospitality, for she paused for a moment, gave me a smile and asked if I were well. This, I discovered, was his first wife and the mistress of the house for she turned and went back into the kitchen to supervise what work was being done.

The absence of young folk and the steady decimation of his people were matters which preyed on the policeman's mind for he returned constantly to the subject, his voice sounding dully in a room that echoed his words, uttered clearly in a steady monotone that changed only when his feelings overcame him.

"These are not our children," he exclaimed angrily as his hand swept round to where the youngsters crouched. "No woman here bore them and no man here fathered them. They are children of our daughters by other men in Port Moresby. They find these men and sell themselves to them and when they have children they are brought back to us to look after while our daughters look round for more men. They never come back themselves because they are ashamed and afraid."

He paused and looked around, but those near him hung their heads and the women never murmured. His voice rose almost to a shout. "We never did things like that before. We fathered our own children and didn't let our women have babies by strange men. In those days we could stop these things but now we can do nothing and we are told that our ways were bad. Our children are not even our own any more."

I had been quietly looking at one of the young lads. He was a fine-looking boy of about seven—tall, with blond hair, blue eyes, and a pure white skin. There was not the slightest outward sign of coloured blood in him, for he had typical Nordic features, a straight nose, oval face and a fine carriage. By any standards he was a handsome youth, fit for any gathering in any modern society, and I wondered how the proponents of racialism would classify him. Yet he was sitting close beside me dressed only in a short green loin cloth and talking quietly to a companion in the Goaribari tongue.

It would have been embarrassing to question these people, but I guessed that he was one of the "Port Moresby babies" for he bore no signs of relationship to any of the old crones gathered there.

Surely the officials knew of this lad's existence, and something could have been done to give him a reasonable education, with training, under more pleasant conditions, to fit him for a better life. Now it was two or three years too late and he was a strange soul who would grow up to be a complete Goaribari in outlook and mentality, with perhaps, in later life, a permanent grudge against the white man who had abandoned him and antagonism against the white race who had ignored him.

These antagonisms do exist and are very real among the people of mixed races. They are a product of the extreme divisions of society in the Territory, between "those who have" and are accepted, and "those who haven't" and are ignored. Those who are related to both white and black vacillate between the two, without leadership and sometimes without direction.

In native society all children are accepted whatever their colour; in white society this does not apply generally. There are exceptions

42

but these affect individuals and this curtain of colour is the basis for much latent hostility.

I have known a fine man of mixed race, with feathers and paint, leading a tribal dance, and who had entirely renounced the white race, and a woman who had inherited her father's money, solely by virtue of being his next-of-kin, and who had scorned all offers of marriage by white men but had accepted a bushman's proposal and was living happily with him.

The sins of the fathers fall on these children because the fathers have lacked the moral courage to acknowledge them. This attitude has, in many cases, been condoned by white society. Let their offspring battle their own way to recognition from village grass huts, but don't upset the transcending superiority of the white skinned community.

Perhaps somebody, with the energy, drive, and persistence of a Lenin might arise from this middle section of humanity . . . someone who might not be side-tracked by the fruits of personal persuasion.

It was at Kerewa village that I heard the stories of the dubu. They were told by the policeman in that shady, dim room, and they were to be repeated by others as I made my way around the country.

"We had a dubu before," he said, "but it became too old and broken so we pulled it down. I have tried to get the people to build another, but we have few young men who can do the work and our children say that they don't want one, that it is wrong and that we should forget about the dubus."

He was most grieved about this and spoke for a long time in a voice tinged with anger and surprise that such a happening could occur during his lifetime.

"They won't listen to me," he kept on repeating. "They say that they have been taught that a dubu is wrong, that they must go, and that the government doesn't want them because they are reminders of the bad days. Why are they told that? This was never the way of our people, and now that the dubus are going, the people are going and there are only us old men and women to remember how strong we were before and how we kept together."

He waved his hand around the blackened interior of the house. "This is my dubu now," he said simply, and I could sympathize with his feelings although I couldn't help him.

The loss of the dubu has had a deep and damaging psychological effect upon these people. Not only has it shattered their last and only remaining link with the past, but it has shown very forcibly that these survivors are the discards of modern times.

The dubu has always been an institution of great importance in their lives—a consolidating force with religious significance, a meeting place for the elders, and a form of council chamber in which decisions of importance for the people could be made. In the past it has served for a variety of purposes; as a sacrificial house, a repository for the skulls of their own leaders and those of their victims, an initiation house and, in more recent times, a club and social centre for men.

For them it has been like the loss of a national shrine as it represented the symbol of authority and power associated with all the traditions of their tribe.

No style of education for a local government council can replace the spirit of the dubu; the Christian Church cannot take its place, for the two are so dissimilar—the church is a place of worship, the dubu a place of association.

The steady and complete extermination of the dubu seems to have been a cruel and unnecessary action towards a people who have long ago given up their warlike and bloodthirsty habits. It does seem suspicious that where mission influences are stronger than governmental ones, the elimination of the dubu has become complete.

From other sources, too, I heard that this process of elimination has received official sanction, for there were many who said, "The government will not let them have the dubu."

We hear a lot about the preservation of old cultures and symbols. Out here, in the west, there has been little preservation. It has been explained to me that the destruction of these old cultures is a form of development, but this contention seems very hard to justify.

Others have told that quite a lot of old symbols and artefacts have gone up in bonfires, and that in some villages there is a line of demarcation between "Christianized" people and "Heathen" people.

It is remarkable, by contrast, that the old "haus tambarams" of the Sepik areas are being replaced by new ones, and that this is being encouraged. One young government officer tried to give me an explanation for the destruction of the dubus.

"The old dances and ceremonies, the Buguru and Hawa'a, were bad things, for during these ceremonies the natives killed people and feasted upon them, and danced obscenely in orgies that lasted for days. All these were planned by the old men in the dubus, and these buildings must go because they still remind the people of the old, bad practices. Now we have local government councils and these are the organizations that must give leadership. We cannot have two competing, one against the other—the old and the new."

I was rather intrigued by his use of the imperative, "must," for

I have visited many local government councils in all parts of the Territory and there are very, very few who display a will of their own and reveal qualities of leadership.

This is a failing which is admitted by the more discerning government officers, many of whom, for the last fifteen years, have been striving to let councils take the torch of responsibility and to exercise their own independent control.

"There is a big gap between what we tell them and what they are prepared to take over," said one man to me at a meeting in the bush. "There is still that big element of unreliability, a fear of responsible authority which should be exercised by themselves. Consequently the government officer is always necessary and he must do duties that, rightly, the council should do for itself. We don't like to make decisions about their own affairs but we have to because they just won't take the plunge."

It appears unusual that a people who have lived for centuries under the authority of their own leaders, many of them very dominant men, should be unable to accept responsibility when it is entrusted to an elected body of councillors. Possibly it is the overlay of an Australian type of governing structure which is at fault—whose realities are not understood because they do not seem to the natives to fit their situation. This weakness can be traced from the local government councils right through to the House of Assembly, and it could be that to impose a western system upon an alien, coloured race with a dissimilar mentality just won't work.

The old-type village policemen, luluais and tultuls, as well as the tribal leaders, were able to work effectively with their peoples. Why cannot a higher-educated type of council do the same?

Again, in Kerewa, I heard tales of the olden days.

"The old days were good," one man reflected. "Our people were together." He shook his head slowly and scratched the stubble on his chin. "That's all finished now and we are left here alone. Our young people go off to Port Moresby and die from puri-puri and disease."

This was an old-timer's view. I also questioned some of the middle-aged men and women. They were all bitter about Port Moresby and regarded it as a place of horror which had swallowed and destroyed their families. "Our children get sick there. The big sick because they run around and sell themselves to men," said one man. He spat on the ground. "Port Moresby is a bad place."

There was justification in their sorrow and bitterness, for I had visited the shanty towns that cling to the urban area and act as magnets to newcomers from these western lands.

Like many young people, the adolescent boys and girls go after the bright lights and the fabulous tales of easy money that are spread everywhere. Most of them arrive with nothing—no money, no ability beyond unskilled labour and no knowledge of the difficulties of obtaining work. They gravitate to the shanty settlements because they have friends there who take them in, feed and accommodate them in crowded houses where sanitation and privacy is at a minimum. They join the mounting army of unemployed and unemployable and are soon disillusioned and have to face up to constant refusals, lack of food and finally accept that they are the great unwanted.

Such conditions soon breed the desire to make a quick and easy dollar, in pilfering, theft, or prostitution, and the Goaribari, because of his social background, easily returns to the practices of commodity trading in women.

In a place like Port Moresby where there are thousands of workers from other districts, all without women and away from their own family influences, there are willing customers.

Shanty-town living means existing in houses made out of scraps from wartime dumps; rusty corrugated iron, discarded timber, and packing crates. It means living with meagre, and sometimes no water supplies; being crowded together, men, women and children, in unhealthy, unsanitary tin houses; sleeping on dirty, infected blankets, with no privacy and with standards of behaviour governed only by their surroundings; fighting, drinking, gambling being commonplace; and with the deterioration of human dignity to a level little better than that of their village pigs.

There are even overflows from these shanty towns into the bush near rubbish dumps where shacks, hammered together in all sorts of shapes and sizes, harbour those who have given up all hope. Such places are hotbeds of petty crime. These shacks are a disgrace to any urban community. How many come here and die through venereal disease, tuberculosis, and other ills is anybody's guess, and few care except the families back in the villages when the stories filter back. Such accounts do not sit well on the minds of old men and women, who remember their children as happy sons and daughters eager for a chance in the big wide world.

I once went to an hotel and disturbed the head of a Commonwealth fact-finding mission from his after-dinner cigar and liqueur to inquire about the results of his visit. "We have seen all we can see," he advised me, "and when we return to Canberra we will be in a position to answer any questions about the social conditions of the Territory."

I didn't bother to go questioning him because I knew what his itinerary had been. From hotel to motor car, to the district office and departmental heads, and then back to the hotel. He had just finished dinner with two selected native representatives and the District Commissioner, and he couldn't talk to the Press because he might be misquoted.

I should have liked to have taken him round shanty town, and shown him a woman dying with incurable venereal disease within half-a-mile of a modern hospital. I had known her years before as a bright, happy, mission-trained girl, but she was dying, ashamed and frightened. She was also beyond all physical help, and nobody had cared.

Is it surprising that the people of the west curse Port Moresby and are embittered over the indifference and neglect of the development of their district? Primitive as they are, they know that the introduction of any industry, even on a small scale, would help stop this disintegration of their families and keep their children within their home boundaries, and thus hold their people together.

As the afternoon light waned, the old woman came in with a small hurricane lamp, lit it, and left it in the centre of the floor. The policeman was still talking.

"Go to the other villages," he advised, "and see what has happened to our people." There was a murmur of assent from those around. "Kamea has five old men and eleven old women and no children. Gouri, which was once an important village, has now only a few old women living by themselves. The village has been turned into a place for pigs. Dubumubu has been deserted. Half of the people have gone to the new government site at Baubaguina and the rest have left to join relatives in other places. Aidia is nothing any more. Just old folk like us."

He noticed my camera and asked if I would take his, and his people's photographs. When I agreed he went inside a room, opened an old cedar box, which bore the marks of many years, and took out his plumes, a head-dress, a wide bark belt and some arm ganas made from fibre. Some of the feathers were killer ones, I noticed—the insignia of a man who had bloodied his spear.

Within a few minutes he reappeared in all his finery, stripped down to a simple shell covering and decorated in the trappings of long ago. He studied himself in a cheap, trade mirror, adjusting his feathers and ornaments with the delicacy of a stage star in the dressing-room.

The children began to laugh and he silenced them. "You see," he exclaimed, "these children do not know what these things mean."

His voice was sad. There were whisperings from the old women in the corner, but they were also silenced with a "shush." For him this was an important occasion, a moment when he could show them all what he looked like as a young warrior. He fondled the feathers almost affectionately, pressing them down with the palm of his hand so that the head-dress draped over the top of his head like a black halo. Others he threaded through his arm ganas, each correctly positioned.

He pushed his hands through the arrow guards of plaited cane with difficulty, as if he had forgotten how to wear them, twisting and turning and comparing one with another. A thigh-bone dagger, yellow with age, he thrust into his wide belt, smiling faintly as he felt it against his bare thigh.

We all moved out into the afternoon sunshine.

He stood alone on the built-up area of hard, clayey mud covered by a scanty carpet of rough, coarse grass, looking out over the channel to the jungle beyond, a shy old man still trying to look like a determined warrior.

In little groups they came and stood and had their pictures taken, the children a bit nervous, two giggling young girls and, lastly, the policeman's young wife. When his first wife's turn came she stood demurely and half smiling and when the shutter clicked she murmured, "Thank you," and walked back into the house.

That night, after several hours of talking in the dark old house, dimly lit by the hurricane lamp, and after an enormous meal of mud crabs and sweet potatoes, I rolled my mat out on the uneven and very hard black palm floor, made my bed, tied a mosquito net clumsily above, and crawled in.

It was not altogether a tourist's romantic dream of a night in the wilds. Below me, in the mud and ooze, pigs squealed and snorted, the smoke from damp wood fires drifted through the house, the stench of decay from beneath and the musty odours of old timbered beams above, hung heavily, while the mosquitoes came along, found a hole in my net, and enjoyed an issue of fresh blood.

When a grey dawn began its first light, the rain came down in typical delta fashion making the waters of the channel heave in slow, muddy swells that burst in froth among the mangrove roots.

The old axiom of "Rain before seven, fine before eleven," came true for by nine o'clock the skies were clear and the sun shone hotly, presaging another day of sticky, muggy humidity. We loaded the canoe, slithered down the greasy poles, ploughed through the mud, and pushed off with the whole population of a little over thirty, waving us goodbye.

The channel was quiet as we ploughed westwards, keeping to the shade of the timbered banks as much as we could, with the steady sweep of the standing paddlers maintaining a rhythm that never varied.

There was nothing but bush, jungle, and patches of sago swamp interspersed with small forests of pandanus. Birds were busy, their calls ringing out from the dense foliage, drowned at times by the raucous screeching of white cockatoos as their sentries gave an alarm and sent the whole flock wheeling high above us.

The water in this inland channel was very still and like glass, disturbed only by the paddles which sent waves and lungfish scuttling and splashing into the soft, muddy banks. Never once did we sight a crocodile, or even signs of one, and only occasionally did the ripple of fish become distinguishable.

Once the paddlers stopped. The leading man stood steady for a moment and then lunged downwards, spearing a mudcrab, though how he saw it through the heavily stained water was a mystery. Another time, we halted under a huge leaning tree, and one of the paddlers aimed his bow and arrow at a cluster of vegetation high on the bark. He fired and brought down a small squealing kangaroo-fox type of animal, which he promptly killed and threw into the bottom of the canoe. It was not until he hit it that I saw it, for we had waited almost a minute for him to take aim and, to my unaccustomed eyes, there appeared to be nothing but fern leaves.

They were sharp, these lads, reading the signs of the forest, pointing into dense scrub and explaining in whispered words what they saw. Once we saw tracks of a pig that had come down to drink, but it either heard or smelt us and it ran off, crashing through the undergrowth as swift and nimble as a deer.

To the right of us the mouth of the Omati River opened, its currents spilling into the waters of the Gulf in distinct lines of small waves. It is a big river, fed from inland tributaries that start in higher country where the limestone formations begin to rise. This has been the area of a lot of oil exploration work in the past. Now, it is abandoned and deserted except for scattered villages well inland.

We rounded the north-western tip of Goaribari Island and still hugging the coast, paddled slowly down towards the gulf waters. From here we could see the open sea with its swells rolling in to splash against the farther bank of the channel.

Still in the lee we edged closer until we were almost in sight of Goare village. Then we turned lazily to starboard, our course set diagonally towards the village of Aidia.

With the south-easterly set of the swells our passage was easy until we were well into mid-channel. Then we began to rock and roll, slightly at first, but more and more as the big swells struck us. Soon the waves were splashing over our bows and flooding the canoe and we were forced to take each swell diagonally, with the canoe rocking alarmingly and the paddles spread out over the waters to steady us.

Although this was the season of the doldrums, the wind was changing towards south-east, and this was the first and only time we experienced it — unfortunately on the only day we had to undertake open water paddling.

Mid-stream the force of the waves seemed to ease, and we moved in what appeared to be a corridor of currents, possibly from the Omati, which broke the power of the curling crests. But on the other bank, near a wide belt of mangroves, there were lines of shallow mudbanks. Here the waves were vicious, breaking and curling over the top of us until we were forced to bail with everything we had to avoid overturning.

Finally, within the mangroves, we stepped out and manhandled the canoe, dragging it along twisting channels between the roots to the sloping beachhead. The choppiness and spray here were just as strong as outside and we were all wet through by the time we waded across to a dry patch of sand.

It had been a long time since I had taken an open water trip in a dug-out canoe. Except for the wetting, the trip had been exhilarating and enjoyable. It is a grand feeling to see the water racing past the bowels of a good, sturdy canoe with a well-rounded beam that rolls easily, and to register the vibration of the seas racing beneath your feet, barely an inch or two away. A long trip can be soporific under the heat of the sun, with the monotonous, unchanging timber and jungle and the hiss of the water as it goes past, for time and fair weather are the essence of canoe travelling and when you have both, nothing could be more pleasant.

Rig up a shade and you can eat, read, or sleep while the world passes by. Your watch may stop and the world may be in an uproar, but that doesn't affect you until you make landfall and reach your destination. You are alone like a passenger on a spaceship, but with no engines to disturb your passage.

Aidia stands well back from the sea, high above the marks of south-east storm waters and surrounded by a high timbered fence of logs set vertically and bound tightly together, giving the few houses that peeped over the top, the appearance of a stockade.

We had just reached the fence when the village policeman

appeared. I recognized his broad leather belt as a relic from former service days. He came towards me with both hands outstretched. "We knew you were coming today," he greeted me, and I stood facing one of my old employees whom I had not seen since I was first in the district.

Sepi was still the thickly built, dour man I remembered, but his hair was grey and his legs were wobbly. I discovered that he was not a village policeman but a local government councillor elected by the people of this distant area to represent them at headquarters.

I asked how he knew of my coming, but he only shook his head and laughed. "My head told me so," he replied, tapping his skull.

So positive had he been of my early arrival that he had arranged for a bed to be made ready and for food to be cooked in a newly-built house next to his own. I knew that the village had been weather-bound for the last few days and that nobody had left, and as far as I knew nobody but ourselves had arrived recently. Furthermore my journey had been unannounced and unplanned and we had just taken a chance of getting through while the weather seemed good.

The village was a new one and only half built. "Our old village is over there," said Sepi, pointing towards a shoulder of land. "The sea has come in fast this year and is washing it away so we have moved to this place. We shall have to move again for the waves are coming right up to the fence and the land is slowly disappearing."

Over on the narrow spit there were the usual signs of destruction. Coconut trees at crazy angles, a few collapsed houses and water splashing over mudbanks that had been firm ground a year before.

He sounded very tired, but despite the slowness of his walk he climbed the rough steps into his house with alacrity—far better than I could do, for they were only rough saplings nailed to two uprights and slanting almost vertically from the ground up to the first floor, nine or ten feet above.

It was a large house but uncompleted. There were no interior walls or partitions. A crowd of men and women were sitting around gossiping, and two women were at the back blowing the embers of a fire into flames.

Sepi sat in a high-backed chair to one side, looking like a patriarch watching his flock. "These are my people," he said, and the words were becoming very familiar. "We are all that is left, all burukus, all old folk."

He had exaggerated for there were at least half-a-dozen young men and women among the thirty or so people gathered there. They may not have been permanent residents and they may have been on holiday, for one young lad spoke excellent English, was neatly and cleanly dressed and, as I found out later, a student on leave.

But the majority were old with the same expressions of weariness as those I had met elsewhere. Two others came in, a man and his wife who had worked for me many years before, and two young widows, one of whom I had also known as a newly married bride.

It was surprising, in this small scattered population, to meet so many whom I had known before. It made the journey easier, for they talked willingly of old times and places, and of people whom we had all known.

I walked over to their house with the married couple and while the wife was preparing a meal of baked crab, I spoke to her husband about the woman, Deti, whom I had seen lying on some old flour bags in shanty town, dying of disease. I knew that this was her home village and in her early days she had always talked about coming home to her mother and sister, and I wondered what the family had heard about her. Surely, they knew that she was dead.

The old man was a bit cautious at first but soon he opened up and told me that none of the family was there. "When her mother heard the news that Deti had died she walked out of the house and sat down on the beach all by herself. People came to talk to her but she wouldn't speak. She sat there just staring out to sea, not crying or anything," he said. "When night came she was still sitting there and although some of the others tried to get her to go inside the house, she refused to move. They left her sitting there for it was a calm night and full moon. She was still there when the village went to sleep, but in the morning she had disappeared, and when they went down to the beach they found the tracks of a crocodile."

I asked about the sister and again he was very hesitant. "She has gone away," he said quietly. "She has gone in the bush and nobody knows where she is. When her sister died and her mother died, she packed all her things and went off alone in a canoe. She was seen at Kikori station, and she was seen upriver at the village òf Amegeau where she slept one night. Then she paddled farther up the river and nobody knows where she went to. They found her canoe on a mudbank. It was empty and her things had been taken. We think she went into the bush on her own, but where, we don't know."

"Did you search for her?" I asked.

"No. Before she left she told us that she no longer belonged to this village and that she was going to live somewhere else. She said

that sorcery had been made on her family and that she was no longer a Goaribari woman."

He was silent for a long time then he muttered, "That is the way of women."

I inquired later at other places about her, at Kikori station from those who had known her, and at Amegeau village, but the response was always the same . . . shaking heads and "we don't know."

This individual incident was typical of the tragedy that has afflicted the Goaribaries with the break-up of the family, the sad harvest of disrupted social customs, the shock of death, and finally dementia and oblivion.

What is worse is the stolid acceptance by the old folk of such circumstances, an obtuse sufferance that these things are inevitable and that there is no way by which they can be combated.

There are other old folk who could tell similar stories but who remain silent. You can see the anguish in their faces when they speak of their children who are away, and in some you can distinguish a look of fear when these things are spoken about, for these are the people who usually have never heard a word from their children since they departed.

Much of their fear is the result of ignorance. They are illiterate and have no means of communicating with their families other than by word of mouth carried by returning friends. Rumours circulate well ahead of any substantial truths, and imagination adds to their miseries.

Often strangers have come to me in the villages and asked if something or other is true about their relatives. Their questions are difficult to answer, for usually one knows nothing and can only give general assurances that all is well.

Aidia once had a large population, as did most delta villages, but this has decreased alarmingly through age, death, and migration. When I arrived, there were about thirty adults, a few children and some young lads. The big village near by, which was now being washed into the ocean, had been reduced to not more than eight houses, ample accommodation for the few who remained.

The two young widows were fine young women barely out of their teens. Both had babies to nurse and both had lost their husbands through accidents at almost the same time.

The one whom I had known before as a single girl and as a young bride came shyly into the house and sat down to feed her baby. She was a plump lass, pleasant looking and well dressed although the black blouse and blue skirt showed signs of being worn for a long time.

Hoisting the Freedom flag in the West Irianese refugee camp near Vanimo, Papua-New Guinea

"She wants to get married again," the old woman said, "but I have told her to wait. She is a good girl and there is nobody here who could look after her properly. She is too young and strong not to have a man but there are no men here who would suit her."

I suggested that there might be some in other villages but this remark was scorned.

"There is no work in this district and the men spend all their time sitting down in the villages. They know nothing and have no money and are too lazy to get out and find work elsewhere. This is a clever girl. She has been trained in housework and her husband had a good job. She will have to go away to find work and another husband. But who will pay for her fare and who will look after her when she leaves?"

I mentioned that the government had welfare officers who might be able to help if they were told about her, but again the old woman replied sharply.

"We never see the government here unless it is to collect tax money or to talk about elections. What do we know about welfare officers? Nobody is interested in us and we are a long way out from the station. Everything we try to do we have to do ourselves. Sepi goes to council meetings but nothing ever happens. It was a good place before but now it is dead, and soon we shall be dead, too."

She bent her head and raked the ashes of the fire while her husband sat moodily staring out over the mangroves and the breaking waves beyond. I looked across at the girl, but she was busily feeding her child and seemed oblivious of our conversation.

Later I spoke to her in English, for she knew the language and spoke it quite well. I asked her what she wanted to do.

She raised her eyes and gave me a fleeting smile. "I want to get married and go to work again." Her voice was soft but it lacked any conviction and I guessed that she had suffered disappointment for too long. "One day I will go away again," she added wistfully.

It would have been futile to offer any encouragement, for what could I say to a young woman who had experienced a lot of pleasure in life and was now stranded on a remote beachhead, back among the primitive conditions she had once left behind? I thought, as I looked at her, how vulnerable she was and how easily the remainder of her life could be wrecked. A young, attractive widow, yearning for marriage and the outside world, eager to please and with nobody to guide her. She had experience and she had confidence but these qualities are not enough when a woman is alone, and she was very lonely there, even among her own folk.

When evening came I sat alone looking at the few new houses

and the protective fence. It seemed somewhat ridiculous that these people, isolated as they were, should have to build a fence around themselves. There were no pigs inside and I knew that they were kept elsewhere; there were no unfriendly neighbours who would attack, and timbered posts, however strong, will not keep out the ocean. But it was the custom, and the fence was built.

There were the murmurs of small groups as they prepared their evening meal and the smoke from driftwood fires mingled in the evening air. The sea had calmed down and there was no wind. As darkness grew only the flickering of small fires and the occasional sound of spoken words indicated that there was human life in this desolation. There were no songs, no drums, no dancing, and the voices droned on for an hour before the village quietened into sleep.

Sepi came along and sat with me, and we talked a little of the people and places we had known together. He sounded tired and weary and I realized that although he was younger than I, he was much older in body and spirit. Before he rose to go he said very quietly, "We are finished. We shall sit here and die just like the others have done and nobody but our own people will know, and only they will care. Why has this happened to us?"

While I was thinking of a reply he rose and shuffled off. I guessed that if intuition had told him that I was coming to visit them, it would have revealed that I had no answer to his question.

As I moved on, from place to place, the full force of the degradation of the delta country and the people became more manifest. The farther we travelled the more unhealthy was the scene . . . nothing but abandoned village sites and the skeletons of once virile populations, now represented by old crones and haggard, wheezing men.

A stranger might well wonder by what means this race of people had once been the terror of their neighbours, had been noted for treachery, cannibalism, killing, and headhunting, and had been feared and avoided by better-armed and equally courageous people.

Two old women came out of a clearing as we passed and stood watching without a greeting or a sign of recognition. They were swineherds, keepers of the village pigs, and their broken down sago-built hut was all that remained of a one-time village.

There were still patches of wildflowers and rows of coconut palms, and betel-nut trees with an occasional breadfruit, and there were still faint traces of where houses had once stood, but these were very few for the pigs had taken over and the ground was churned up into wallows and puddles of slimy mud.

"Why do they stay here?" I asked a paddler. His reply was simple. "They have nowhere else to go. This is their home."

Farther on there was one house perched beside a stream. Two men and three women lived here, and a small naked boy ran out to stare at us. His body was covered with sipoma, a loathesome skin affliction in the form of a ringworm and brought about by filth and lack of hygiene.

A woman, clad only in a dirty ragged grass skirt, bony, thin-chested and with withered breasts, called out to him. She, too, was covered in this skin disease, and she stood and scratched herself as we passed.

And so it went on, day after day, and there were times when, at night camps in vacant houses, there was a fear that we, too, would contract some disease and this fear overrode all other alarms of snakes, scorpions, spiders and other crawling things of the night, for decay was in the timbers and death had passed many times this way.

I realized that the census figures I had fortunately collected at Kikori station told only part of the story. These were the figures of a census taken during 1966/67 and totalled slightly over 2,000 people for the Goaribari area alone, which is reputed to have a population of from 11,000 to 15,000. The totals could be greater but these are the variations I obtained from different sources.

The overall birthrate of the census areas was given as 4.2%, and the deathrate as 4.6%.

There could be doubt about the birth figures, for I remembered what the policeman at Kerewa had said, "These are not our children. They are those of our daughters by other men in Port Moresby." But there can be little doubt about the death toll, for in some of the backwaters there must be many who die and the deaths are not recorded.

"Crocodiles, old age, and sickness," the ancient had said, and a lot of the victims must have met their end in dark corners that few knew about.

Next door, in the Lower Turama region, totalling only 668 people, there was a natural decrease of 5.09%, with births at 2.09% and deaths registering 7.18%.

How long are these few people going to last with a natural annual decrease of 5.09% in their numbers?

Age, infirmity, sickness and accidents will take a greater toll as the years pass and the 0.4% decrease in the Goaribari area alone could mean that within ten years this population may vanish.

This is a region that has been officially labelled "Depressed" and it can be attributed to two main causes; over-recruitment of male labour in past years, and a complete lack of any economic incentive to keep the people together.

I searched in vain for any signs of positive development and found only one. And that was of doubtful integrity.

I had been questioning a government officer on what were the policies for future economic development in this region, and he replied very guardedly to my questions, so cautiously, in fact, that I knew, and sensed, the uncertainty in what he was going to say.

"We are planting 200 acres of rubber to help the people," he replied, and when pressed for fuller explanation added that the planting had only just been started and the completion of 200 acres was still a long way off.

Beyond that there was nothing.

It has been stated officially that rubber growing can be used by subsistence farming people to supplement their income without necessarily becoming a main cash crop. This argument appears to be rather specious when compared with the facts.

Rubber takes six or seven years to bring any economic return and then it is only a very small one and the costs of maintenance and production are tremendous. At the moment it is one of the most depressed commodities on the world's markets, and Papua-New Guinea's contribution is so insignificant that, as one Singapore buyer said, "We just toss it on the heap."

Apart from having to compete on the world market, rubber also faces growing competition from synthetics, and to make any notable addition to income it must be produced with the best of yielding stock, on large acreages, and under the most efficient management.

Substantiation of this criticism comes in the latest five-year, $1000 million development plan of the Administration which projects from 5,000- to 10,000-acre holdings of rubber in the Madang District, and there is no surety that these will succeed, even under Administration management, for the term "experiment" is used as a cautionary qualification.

So with a population of about 11,000, scattered over about 10,000 square miles of swamp country, 200 acres are not going to improve many peoples' standards of living even if they live long enough to see the actual latex being tapped.

What is going to be done during the intervening six or seven years is anybody's guess.

However, it is yet another statistic to be included in the annual report, which is some achievement.

About fifteen years ago, the present District Commissioner of the Gulf District, Mr J. J. Murphy, was commissioned to carry out an investigation of some of these depressed areas, but nothing has been heard of the report he submitted and it probably lies buried in some Administration pigeon-hole.

Time did not permit me to meet Mr Murphy, so I wrote to him afterwards asking if he could assist me in locating his report. He replied very cordially that he had not kept a copy of it but suggested that I approach the Administration on the matter.

On my return to Port Moresby I tried to get the report from official circles but the quest was hopeless. Few, if any, had heard of it, and very few cared.

Why Port Moresby should abandon these western areas is hard to understand. All agree that there should be some development and all agree that nothing is being done.

At Kikori there is a school, a hospital, and a government station with what appeared to be an overload of police. Recently a light-plane strip has been completed but this can be regarded mainly as a government convenience and will do little to encourage economic progress where the basic essentials for trade do not exist.

Mission influences have made a greater impression than the government. This, after thirty years' absence, is plainly visible, for government activity is centred on law and order while mission work is based more on social reforms.

The government station's establishment of native police is tremendously expensive when compared with the productive aspects of administration which are practically nil, and this imbalance was reflected everywhere in the areas over which I travelled.

This, plus the maintenance of official prestige in the area, which must be exceedingly costly, indicates that the Administration is not sure of itself in the Kikori delta region. It has a problem which it seems it is incapable of handling—that of a depressed and under-privileged people living in a depressed and under-developed land.

Some indication of the way in which officialdom works is shown in a letter to a newspaper from a local resident of many years standing. The writer complains that the government will not seal the new airstrip apron and this means that, for a major part of each year, it will be unavailable to aircraft "due to the extremely heavy rainfall which averages about 250 inches a year."

He also complains about the Administration's decision to close down a near-by lime kiln and to import lime from Australia at twice the cost, a remarkable disclosure of official thinking.

When I visited this kiln, at Mati, a few miles above the station,

58

it was producing about ten tons of lime each week which was then being used on the construction of the airstrip. I was told that this would be taken over later by the local government council as the nucleus of a local industry.

This suggestion appears to have been dropped, although the whole vast region is a natural reservoir of limestone, which is used considerably by mission bodies for their own requirements.

The low level to which development in the delta had fallen can be assessed by the amount of concern experienced over the closing of one small kiln, which would be a minor matter in any region that had other sources of income.

Here there is none.

It is ridiculous to say that nothing can be done with the place, as I have heard government officials remark. Many of them have done nothing more than fly over the top of it, in a hurried return trip from Port Moresby.

The only industry of any consequence to the people since the war has been a mangrove bark industry established at Aird Hills. This lasted for a while and then folded up.

According to John Senior, this was an excellent introduction to an agricultural industry for the village people, and one fitted to their temperament and capabilities. They could move around the mangrove forests in their canoes, stripping bark from the trees, paddle their loads direct to the factory, and receive payment on the spot.

It provided all of them with an occupation—even the kids could cut bark—and brought a steady, small income to help provide food and clothing. Mainly, it provided them with something to do, organized on the basis that the most energetic received the greatest rewards. There was always a hope that an industry such as this could be expanded, or that other industries would start.

The reasons for its closure are not too clear. In the delta, one can hear a number of reasons, any one of which might be correct.

This was the first real industrial undertaking since the halcyon, pre-war days of oil exploration when this area was one of the main fields of operation. Then, there were many hundreds of local people employed on good wages and conditions, and the effects of this spread far and wide and gave benefit to groups in distant hamlets as well as creating a busy centre of the main station area.

The closing down of much of the active field work and the reduction of the camps at Middletown, Barikewa, Kuru and other gas finds to static areas with skeleton staffs was the delta's severest blow.

Uncertainty of the future still remains, although the companies retain their large permits to prospect and explore. But this industry, if it ever reopens, would be a multi-million dollar industry and would at once put the delta back on the map of prosperity.

It is to the smaller industries that we must look, the ones in which the native population can participate as producers and suppliers of labour and materials.

The growing of rice, sorghum and other cereals is possible, and it would also be possible to process these commodities by means of secondary industries suited to the capacity of the crops.

One hears far too many objections against such endeavours. The more usual are, "It would not compete on world markets," "Costs are too high," "Transport difficulties," "Lack of markets," "Shortages of skilled staff," and a continuous stream of what amounts to nothing more than excuses to avoid the responsibilities of action.

The Territory is being subjected to such an overload of scientific planning that the practical results are lost in a maze of research, investigations, reports, and committee meetings. All of this country's agricultural possibilities have long ago been subject to practical tests. Some have succeeded, others have failed, and there are records to prove it, but this does not prevent every new suggestion of growing some commodity from being overwhelmed by scientists and investigators whose cost is astronomical and whose results are carefully filed away in manilla files.

Practically all the possible commercial crops were grown and tested at the old gaol site at Hombrom Bluff and the Laloki during the years of the first world war by one man with a few native assistants trained by him. He discovered what could be grown and what could not, the returns per acre and the money values at existing prices, and he was not a trained agriculturist.

Here in the west, the limited capabilities of a department which is to reap $65 million during the next five years, rests upon a paltry 200 acres of rubber.

Surely in the many thousands of square miles of nipa and associated plant life, a paper or hardboard industry could be founded, and there are large timber stands in the inside country which could be used, if not as a main industry, then as a subsidiary one serving local needs.

Limestone, clays, and ochres exist throughout the region, and when one enters the higher rainforest country there are untapped and unlimited supplies of copal gum. All these have industrial uses which could be developed as local industries.

I have, myself, collected a flour bag full of resinous gum from trees within an hour by just walking around the forest and gathering it, and the price quoted for my little sample was £80 ($160) a ton in 1937. Nowadays it would still be of value, even though prices have dropped considerably.

Official developmental planning seems to be getting farther and farther away, beyond the far horizons, and ignoring what is at its feet, a pattern that can only result in economic suicide for such depressed areas as this. Meanwhile the import-export gap widens and there are calls for greater co-operative efforts from the people and the unspoken threat of higher taxes.

In a region like Kikori and its surroundings, where there is little but mud and misery, the people are not greatly concerned about competing on world markets. They would be perfectly happy if they could get something extra to grow that would add variety and substance to their diet; or produce a crop that could be sold, easily and directly, to bring in a few extra dollars; or even if they could secure daily work to supply their daily bread.

Economic rules cease to function when you are living at subsistence, or below subsistence levels, when life under the new system means the break-up of the family, the loss of your children, with neglect added to misery, with vacuous promises that have no relation to your immediate needs and which, more often than not, fail to materialize.

Their wants are simple and to augment them would cost but a fraction of that being spent on grand plans and projects. Mention development today and you are presented with a misty coloured picture of the future and talk of millions of dollars, and if you persist in seeking details of depressed areas and peoples then there is silence, broken only by the rustle of humanitarianism as it slides out the back door.

That is why there is disease, death, and degradation in the delta. It would be futile to expect any other results from the long lack of interest and neglect that it has received.

If ever there arises an intellectual leader from among the Goaribari people he will probably say to the central government, "Build a fence around us and leave us alone. We can do better by ourselves."

And he would be fully justified.

All things are relative and I suppose enjoyment must be viewed from that aspect, too, so I am not wrong in saying that one of the relatively enjoyable recollections of the past is that of a personally conducted visit, and a community conducted exit, at one of the chief old-time ravi houses of the Purari Delta.

The relativity applies to my complete innocence at the time which brought about my rather forceful exit, a sight that must have been very humorous to some of the bystanders.

This journey began at Port Romilly when Charles McKinnon, manager of the sawmill and the man under whom I then worked at Kikori, suggested that I take a canoe, a paddler, and an interpreter and go upriver to one of the biggest villages to buy sago to feed his work force.

The village was Ukaravi, a huge spread-eagled affair set back in a maze of inland channels and surrounded by vast swamplands. It was a consolidation of three large villages and carried a total of about 4,000 people; a city of women, song, and betel-nut chewing, remaining true to the old traditions of sorcery and bloodletting, and obeying the dictates of their overlords, the gentlemen who conducted the magical rites.

There were dubus and ravi houses in confusion and a surfeit of puri-puri artists and sorcerers who formed an active and greatly respected section of the community.

The absence of any form of Christian mission was hardly noticeable among the large variety of local religions, which provided for a complete range of tastes, from the exotic to the erotic, and, under the prevailing circumstances, the absence of a Christian religious influence was almost a prudent omission.

The individual villages sat on mudflats, which were firm enough to walk on but, like the whole surroundings, were not too salubrious. They were constructed after the fashion of a town planner's nightmare.

Progress from one village to another was by means of floating logs, spongy with age, slimy, treacherous, waterlogged, and bordered on each side by stale, stinking areas of decomposed swamp matter, bubbling with gases being released from the filth beneath and the refuse thrown from the village.

There was no sanitation, and pigs, ducks, children, and dogs wallowed happily together in the slime. Everybody seemed contented and happy and couldn't have cared less about the fevers, agues, and intestinal complaints emanating from the surroundings and which brought periodical decimations of the numbers of the very old and the very young.

With crocodiles thrown in to liven things up—for good measure—it is surprising that anybody survived three months, yet populations had lived in this area under similar conditions for centuries, and had probably developed a fair degree of immunity.

Tripping along the floating logs was an intrepid feat which I managed with the combined aid of the paddler and interpreter, fore and aft, while the town looked on. They probably thought I was a bit of a cissy for holding on to somebody, but not being prehensile, and being repelled by the possibility of slipping into the muck on either side, I didn't care what they thought.

There were dubus for almost everybody. They were there for the older men, the younger ones, for the children's initiations, for the widows, and apparently for anybody else who wanted the use of one.

We came to a narrow track, and walking along it, we came abreast of a dubu for females and were nearly overwhelmed by the crowd of women who emerged. Some were daubed with ashes and plastered with soot and charcoal, and some were just filthy.

Young and old, they came streaming out and hailed us with what must have been cries of joy. Daubed in charcoal and mud, and wearing long, ragged grass skirts to their ankles, they were an unprepossessing lot, and being some of the great unwashed, they stank to high heaven. One could imagine the solidity of the atmosphere inside the house.

Some of the younger ones had that wild and woolly look in their eyes and as we pushed through them, their hands clawed at our clothes and their tongues babbled. It was no place to linger and we kept moving.

The interpreter sidled up alongside and whispered, "The women want you to go into their house and talk to them," which I regarded as rather an understatement, and promptly ignored, in view of the clutching fingers and harsh breathing from our would-be hostesses. We had apparently landed at the wrong end of the village.

The main ravi was a tremendous building dominating the whole scene, its high, wide, open eaves resembling a crocodile's mouth and long, squat backbone. It must have been at least two hundred feet long and sixty feet wide and sat straddled on dozens of spindly looking wooden piles.

We climbed the steps and entered into a central passageway with small, individual cubicles on each side, each one housing a small initiate and his mentor. The boys were mere children, none appearing to be more than ten years old and some, much younger. This was a nine months' preliminary training period during which time no woman was allowed to set eyes on them, and their mothers came with their meals each night and pushed them through a small doorway at the back.

At night the lads were taken out for exercise, their heads covered with basketware, and shepherded by their uncles who shouted warnings to the women to keep out of sight. Girls screamed and ran away, and women always found jobs inside for fear that the curse of looking on these lads might bring on wasting diseases, with the aid of spears and poison.

The skulls of crocodiles hung on the walls of each cubicle. They were trophies of the hunt and mementoes of the youngster's ability. The boys sat quietly, cross-legged, on mats, their faces painted with pipe-clay in tribal-related designs and their hands clasped at their waists, as if in prayer. The fact that a white man was standing looking at them had not the slightest effect on their attitude of indifference and they seemed like little decorated dolls on show.

For them, this was a serious matter, a time of early preparation when they would learn patience and obedience, so that later they could stand with fortitude some of the more excruciating ceremonies for initiation into manhood.

This is a mental process—brain-washing is the modern term—and for nine months these young minds are steadily impressed with the facts that govern their tribal life. I doubt whether they have any light entertainment, whether singing, dancing, playing, or shouting. No games that other kids enjoy; no freedom of movement beyond their nightly exercise; nothing but the four walls of a small cubicle and the incessant voice of the mentor drilling ideas into their minds. There would be a feast and a big dance when they had completed this course, but for nine months, nothing else but tribal lore.

By this time the paddler had gone back outside. Together with the interpreter I left the lads and pushed on down the passage through a long fibre curtain and into a large room containing dancing masks, spears, and the paraphernalia of a primitive man's world.

We moved on again through another hanging curtain and into what was a store room, untidy with odds and ends lying around, such as bundles of food, firewood, and a sundry assortment of mats, ochres, and ceremonial wear.

Still moving, we pushed through a third curtain, a huge ceiling-to-floor sheet of woven matting, stained a brilliant red and wide enough to cover the whole of the last section of the house.

High above our heads swayed a massive figure of a whale made entirely from cane and suspended from the beams by fibre ropes. Cages and huge masks filled the walls. A big wooden bullroarer stood in a position of honour, surrounded by bundles of feathered lances of long bamboos. There were hunting spears and bows and arrows in profusion, with a collection of stone pineapple clubs stacked roughly alongside a long, cane box. Closely plaited, it was shaped, and looked, very much like a coffin.

64

Quite a lot of the objects were hard to distinguish, for they were packed so closely together, the majority made from woven cane which had been plaited into various shapes.

I had heard before of the weird rites and ceremonies of the Purari, many of them related to similar ceremonies of the Gulf and delta areas. I had spoken with the Government Anthropologist, F. E. Williams, and read his books and pamphlets on this area in which he had done a number of intensive studies, and I had spent quite a number of interesting hours with him, just listening to his accounts of ceremonial rites, and the behaviour and mysticism associated with many of these objects.

The Purari people were then a fertile field for the anthropologist. In the interior they had been comparatively untouched by mission or government influences, and the old customs and decorative rituals still held sway over the people. Such influences had evolved through generations, since the coming of humanity into these desolate regions. They had been affected by inter-tribal wars and other tribal cultures but had remained free from the outside pressures of civilization.

Here was a collection of objects which in today's hungry curio market would be worth many thousands of dollars. At that time, apart from museum research workers, there were not many people interested in them. There was a more sympathetic approach to primitive culture, and the dollar was not so almighty.

No strangers could have purchased these objects, for they would never have been allowed to leave the ravi. They were the religion and emblem of their ancestors, repositories of good and evil fortune; objects that commanded obeisance and obedience, untouchable to the majority and not to be observed by them.

It was conjectural to consider what impression Christian evangelism would have made upon the fetishism of these beliefs and there was no forewarning that, within a decade or so, most of it would be destroyed or taken away, through the effects of war and through the advance of missionary zeal.

Yet, to some degree, paganism still prevails in places, and the bullroarer is a far greater instrument of veneration than the church bell. I have seen the fanaticism of primitives roused by a medley of trumpets, drums, and bullroarers; I have seen women run screaming into the jungle rather than face retribution from a feathered and painted sorcerer, and have heard them singing in the darkness, across the slopes of a jungle valley, in gentle, lilting refrains that echoed from hill to hill as the sacred flutes piped their message into the night air.

65

So engrossed were we in what we saw in the ravi that neither of us heard the rush of feet but we certainly felt strong hands on us and saw the shouting, gesticulating crowd of men that surrounded us, all pushing and grasping, with anger and hostility in their voices. Grasped by about a dozen, I was lifted up and carried through the house to be dumped unceremoniously at the foot of the ladder outside. A few seconds later there was a whirl of arms and legs and the interpreter came sprawling beside me. Other hands picked us up and led us, firmly and forcibly, to our canoe tethered at the edge of the swamp.

A voice whispered in my ear, "You should not have gone in there. It is taravatu," a piece of wisdom that would have been handy a few minutes previously. Another voice, this time more urgent, said, "Get into your canoe and go," a point that was taken expeditiously and we scrambled into our craft, yelled to the paddler, and pushed off. On the mudbank the crowd were still stamping their feet, waving their fists, and yelling obscenities but I noticed that nobody seemed prepared to take a canoe and chase us.

We had come out of it with a couple of slight advantages. The ground had been soft and resilient, thanks to the mud. If they had only thought, they could have carried us another five yards and dumped us into the bubbling, stinking, festering swamp.

I lost my hat, my trousers belt had snapped, making things a bit uncomfortable and embarrassing, and the buttons had been ripped off my shirt. The interpreter had suffered the indignity of completely losing his pants and he was now clutching the torn remains in an effort to appear modest, and with a nonchalance as if being man-handled and losing your pants was a minor, daily experience. Only the paddler had escaped. He had seen the affair from afar and had scooted back to the canoe and was laughing so uproariously that he couldn't paddle.

It was the interpreter who got us back over the swamp. He threw the remains of his pants in the water, grabbed a paddle, and standing up with his singlet well above his waist, stroked like mad, accompanied from behind by the jeers and shrieks of the charcoal bedaubed old women who had tried so hard to entertain us.

We reached the other side and shot into the nearest shrubbery, pushing between mangrove roots into clouds of mosquitoes, caring for nothing. If there were any crocodiles under the scum they must have moved out of our way, for we soon got blocked among the tangled roots and were forced to get out, wade through the slime, clamber over roots, and manhandle the canoe into deeper water.

Five minutes later, and still well under cover, we paused for breath and in answer to my, "What the hell happened?" the paddler pointed to the interpreter's naked limbs and began another session of uncontrolled laughter.

As a buying expedition it was not successful but there had been moments of interest, and when I reported back to the mill, and Charles took stock of our appearances, he asked, "Did you go into that ravi?"

To my feeble nod he replied, "Christ, you're lucky. They're in the middle of a ceremonial session. I should have warned you against it," and went off to ponder over his depleted ration stocks.

We had been lucky. If we had accepted the invitation into the women's dubu our initiation would have been the hard way.

Two days later I was heading back to Kikori and the quiet, subdued, rural atmosphere of head-hunting and cannibalism. In future, my studies of esoteric ceremonials would be done in museums, for you can still go home with your pants on, and there are signs, "quiet, please," which is an excellent form of discipline.

journey into hope | 2

THE VARIOUS SCHOOLS of opinion regarding the native people's capacity to attain standards of political authority and business responsibility, at highly qualified, professional levels make an interesting study, not only of native capabilities and potentials, but of our own western attitudes towards a race of people who are, mainly, illiterate and primitive and of whom the most advanced echelon is not yet two generations removed from its old traditional modes of living and thinking.

The complexities of such human development are so many that they discount the arguments of that faction who maintain that a responsible government, run by their own people, is possible within a relatively short period.

The reiterated demands of the United Nations for Australia to set "target dates" for political maturity are unfortunate in that they detract from the main purpose of self-government, which means an acceptance of full responsibility, and obstruct the machinery geared towards ultimate independence.

Possibly scientific and academic reasoning can produce satisfactory answers to the problems, although these are, fundamentally, beyond the realm of academics, for the difficulties are ones of human nature, having a genetic basis—ingredients which cannot be measured by a yardstick or fitted into the framework of idealism.

It would be physically possible, but morally wrong, to hand over the reins of government to an intelligent section of the people in five years. The results would be calamitous, not so much in terms of the material waste and loss, which is replaceable, but in the psychological impact of responsibility being thrust into their hands; responsibility which they would be basically incapable of handling.

The problem goes far deeper than the attainment of literacy, accompanied by political and administrative training, for there is still a barrier of primitive relationships and thinking which affects the most advanced and intelligent sections. This will have to be overcome.

For example, I know one man who holds a very high position in the country. I know his background and that of his family for over a quarter of a century. I know the tremendous efforts he has made in improving himself, mostly without outside assistance, and I know his personal responsibilities and disabilities.

Yet I have often sat with him in his more private moments and have been surprised to hear him outline some of his own attitudes and come to conclusions that were based entirely upon primitive reasoning, solely because the rules governing his old traditional society have dictated the decisions.

They were in conflict with his adopted western mode of living, and against the tenets of his training, but their roots were in the generations of his own people and they had to be recognized.

This is not an isolated example; it applies generally. It is something that education and training have not yet eliminated, and it will continue until environment and circumstances force a divorce between the old ways of thinking and the new. When that occurs there will be positive progress towards political independence.

Who knows how long that will take? One, two, or even three generations, and then only by the most advanced section, for the mass may still be struggling, a hundred years from now.

It is something that the people themselves must do. It cannot be forced by an overlay of foreign political benevolence through the United Nations, the Department of External Territories, the House of Assembly, their own local government councils, or through selected individuals.

Yet the germ of independent political awareness is there and becomes manifest in numerous ways, sometimes crudely, sometimes by stealth, and on occasions, by open protest, but it can never fructify because of the anchor of traditionalism and the heavy, foreign political veneer that covers the Territory and all its peoples.

There are extreme measures that could be used to hasten the process, such as the complete segregation of the very young for upbringing under our own concepts, or a programme of outbreeding the present races through the introduction of a more virile and mentally progressive race, but these are contrary to the principles of humanitarianism.

The basic and most enlightening political field for studying indigenous awareness is the present form of the local government councils. The council is a crucible wherein the expressions of the ordinary people meet, with almost equal importance, the policies of central government, and the strength and weaknesses in the character of the native people are thrown into sharp relief.

One can witness the influences brought to bear in overriding their objections, although I have found, in travelling quite widely, that the general tenor of local government councils is one of acquiescence to authority, and at times it is one of supine consent.

Occasionally one finds the reverse, where the representatives are men of character and perseverance, who follow the wishes of their people, show initiative, and guide them into channels of social and economic productivity, even in matters which do not comply with the official viewpoint.

It is a rare phenomenon but it does occur, and as an example I would quote the work and development of a small, rather isolated council whose birth, in 1961, indicated no new or startling departure from standard procedures but which, in four years, had demonstrated its ability to govern by the people and for the people, and to pursue this course with a minimum of outside aid.

In fact, there were periods when it was discouraged, an attitude which ultimately accumulated and resulted in a withering away of its greatest effort.

The council concerned, the Siau Local Government Council of Aitape, in the West Sepik District, is a body in which I have been interested for years. I have watched its steady development from a small, almost insignificant unit into an organization of considerable economic substance.

A background review of its situation has considerable relevance.

Aitape is an oasis on a coastline that stretches monotonously from Wewak to Vanimo on the north-west mainland shoreline, and the settlement shows the only break in a panorama of long, drab stretches of forestland, swamps, scrub, and rivers, bordered by a narrow strip of grey-black sand.

Only the western deltas of Papua are less inspiring, for there is an immensity of forest and jungle covering the contours of the land which, to the tired eyes of an air traveller, is recorded only as an endless olive-drab carpet of vegetation, a scene which soon dims the eyes and dulls the senses.

There are scattered villages, sometimes hard to distinguish because they have taken the camouflage of their surroundings, and there are river mouths spewing brown, fan-shaped, semi-circles of mud into the blue ocean.

I have made this journey many times, in all types of aircraft, and

70

only once do I remember seeing any beauty in this land while flying, and that trip was made on one of the workhorses of the outback, a small, single-engined, light plane, piloted by a mission brother and under the ideal conditions of a perfect evening.

The sky and air were at their best, clear and pure, and the rays of the setting sun lit the countryside in intense, oblique contrasts of greens and blacks with the ramparts of the inland mountains standing high beneath mushroom spouts of billowing cumulus.

They were black and ugly looking and foretold heavy night rains, but they were tipped with orange borders against the blue sky and they enhanced rather than detracted from the glories of the evening.

We travelled peacefully, free from turbulence and flutter, low over the beachhead and jungle, watching the easy, almost weary, splash of the waves over the coral shallows as we swept with abandon down past shoreline villages whose inhabitants came out to wave.

This was the Sepik coast at its best, showing a softer, almost enticing aspect, contrary to its usual gloominess. To starboard rose the islands of Ali, Tumleo and Seleo, three sentinels in the channel which leads into Aitape. Beneath was the sea, a vast sheet of glass with the multi-colours of reefs showing through like intricately composed paintings, shimmering pictures in green jade, coral pink and aquamarine.

We rose to skirt the headland behind the town, circled, and touched down just as the first lights appeared in the white smudges of houses.

I had first come here in 1964 and had been captured by the innate spirit of comradeship and hospitality in all sections of its community, and by the old-time air of contentment which radiated through the settlement.

The place has a legacy of eighty years of civilization, from the time when the Germans first came to this coast and set up their trading and administrative bodies.

Across the mouth of the creek which splits the town still stand some old concrete piles which once carried an early bridge, and up on the steep hill behind is a weatherworn, concrete blockhouse said to have been used in the early days as a gaol.

There are still people who speak fluent German; aged and feeble now, they are always eager to hear words of their first European tongue. One old patriarch had been an orderly of the first German senior official, and on Ali Island I met a matronly woman who had been a housemaid with a German family. Both spoke the language fluently, the woman in a soft, Bavarian dialect without a trace of faltering.

The people hold strong memories of those German days, many of which have become traditional for the younger ones, and one of the most impressive evenings I have ever spent was on the sands of Ali, with the missionary and the villagers grouped around under a full moon as two old men described the first coming of the Germans as their fathers and grandfathers had told it to them.

There was fear, they said, as the white strangers stepped from their boat, and panic swept the people as the visitors walked slowly up the beach towards warriors who were standing ready with bows and arrows.

"Some of the women ran into the sea with their children, and the men moved behind the rocks ready to fight," one ancient said. "The Germans had guns, which we knew nothing about, and they fired them up into the trees above our warriors' heads."

He pointed to a white pile of rocks near by and then up to the overhanging trees.

"That is where it happened," he said, "but there was no fight because our leaders saw that these people were men like ourselves and they wanted to hear them speak, so our men laid down their bows and arrows, and the Germans laid down their guns, and then they came forward and put their hands on our warriors' shoulders in friendliness.

"My father was a little boy then and he was taken into the sea by his mother."

Memories of the Germans live strongly among these people, and they speak of them as their friends, and of their relations with them as times of happiness and work. A stranger gets the impression that some of the older folk still feel that they are German subjects, so closely do they speak of them.

One is apt to forget that these people have experienced three kinds of foreign masters, the Germans, the Australians, and the Japanese, and over the years they have become shrewd judges of national character.

They speak little in comparing one nation against another for perhaps there have been too many contrasts and they are tired of adjusting themselves to a changing pattern of government.

Behind the house where I was then staying, a long, damp tunnel bored its way into the hill and twisted off into a maze of passages, too dark to follow and too wet for comfort.

This had been made by the Japanese as a shelter against Allied air raids, for there had been an army headquarters on the site where the house now stood, naturally hidden in a small depression below the hill and sheltered by timber.

More than once I tried to get the reactions of the older men to those wartime days when the Japanese were masters but they would never respond, and more often than not, would give me an expressionless look and turn away.

The stories of the old men took my mind back to two moss-covered tombs standing on a sparse patch of foreshore grass some miles eastwards of Aitape, where I had been less than a month before.

Here, long ago, a Catholic father and a lay brother had been landed with supplies as an advance party to build a hut and lay the foundations of peace and good fellowship among tribal people who had never before seen white men.

Three months later the vessel returned and when those aboard went ashore they found neither hut nor welcome. But they did discover two neatly piled heaps of human bones near the spot where the two missionaries had landed.

These incidents show that different groups of native peoples had quite different reactions to the same subject — the coming of the white man; what one group regarded with wonderment, the other treated as a gastronomical delight! Yet to us, both instances of the white man's coming would appear to be similar — part of western man's invasion.

The Siau Local Government Council now controls the whole of the Aitape sub-district which, administratively, comes under the district headquarters at Vanimo.

In its eight years of existence it has passed through the usual kinds of council troubles, lack of understanding and responsibility; lack of response from the people who are invariably suspicious of new ideas; lack of contented staff; and the inevitable lack of money to finance its projects.

Council income initially was not large, and by 1963, two years after its foundation, its income had only reached $5,000.

By 1967, four years later, the figure was $34,000 which is a very good indication that the suspicions and reluctance of the people under its care had been overcome and that the work of the council had not only met with their approval but had received their full support.

One of its outstanding characteristics was the adoption of a progressive economic outlook from the very start, and it oriented this attitude strictly towards the people's land and its development.

"Land" is one of the most serious matters that concern native people, for it is their inheritance, all they have as their security, a fundamental part of their lives and significant in history and traditional beliefs. In these days of exploitation and development, it is their only marketable commodity, surpassing their incomes from cash crops and other sources.

This principle is not restricted to the Aitape people but applies throughout the whole of the country, with the strains and stresses of land problems increasing and magnifying to such an extent that future land troubles are bound to arise. These could easily become the germs of internal revolt. Indeed the elements of such troubles have already become apparent and they are very likely to intensify to an extreme degree.

The fact that the Aitape people pinpointed "land" as the target of their main activities may not be so remarkable in view of the importance that this occupies in native society, but the manner in which they promptly dealt with this revealed a capacity for leadership and a determination which few other councils have shown.

One of the basic motives prompting such determination is the manner in which all native land purchases are made, and have been made, since white settlement began. They are all channelled through the Administration only, by a system which has not only become antique but which exhibits colonialism in a most blatant form.

All land required for government or outside purposes, in industry, agriculture, business, et cetera, can only be purchased, on a lease basis, through Administration officials.

There is no direct contact between native owner and the prospective purchaser, as in bargaining, except for any private preliminary agreement between the two parties but which has no legal standing and is not binding.

A purchaser of land must apply for the section he requires to the Administration, through the local district headquarters, and pay an application fee. This is forwarded to the central government which directs that district officials make local inquiries from the owner or owners, as to their willingness to sell, not to the applicant but to the government, and the price to be paid, on agreement, again by the government.

If this is completed, satisfactory to Administration interests, the land is officially gazetted for tender, usually with a set price which bears no relation to the purchase price. Ultimately the applicants go before a Land Board which decides to whom it will allot the land and the conditions of the lease, which may extend for periods up to ninety-nine years.

These conditions include annual rental, improvements, periods for reassessment, and any other special reservations that may apply, and the price agreed upon is then paid to the Treasury, for the land is now government owned and irrevocably lost to the original owner.

The official attitude has always been that the Administration is the protector of native land rights and that the circumstances and future needs of the people must be preserved, and by implication, that any possible fraudulent actions by an outside purchaser will thus be prevented.

The system was probably very sound during the early years of settlement and until 1945, when a postwar Administration came into being, but the passing years have shown an increasing number of weaknesses and inequalities, many of which border upon unfairness to native land owners.

The present system is completely out of date and has never been re-adapted to suit the advancement of the native people and their growing awareness that their own land contains potential wealth.

Nor does it comply with their own desires that their land should be developed in conjunction with themselves and without the inevitable and complete loss of title which now prevails.

The whole official attitude towards land is a presumption upon the character of the native people, for while the Administration recognizes that individuals may invest and operate businesses, may accept graduated responsibilities in government, may hold professional appointments, may represent their people overseas, may become actively engaged in transportation, trading, and agriculture, and may advance to any position for which they prove capable, the government's position on land affairs shows plainly that it regards the native people as incompetent to handle this type of business.

In fact, by its complete sovereignty over all land—and this includes freehold grants, which have now become a misnomer—the government's attitude can only be described as one claiming infallibility, for it controls all the media of land operations and will listen to no argument.

Proposals and demands have come from many sources for a readjustment of land methods to ensure greater and wider participation by native owners and a fairer result in land dealings, but the Administration has always staunchly rejected them.

The loss of their land in perpetuity by native owners is a national tragedy which should never be allowed, for once the land is purchased, at Administration values, it remains for ever the property of the government and will never, under any circumstances except those of a revolution, be returned to its original owners.

I once led a deputation of Hanuabadan elders to the Director of Lands with a request that certain blocks near Government House, purchased some time during the 1880s, and still not being utilized by anybody, be returned to the people who were willing to pay the Administration its own, current valuation.

Hanuabada had long been an urbanized village community of Port Moresby and it had constant land-pressure problems which must increase because of the expansionist pressure of the capital, but these village elders were told in no uncertain terms that they would never get this land back.

It is still there, scrubby and derelict on the side of the hills, unused and unwanted these last eighty years.

The position now is that the Administration is the biggest real estate operator in the country, and it is untouchable. No wonder it won't review its own system.

Many prominent people have called for direct leasing between native owner and prospective purchaser, without government handling, on a limited-lease basis.

Others have called for share-farming arrangements, both parties working together, with the land to be returned to its original owner at the end of a fixed period, complete with any improvements which may have been made.

It is maintained that in the case of disputes a land conciliation committee of all interested parties, with the government as a neutral participant, could be formed as a court of appeal.

These pleas have got nowhere; the Administration gets the land and it holds on to it. It is raw feudalism under the cloak of progressive civilization.

The native people are fully aware of this and they appreciate the fact that without financial capital they are unable to improve their land to the extent that foreign wealth can. This realization has resulted in an attitude, becoming very prevalent, that they will retain their land and develop it on a mutually co-operative basis within their own means.

I have heard leaders exhorting their people not to sell any more of their land to the Administration, no matter what the reason may be, and there are distinct signs of a revulsion among native people to the further disposal of any land.

The result is that the Administration is now having to employ the methods of forcible resumption, which it is prepared to do, but which could prove as dangerous as handling soupy gelignite.

This long dissertation on land matters is necessary as it highlights the attitude of the Siau council, and their people — their determination to exploit their own land in their own way. Their ideas stem from German times when settlers were given blocks of land and assistance in becoming established. The descendants of these settlers, today, are independent farmers of considerable standing, and still owners of the titles to their soil.

From Aitape, a vehicular road runs directly inland for a distance of about twenty-two miles. It penetrates an area of richly fertile country, rain-forest land, undulating, well-watered, and according to figures given me, with an available area of 50,000 acres.

If this whole area were scientifically developed it would prove one of the most productive in the whole Sepik complex and could, in agriculture alone, provide wealth and economic stability for a district which has always been on the economic breadline.

It is settled by scattered native populations living at subsistence level, perhaps a fortunate people, for their food problems are few as the fertility of the soil provides plentiful and bountiful harvests.

It was in this area, and at the end of the road, that the council created its settlement area, with individual families taking up blocks of from twenty to twenty-five acres each, to build their homes, make gardens, market their produce, and it was hoped, eventually to plant areas of cash crops of cocoa or coconuts.

It was a far-reaching scheme, for the council had envisaged that in time the community would have its own school, medical-aid post, stores, transportation, and would, in all respects, become a productive, almost self-sufficient group.

Expansion from agriculture to light village industries was also planned as, close by, the Catholic Mission had commenced instruction in the manufacture of cane furniture and "blinds," the latter a wall-building material made on home-made looms from local bamboos and canes.

The scheme was not confined to the local people only but embraced the people of the mountain areas beyond, folk of the Lumi sub-district who were interested in moving down to the lowlands and taking up farming land because of the limitations and poverty of their own mountain soils.

The Lumi local government council backed the scheme and encouraged its members to give it their support, many of the families moving down and taking up blocks.

The breadth of reasoning, overall, shows that the Aitape people, at any rate, had a clear recognition that labour, land, and productivity are the keys to prosperity and that, combined, they created a form of independence by helping the farmer and married folk and instituted land investment and an assurance of future security— the essentials for any community that wishes to advance.

It possessed an element of social stability as well, and one that is becoming vitally necessary in these days of expanding education and the attractions of urban living, for it kept the people together and prevented the drift of the younger generation to the towns in search of elusive work and wealth.

The realization of this struck me very deeply for I had seen the decimation of the Papuan delta people, brought about mainly through the departure of the better-educated young people, with the resultant break-up of family life, and hastened by the lack of local economic alternatives.

Here, in Aitape, was the framework of a project which could be a power in avoiding such degeneration and degradation.

On my visit in 1965, the settlers had been on the land for about four months, time enough to show if the scheme would work.

On each side of the road were new and neatly built houses, lined correctly and squarely, each surrounded by its garden of vegetables with the boundaries of the area being pushed back into the forest.

Large patches of fallen timber covered by a tangle of brown, withered jungle growth were awaiting the torch.

Some newly acquired allotments showed areas of blackened, burnt earth where clearing was still under way and there were gangs of men heaving on long poles against the lopped, fallen trunks of trees while others with axes were clearing the lighter timber, stacking it for firewood or for burning.

The sapling framework of houses dotted the country, and the rich, brown earth had been turned, cleaned, and planted with root crops and grains. On every hand were the pioneering signs of people labouring to make their small world a productive one.

They brought me samples of their vegetables: corn, cabbage, sweet potatoes, carrots, leeks, watermelons and pumpkins, which were all strong and of good colour, far larger than similar vegetables I had seen on the coast. Here was good, virgin bush, mulched by annual accumulations of leaves, organic matter, and detritus, fed by seasonal rains, and building itself up into a little Eden awaiting the hand of Man to help it to bear.

Already these people had reached the stage of becoming almost self-sufficient in their food needs and they were producing extra crops to take to the Aitape market for sale or exchange. They were a happy folk, proud of their achievements, vigorous and hopeful, with an attitude far different from the stultified, lethargic one so often found in village communities.

In the psychological field alone, the scheme had raised their morale, given to each a feeling of self-reliance, created a community spirit, and had brought the incentive to work and prosper to this sector of the submerged nine-tenths.

78

These are achievements which are too often overlooked, particularly in schemes which are born with a flourish of trumpets and later languish because the spirit of incentive has been allowed to wither. They are factors which emerge early in all native endeavours and require the careful development that one gives to newly-formed plants.

Accompanying me was Kevin Goodwin, a resident of Aitape for the past fourteen years, a trained carpenter and building master, and a man who has long studied the interests of the native people and has encouraged them to use their abilities for their own social and economic advantage.

He was then acting as a council adviser in the practical fields of constructional work and the training of its members, and had been behind this settlement project from the beginning, spending as much time as he could out in the bush helping the people.

Kevin has a very pragmatic approach to most things, and works not from theory but from the results of his own practical experience which have come from a hard and difficult life.

"This is one of the finest things these people have ever done," he told me. "It is a development of their own life, a method by which they can work and go on through mutual co-operation. It is, in fact, the most logical step upwards from village life, the next stage from subsistence agriculture, geared to their own land and using it in a way they can understand and appreciate."

On our arrival a number of men had run out and greeted me as "Master Mark."

At first I thought it was their own interpretation of "Mac," but Kevin explained that they thought I was a government surveyor who had come to measure their land and put marks around the boundaries.

Much to their disappointment I had to tell them that I was a private individual with no qualifications or authorization to survey their land.

"They have been waiting for a surveyor in this district for nine years now," Kevin said. "Year by year they have been promised that their lands will be surveyed and properly marked but nobody comes to do it although they are still hopeful."

This was the first indication of upset I had seen, for by the size and scope of the venture, it had appeared that, behind it all, there had been some professional direction and assistance.

When I inquired about this I was told that it was purely a council enterprise.

"They have received no assistance and certainly no encourage-

79

ment from the central government. What you see here is the work of the council, the people, and some unofficial aid and interest from other people who realize the value of the project and have a personal desire to help the people.

"They could certainly do with some help but they have been left alone to work out their own ideas."

Later, I spoke to many Europeans in the district and they all replied enthusiastically, praising the council and the people, although some of them had reservations.

"It may not last," a plantation man told me. "It is too isolated and without a reserve of resources, and it depends mainly upon the morale of the people and how long the council can remain an effective force towards its development. The idea is excellent but it needs official support. Unfortunately, these people are on their own, and the spirit of enterprise can weaken very quickly."

They proved prophetic words, for a few years later, I again visited the area and found that what this man had said was becoming true.

There had been other developments and they had almost meant the death-knell to this small, individual community.

One did not have to look far to discover the chief cause which had brought depression to the settlers.

It came, in a typically oblique and confused pattern of official behaviour, through the report of a survey carried out some years previously by the C.S.I.R.O. scientists and filed with the Administration in Port Moresby.

The findings of such reports are seldom made public unless some special development or an investigation demands it, but it is an accepted fact that routine surveys, particularly on the subjects of land and agriculture, continue from year to year and that these influence future government policies in relation to national and district development.

The facts that this survey revealed and reported upon would, one would naturally suppose, have been a sufficient guideline for further development that might eventuate and would have been most applicable, and of tremendous assistance, to the council and the people in their scheme of rural settlement.

In retrospect it poses the question, why was this report not used to give direction and assistance to the people?

There was no answer to this until 1968 when, through its own actions, the Administration, while not giving a direct reply, gave a more substantial explanation, and a more truthful one, by purchasing 400 acres of land in the same area as the original settlement for the

80

purpose of establishing an indigenous land settlement scheme, each individual settler having from forty to fifty acres of ground.

The area concerned is across a river, some distance away from the first group, although in the same locality, and to emphasize its decision to proceed with land settlement, the Administration also announced that an agricultural extension station would be built to help the new settlers.

Why a new settlement should be established when one existed and was working well, and why the enlarged assistance of an agricultural station for the original settlers was not proposed, are conundrums which are never answered.

The interpretation that seemed to be general at the time was that because the land of the original settlers did not belong to the government, no aid could be forthcoming, and the natural conclusion was that unless you sold your land, you got no help.

On the other hand, to treat the government as an outsider in land development, no matter how competent and enthusiastic you might be, would be no way of fostering native economic advancement.

So the original settlers languish, a survey of their land still unfulfilled, their efforts and hopes overshadowed by government sponsored opposition next door, and the spirit of enterprise slowly dying from inertia.

Now the government owns a block. The landowners have been paid and have forfeited all future rights to reclaim it.

Departmental soil survey officers are pursuing their investigations, surveyors are putting in the pegs, public works men will come and erect new buildings, roads and a paraphernalia of equipment will be provided, and there will be flying visits from Vanimo, by chartered aircraft, to pursue a proposition which the people had already established by their own efforts years before.

Only the mission up the road has the slightest interest in the old settlers, for cane industrial work has been added to their present activities, and this is bringing in small sums of money for their work.

The long-term plans for a school, an aid post and stores, for transport and other amenities and services have faded, and in a year or so the settlement will degenerate into just another village group.

Just what part the council now plays in its land settlement scheme it is hard to say, and whether, like the people, it has given up hope because of neglect and lack of support is debatable, for its activities have widened and its wealth increased, and money is being directed into schools, health centres, road building, and the airstrip, which are expensive items to handle even with a percentage of official, financial aid.

On roads, transport and the Tadji airstrip, an old, wartime base, the council spends 53% of its budget, but the roads being pushed through virgin bush country do little to encourage further land development and are costly to maintain.

The land areas bounding them are native owned and the people have little inclination to sell this land to the Administration under the present system, while the Administration, in turn, shrinks from developing land that it cannot buy outright.

By what methods, other than by political idealism, the people are to be advanced to the responsibilities of self-government while the land development situation is in such a chaotic mess, it is hard to imagine.

Direct private approaches to native landowners, for mutual development, are not permissible, and if they are attempted, have no legal backing. The native peoples' own schemes for development are cold-shouldered. The Administration wants to own the land, and this the people are becoming more hesitant to accept.

The council is still leading in agricultural development but in a different manner.

The emphasis is now on coconut planting and the copra-making industry, for here is a product that will return revenue and has none of the uncertainties of a co-operative farming venture while copra itself is an income earner for official bodies.

More land is being utilized by the people in extending their plantings, and the council is giving aid in the transportation of products by road and sea through subsidies, one of which applies to freight costs on locally-built vessels.

This latter is a new industry, not council inspired, and is being directed and encouraged by a Catholic priest, Father Dom, out in the islands of Ali, Seleo, and Tumleo.

These islands people have generations of craftsmanship in canoe-building and they make sea-going vessels with a central hull and two large outriggers which are fine vessels, easy and safe for coastal journeys.

Lately, with the addition of outboard motors, they have been used extensively in freighting stores and passengers between the mainland and the islands.

I went with Father Dom to the foreshore of Tumleo and walked among a small forest of twisted, stunted trees. Their trunk and branch formations appeared like badly affected rheumatic joints, gnarled and twisted out of natural uniformity.

He bent forward and traced a finger round one of the joints. "This is what these people use for the framework of their canoe hulls," he explained, "and this one would be an ideal piece for the section joining the keel to the bow. I have watched them searching among these trees for hours, looking for the one suitable piece. They are artisans in their work and they have very practised and selective eyesight. They use only the best."

Father Dom had been trained as a shipwright and he quickly recognized this natural talent among the people. Soon, he began training selected men in modern boat building and now a small local industry has become firmly established.

Just before my arrival they had built a twenty-six foot workboat, to carry three tons of freight and powered by an eighteen-horse-power diesel engine. The council was then operating it and there was talk of building bigger vessels.

From the islands to the inland again, this time to Pes village and mission station, a few miles from the first settlement, where Father Leo, from Rome—a vivacious and active man, short, solidly built, and gifted with an amazing number of talents and skills—is showing what can be done by one man, through good supervision and encouragement, in teaching the young men of the area the accomplishments of small industries.

He met us as we stepped from the jeep and immediately took us over to his cane furniture factory and explained the whole process of the work, from the selection of certain types of cane, cut and sold by the villagers, to the cleaning, moulding, fastening, binding, and completion of the article.

There were lounge chairs, planters' types, stools, small side-tables and patterns for a wide variety of household furniture.

From there to his new house, a two-storeyed, cement, brick, and timber building complete with all modern fittings which he and some of his assistants are constructing themselves.

And then, for a few hundred feet, to where the foundations and framework of a new church stand, barely half-completed but growing, day by day, under his expert hands.

One hour at the station and you realized his amazing list of accomplishments, most of which I was able to jot down.

He is a builder, carpenter, stonemason, steel constructional worker, mechanic, radio operator and maintenance man, plumber, electrician, drainage expert, school supervisor and teacher, medical assistant, vocational training instructor, and printer.

These are apart from his duties as a priest in charge of a remote station with a scattered population, for whatever job comes up, he tackles, and his many years of experience in the bush have exercised to the full his self-reliance, energy, and determination.

83

It is Father Leo who started the blind-making industry in one bush shed with a few home-made handlooms. This industry has now spread to the surrounding villages, where there are many looms, and the older men and women toil patiently to produce these plaited sheets of prepared cane to be used down in Aitape, and elsewhere, in the construction of cool, cheap houses, storerooms, and other buildings.

"I am trying to get some Japanese-type looms, more suitable for this purpose," Father Leo said. "There is a wide range of equipment suitable for cottage industries, and when this industry is established firmly, then we may be able to start another."

He shook hands with us and turned away, for a very worried man stood near-by with a truck whose engine wouldn't start, and the last we saw of Father Leo was a glimpse of him with his head under the bonnet as he gesticulated to the driver to press the button.

"The Aitape people are different," a District Commissioner once told me, and this is well impressed upon the visitor who goes to see just what these local people can do.

They are a friendly crowd and welcome those who show interest in their work.

At Yakoi, close to Aitape township, are the descendants of the original settlers placed on land blocks by the German Administration.

They were originally from Ali Island, and now each family has its own block fully planted with coconuts and cocoa. During the year 1967-68, the group of 280 men, women, and children produced 91,700 lbs of copra from their trees and quite a healthy harvest of cocoa beans.

A lot of the men are working at other jobs around the district; their families maintain their small plantations, and there are some individuals who have established stores, a bakery, and other small businesses on their blocks.

There is, in the Yakoi community, the distinct attitude of independence, seen in their work and general deportment. They are individual producers with incomes sufficient to maintain good living conditions and they are not dependent upon outside aid.

Many of them send money over to their relations still living on Ali Island, and much of this money is being invested in European-type houses complete with all services.

The island's people also have plans to encourage visitors and tourists to come over and stay with them. They are planning modern bungalows and a swimming pool, for Ali is one of the lovely spots along this coast, with wide, sandy beaches and good fishing and

A West Papuan of the Indonesian Police Force who fled to the refugee camp just beyond the West Irian border

swimming, ideal for those who wish to get away for a few days and enjoy quietness, sunshine, and salt water.

The people of Ali are another facet of the population of these Sepik areas. They show an admixture of foreign blood in their finer textured skins, lighter than the Sepiks, their thin ankles and wrists, and the slim build of a lot of their women.

They are proud of their heritage and clannish in their love of family and homeland, for no matter how far the Ali people roam, they will always, sometime, return to their island.

There are relationships along this Aitape coast with the people of West Irian, those of Papuan stock who have, over the centuries, traded and intermarried.

One can find relics and heirlooms in some of their houses which have passed between the two peoples long ago, all carrying messages of inter-family and inter-tribal responsibilities.

In these days of turmoil on the border there are many whose sympathies lie with the West Irian refugees who are crossing into this country, for to many Aitape families there are ties of long standing and memories of friendships that existed long before a boundary line was pencilled on the map.

Geography has placed many disabilities upon this Aitape enclave, for it is remote, hemmed in by the ocean, on a beachfront that has no harbour or safe anchorage in bad weather. A lot of the littoral belt is swampy, and only the fringes of development touch the area, for there are no roads leading to it.

Yet the strongest characteristic of the people is that spirit of self-help, a continual striving to launch out for themselves, and a determination to share in the benefits that others, in more favourable localities, enjoy already.

Their greatest asset is their land, for it is plentiful and bountiful and they know that within it lies wealth in food, in agriculture, and in minerals, for there are seepages of oil still flowing, and quite recently, copper and gold have been located and are now under investigation.

One must respect them for wanting to use their resources for their own benefit, preferring to work out their own destiny through hard, manual labour rather than hand their heritage passively into foreign hands for ever.

They have been tempered in the fires of too many administrations, of the Germans, the Japanese, and the Australians, and they know the weaknesses and strength of each. Perhaps there has formed an ingrained belief or confidence in themselves, with or without outside help, which the passing decades have served to make stronger.

The unfinished bush house in which the Author 'lived' during his stay in the West Irian Refugee Camp

Yako Refugee Camp at Vanimo was established after Indonesian raids on the border camps near Wutung Village

It is this element of self-reliance that is steadily growing among all the native people, a natural phenomenon that, when it has developed sufficiently, may well form the basis of national unity.

The people and their land are the two principal sources of national growth and identity.

If they co-operate in their mutual development, each complementing the other, a nation will be formed, but separate them, or play one against the other, and there will be disgust, chaos, and possibly revolt.

3 | journey into genesis

DR BILL CHAWNER reached into a drawer and passed me a .38 revolver.

"Have a bang in the air with this if they worry you," he counselled, "and if they get too close, pepper their backsides with buckshot, but don't hurt anybody."

He failed to explain how I was going to get them to turn round. Did I make circular motions with my finger, or wait until they got tired of looking at my face?

And what about his, "don't hurt anybody"? I'm not a hotshot. I have got myself a feed by sneaking up on ducks, and I could probably hit the side of a barn, but I would think twice before letting drive at a pair of black buttocks because I think it might do something more than hurt. And if you were looking at them from the stern view, they'd be running away, which would be happier for everybody concerned.

This was part of the kindly advice handed out to me just prior to my leaving for the Upper Strickland River country (in 1937) where my job would be to prepare advance camps for field parties following on later.

What the local inhabitants would be like was anybody's guess. Uncontrolled territory was on one bank of the river, with semi-controlled on the other, and you sorted yourself out when you got there.

I subsequently found that the gentlemen of the uncontrolled side were far more friendly than those of the semi-controlled, not that there was much difference between them, but it meant that you just couldn't judge by the official nomenclature.

I had been hauled into the drawing office at Daru by old John Muir, the chief geologist, a fine Scotsman with a world-wide

87

reputation, and a man with a fatherly disposition towards all who worked under him.

Unknowingly this was the last time we were to meet. He left for Australia the following day and dropped dead outside Sydney's G.P.O.

Bill Chawner spread a map over the table and idly fingered a pencil.

"When you reach Kiunga," he instructed, pointing to a dot five hundred miles up the Fly River, "stay with Brownie for a day or so and pick up whatever extra gear you need. He'll make all arrangements regarding ration supplies and communications, although your main schedule will be with the coast here. Call at least once a day. We don't want to send out search teams looking for you."

His pencil wandered off into a blank space. "You'll only get as far as here on the Elevala. Too much shallow water and rocks up farther. From here you'll walk across to the Strickland, and when you find a camp-site, get it fixed up on high ground somewhere over here." This time the pencil wandered aimlessly over nothing.

Geoff Barrow, another senior geologist, who had recently arrived from Venezuela, and was to be in charge of this new area, added a couple of words, "I'll be around your way in about four months. I'll meet you there."

Bill was in charge of the Upper Fly, Ok-Tedi, and Palmer Rivers area; Geoff had the Strickland and the limestone country northwards.

This last was a new area, a practically virgin part of the earth that had been seen by few foreigners. Government patrols and a few individual prospecting groups had been there infrequently, though most gave it a wide berth.

The most recent party had been that of Jack Hides and Dave Lyall, a disastrous trip which had resulted in a hard struggle back to the coast. Dave died at Daru and Jack, in Australia some months later.

Karius and Champion had been that way in 1927, ten years before, but there was little to mark their passage except spidery lines on maps and a few notations.

Many had come out feet first, as I was later to do, some to die like Lyall and Hides, others to be ill for months, or like Karius, to carry the ill-effects of their experiences for the rest of their lives.

Yet, in places, it is a beautiful country and the river is inspiring, but it is sullenly hostile with an unfriendliness that one can feel. It is big and strong in every way, and you feel Man's insignificance as you stand in the middle of it.

So the revolver was packed away in the patrol box to be fired only twice the whole time I was away. The first occasion was that on which I put a bullet through a death adder, and the second, when I almost put one through my own head.

This was one time when I realized that a moment's carelessness with a firearm can be more dangerous than a lifetime with primitive, savage people, and if I had succeeded in blowing my head off and tumbling into the river, eighty feet below, the police corporal standing beside me might have had a hard job proving that he hadn't shot me.

We had both been handling the weapon and my hand had fired the trigger.

We looked at each other with a deep understanding as I handed him the revolver and told him to take it away. After that episode I never touched it again.

On a small chartered launch we pulled out of Daru at dawn and headed across the passage towards the mainland and Parama Passage in a morning swell that rolled our gunwales over and under.

There were two of us, apart from the skipper-owner, Dick Ely and myself, and there had been a party the night before at Lennie Luff's place, so the choppy waters were not conducive to comfort.

Dick lay inert on a bunk. I shook him, and he opened one eye, scowled, moaned, muttered something nasty, and went back to sleep.

I was surprised to see him so much the worse for wear, as he was a tough, hard-living chap, had served five years in the Foreign Legion, had battled round the world, and reckoned he had never said "No" to a drink, a conviction which he had stoutly maintained at the party, and he was suffering for it.

He was a man with a cherubic countenance and two bright blue eyes, rather florid but benign, an appearance which had caused me to mistake him for a missionary when we first met, a natural error seeing that he was drinking lemonade at the time and was on one of his periodic bouts of reform.

He corrected very smartly my impression of him and my idea of his taste in drinks and from then on we had become firm friends. We had both travelled, had a lot in common, and knew our way around under most circumstances.

By the time we reached Madiri, Dick had recovered sufficiently to put on a clean shirt, had shaved, and tidied up, so we went in to enjoy one of Mrs Cowling's hearty breakfasts of roast beef, Yorkshire pudding, dumplings, cabbage, and potatoes for the first meal of the day!

Madiri was a recognized stopping place that nobody passed by if Mrs Cowling was in residence.

"You must have something to eat," became a rule of the river, for she was a great believer in home cooking and eating, just as they did in England way back in 1800 or something.

Queen of the River in every sense, she was a grand old lady with strict Victorian traditions, including antimacassars on the chairs and bric-a-brac of porcelain on the shelves. It was a real 19th century atmosphere mixed with accents from the Yorkshire dells, and Queen Victoria never had it so good as guests did at Madiri.

Above Madiri we entered the swamp country of the Suki people who live in trees, and the Tugeri tribesmen, a fearless and warlike crowd who wander at will.

The Suki tribe is an odd group, and it would be hard to imagine more grotesque people. They are a shy folk and keep out of sight, but if you are fortunate, you may see a clustered house in the branches of a tree and catch the smell of wood smoke rising from their bark canoes as they paddle among the reeds and high grasses.

On hard, dry land they are helpless and appear as animated images of Donald Duck. They are stumpy and almost gnome-like, with heads and torsos like normal individuals, and deep, heavy chests, remarkably developed biceps and long arms.

But below the waist they are deformed, with legs, knees, ankles and feet shapeless and flabby, twisted and distorted in the effort to bear their heavy bodies. Their walk is a wobble — painful to watch — and one can sense their embarrassment and helplessness. Swamp mud and water are their natural elements and some have never stepped on hard earth; consequently they grow with bones misshapen, muscles like jelly, and sinews that have little control.

In the water they can move like newts, skipping with a speed that is amazing, and scuttling up the vine-made ladders of their tree-homes like simians.

One question that was always in my mind was how parents kept their kids from falling out of the trees into the water, a domestic problem that must have a lot of the mothers worried.

The Tugeris are another kind. Killers by instinct and partial to raiding small, unsuspecting communities, they murder haphazardly and leave their victims as mutilated carcasses among the smouldering remains of their houses.

Calculating and cruel, their home is anywhere on the border, and they raid indiscriminately.

A week before we had sailed, there had come a report to the District headquarters in Daru of a raid on a small village, and there was considerable commotion going on, for nobody could tell if the raiders lived on Papuan territory, or as it was then, on Dutch New Guinean soil.

Now the Indonesians have the country, but that wouldn't make much difference to the Tugeris. Killing is their game and the odds are invariably in their favour.

The estuary of the Fly River is fifty miles wide, a mighty piece of ocean with waters that can be as turbulent as any in the deep sea. The flow from this river turns tide patterns into crazy crossroads, with currents going all ways, bringing high tide at one spot and low water half a mile away.

During the war I paid a brief visit here on army duties and found wreckage and flotsam from the Coral Sea battle which had been carried hundreds of miles and had gathered among the swamps and mangroves of the Fly delta.

Gus O'Donnell, then acting as District Officer, showed me what had been collected at Daru: lifeboats, the wreckage of planes, and thousands of woven, cane shell-containers, with enough timber, according to Gus, to rebuild the whole of Daru.

Most of it came from the American aircraft carrier, the U.S.S. *Lexington*, which I had witnessed being commissioned in New Jersey Naval Yard many years before. I had seen her debut and now I was witnessing the residue of her destruction, and much of it was still lying scattered along the southern flanks of Papua.

Only a comparatively short distance up the river, it narrows to a bottleneck and you crawl steadily through a channel, close under the overhanging trees of the left bank. Then it broadens out and you enter the main flow, following the bends and twists of two low banks of timber and jungle like twin strips of chlorophyll.

They are broken by vivid red splashes from the drapery of D'Albertis creeper festooning the trees, and in the occasional, searching beams of sunlight you may see the flashing plumes of a Bird-of-Paradise and hear its raucous screams.

Blue-crested Goura pigeons sit in pairs and gaze sombrely down at you, finches and sunbirds wheel and buzz by, and hawks circle high above, planing in the air currents without a flutter of their wings until they see a possible victim down below, and then they drop like stones.

There are egrets and cranes in the river, and sometimes a flock of ducks whistling overhead on their way to the feeding grounds.

One evening we came to the border of Dutch New Guinea and dropped anchor for the night below the village of Domangi.

As the chain rattled out, a canoe crept out from the trees and headed our way. It contained one paddler and one passenger and when they reached the ship's side, out clambered a tall, cadaverous looking European, bearded and bony.

Dick, whose eyes and mouth were wide open, exclaimed, "Good God! It's Robinson Crusoe," and our visitor certainly looked a replica of that celebrated gentleman.

He appeared to be in his forties and wore a tattered and decayed shirt, a loin-cloth which might have been any colour, sandals, and a hat made from wallaby hide, the latter perched on his head like a cone, and he carried a real, old-time muzzle-loading shotgun, a museum piece if ever there was one.

From the canoe he heaved out two old-time, four-gallon kerosene tins, some rawhide straps sewn with sinews, some animal skins, bundles of food wrapped in sago leaves, and a couple of smoked pigs' legs. It looked as if he had come to stay.

Laurie, the skipper, went forward to greet him, shook hands, and received something muttered through the beard of our guest as he squatted on the deck.

It turned out that he knew no English, or Pidgin, or Motu, and apart from headshakes and smiles, our acquaintanceship stood still until Dick happened to curse in German and the stranger took notice. From then on our conversation took on a relay of staccato words and phrases from German, Dutch, and French, accompanied by signs.

In retrospect it is easy to write of him now, but that evening, and almost all night, we struggled to understand a white man, highly educated and able, who had transformed himself into a primitive bushman, and the transformation had been so complete that he no longer recognized his European identity or language, nor the sympathetic understanding of his fellow Europeans.

He showed an almost ingrained, elemental fear as he stuttered the words and then paused, grasping ideas that he was trying hard to recall, for he had the look of the hunted, and the manner of one who shuns his fellow-men.

He was a Dutchman, who, after graduation, had chosen medical missionary work in Dutch New Guinea and on his arrival in Merauke, had been sent away inside the country to one of the most primitive of areas, among people who were nomads and viewed all strangers as enemies.

Left to his own devices he had settled with one of the tribes, learned the language, and lived as they did. Over the years he had ceased being a European, and soon he had chosen not to think as a European.

The mission had tried to keep in contact with him by sending parcels of food and drugs through jungle trails from village to village to the borders of the unknown country where he had settled. Some never reached him, and of those which did, he kept what he immediately required and gave the rest away.

Powder for his gun he secured through Malay bird shooters, bartering for it as the natives did.

There was plenty of gold in the Digoel River, he said, only two days' walk from where we were anchored. The bushmen brought it to him but he had no use for it and turned it away.

He trapped animals for their skins and food and made his packs and straps from their hides. He enthusiastically showed us how he operated his gun, but he was out of powder and the demonstration was by signs. He said that he could use bows and arrows as well as the natives and normally did so.

We offered him food but this he refused, as he also did cigarettes and tobacco, smoking his own dried tobacco leaf which he took from his pack, lighting it from a firestick his paddler brought aboard.

The smell of coffee cooking in the galley broke down a bit of his restraint. He greedily drank two cups and shyly accepted a tin of grounds from our larder which he stowed away among his goods.

Why had he come to us?

He explained that a big sickness was sweeping the country and many of his people had died. Those who had survived were afraid and had fled, many of them going across the river into the swamps on the Papuan side. Now he was trying to collect them all and he had broken down the barrier of isolation because he wanted us to take him upriver to where the big swamps began.

He had seen that we were not Dutch people. He was afraid of them, because if they found him they would send him back to the coast and thence to Europe.

There was an evil spirit in the country and the people had asked him to aid them. Would we take him along?

Later we discovered that an influenza epidemic was sweeping the country and that there had been many deaths. The villagers were frightened and there was wailing and keening in every community.

For three days and three nights he had sat beside the river. Our arrival had solved his problem, for he would not venture too close to riverside settlements in a native canoe. That night he curled up on the forward deck alongside his companion, having refused the offer of a bunk and the invitation of blankets and a mosquito net.

We sailed again at dawn while he and his companion sat silently watching the river banks. He accepted only coffee and took a morsel of his pig meat to eat. By noon we had come within sight of the big Dutch outpost of Asoeur which sits on a high red bank of clay, and the boom of drums told that we had been sighted.

Our visitor rose, signalled us to stop, and with his gear, clambered back into the dug-out. Without a word they paddled away, heading for the high swamp reeds on the Papuan side. Before they disappeared there was a wave of a hand, and then they were gone, leaving us wondering what manner of a human being this was who could throw culture and civilization into the discard and take up the life of a roaming savage.

He had not told us his name. Perhaps he had forgotten it, or didn't think it worth mentioning, although for one night and half a day he had touched civilization and comfort and had temporarily enjoyed some understanding from people of his own race.

I wondered how it had affected him. Would he think of it and yearn for more in the dark, lonely hours, and would he try to venture again into the circle of civilization? Or would he wait for his inevitable end as a body propped up on a bark platform for the birds and the insects to eat, and the wind and the rain and the sun to bleach until his bones were fit to be thrown into a bushman's charnel house?

Did the bushmen think he was really one of them or did they wonder still why he had come among them, just as we were wondering as we went on our way onwards towards Kiunga?

The people waved and shouted as we passed the village of Asoeur. There was one stout white man, in white shirt and shorts, who also waved, and pointed across to the swamps where the canoe had gone, but we sailed on and were soon back once more in Papuan waters.

The Fly, for almost 500 miles, is a languid river affected only by heavy rains in the mountains and the seasonal monsoon storms. It is comparatively flat country until D'Albertis Junction is reached, and here the foothill country starts, and the Fly breaks in two, the right-hand stream remaining the main one and the left-hand branch becoming the Alice.

A long way north, in the Hindenburg Ranges, on the Papua and New Guinea border, a multitude of limestone streams pour down from the gorge country forming the Wok Feneng, which in turn cuts into low sandstone hills covered in forest, to join with the Palmer from the Emu and Blucher Ranges in the north-east. On it goes through other hills and rapids and sandstone bars, fed by the Elevala which later leads into the Fly.

We turned to starboard away from the Alice and within a few

hours reached Kiunga, our main base camp, our destination, and a very welcome change after being cooped up in a small launch for seven days.

Kiunga was then a series of small thatched huts sitting on a steep slope which slid straight down to the river. There was one small jetty, and on the other bank, almost opposite, was the airstrip, a reclaimed area of low-lying ground, inclined to flooding and sogginess, and a long way below bowling green standards.

It was out of commission, for the remains of a tri-motor Junkers occupied the centre, wedged tightly in the soft soil with its tail high in the air.

The Ward-Williams expedition had used this camp as its headquarters and flying base on a gold and mineral quest which had failed. They had left, and the old camp had been renovated as our main base on the river.

One constant visitor was Dick Archbold, a millionaire, Standard Oil beneficiary and zoologist, whose parties operated out of Western Papua in his flying boat, the "Guba," and later in a U.S. Navy Catalina, the first of its kind to be seen in the country.

With the Archbold Expedition and our own oil-exploration companies working at the same time, considerable confusion existed in the minds of some people as to Archbold's relationship with the other companies.

"All I know about oil is that it is refined into gas and used to drive airplanes and automobiles," he was known to have remarked to one worried gentleman who had some oil scrip. He was a brilliant man but his health was sadly affected by sleeping sickness, contracted in Africa.

Bill Brown was general factotum at Kiunga. He was one of those chaps you meet in the bush who does everything, fixes everything, knows everything and becomes indispensable to the place.

As unofficial lord mayor he was listened to by all and sundry, including his wild and frisky neighbours who lived somewhere over the hill at the back of the camp.

These, in their jubilant moments, would muster in force, come screaming down the hillside, gallop through the camp waving axes and spears, let out their national war-cry, and turn and shoot back up the hill.

Brownie was used to this and regarded it as just a burst of youthful spirits but it happened so often, and so unexpectedly, that to a newcomer it brought moments of apprehension. I was never sure when they might fail to turn the corner. At the speed they travelled, and with a little more enthusiasm, they could have made quite a mess of the buildings and the blokes inside.

It never happened but it would have been an interesting experience for anybody on the sidelines.

Despite its mini-stature—four long houses and a couple of huts— Kiunga was always marked on maps in letters equal in size to that of London. They had plenty of blank space for this, and once, in Australia, when I pointed out the place to an interested listener, he asked, "What's the food like at the hotel?" and just couldn't believe that it wasn't used as a week-end tourist resort.

For us it was the big town; important as our supply base; our radio city with Brownie's voice coming in clearly on out-station sets; and a place to gather before we returned to the coast.

My thirty carriers, mostly Goaribaries, and eight armed police under a corporal, were waiting for me, so after three days of odd-jobbing, we loaded the canoes and with George Christie, from Kiunga, as guide, set off up-river again, the Elevala staging camp being our destination by nightfall.

This was the farthest point we could reach by water. From there on, we walked. The Elevala camp was a very makeshift place. Two tent-flies to camp under and a thatched shed for cargo. It was comparatively new, built mainly for the Strickland River teams, and only George Christie had used it in his walkabouts from Kiunga when searching for tracks that led north-east in the direction that we would eventually have to go.

George's job was to see us to the big river, to help us settle into camp, and then to return to Kiunga. The prospect of a ten days' hike there and back didn't daunt him in the least. He was a good bushman and a fast walker with plenty of stamina, and like a lot of others I've known, invariably travelled on one good meal at night, with cups of tea and dry biscuits during rests throughout the day.

George's maxim was that you needed food when resting at the end of the day to build your body up for the next day's work, and once you started to walk, you kept on walking until your feet, legs, and body began to cry out for a spell. It was tough for the first few days until you became broken in, but it worked after that when your body and lungs had hardened to the extra exertion.

On that first night the latticed beds at Kiunga seemed like feather mattresses when compared with the draughty canvas sleeves we had been using. It began raining after sundown, became colder, and whichever way one turned, the draught seemed always to be coming the wrong way.

Sometime in the middle of the night our beauty sleep was shattered by a rifle shot. George and I were out of that tent like whippets. I noticed that he had his revolver. Mine was still snugly warm in the patrol box.

A disturbed police guard came over, and pointing to the tethered canoes, stuttered something about someone crawling out of the river and climbing into a canoe. He had shot it and it had splashed back into the water. He swore that it was a bushman.

The rain had gone and it was bright moonlight so the police, plus some frightened carriers, cut some long sticks and began prodding the bottom of the muddy river.

George wasn't impressed by the bushman story. "Just a bloody crocodile," he declared and we went back to our slumbers.

With the police and carriers fed early next morning, we sent them ahead to cut a track through what appeared to be some solid country. George and I sat in camp checking the loading of stores.

"No need for us to go out for an hour or two," George assured me. "Let them have their head. They know the way. Besides, this will be a short cut. Save ourselves miles of walking."

Getting on towards mid-morning we decided to follow up the line and see how they were going. George was sure that the track had been cut almost to the old pad by this time. "They might even be through by now," he said, "Then it will be straight ahead and in camp by four this afternoon. Nice and dry with plenty of good water."

The sounds of slashing and chopping with a medley of yells came from ahead. They were still at it, and were still going when a halt was called for the midday meal. On they went in the afternoon until three o'clock when George, rather worried, went to take personal command.

Half-an-hour later there was a yell of triumph. They were through. I pushed through the smiling police and sweating carriers and found George standing at the side of a river a few hundred yards upstream from our old campsite. We had completed the circle and George had been right; it was nice and dry, with plenty of water. It was the same camp, the same water!

We hacked our way along the riverbank just as a canoe, paddled by two old women, passed quietly up the opposite side. Amidships, and sprawling awkwardly across it, was the dripping body of a man. The police hailed them but they increased their speed and passed on without answering. It could have been the something the policeman shot the previous night. We had no way of finding out.

For the first time we put double guards on that night but nothing happened and when morning came we made an early start, taking the old pad to get clear of the hoodoo that made our carriers run in a circle.

Short cuts were out, and despite the witty jocularity of the police, George was not amused.

We reached the western bank of the Strickland in five days and nights and by some strange freak of nature, they were days and nights of perfect weather.

We saw no bushmen until the second day out and the first we knew of them was a rustling in the grass alongside of the track, the sounds of padding feet, and some sharp, staccato calls. When we stopped for the usual pannikin of tea they came creeping out of the undergrowth, one by one, whistling by in-drawing the air between their teeth, and smiling as they collected in a bunch and watched what we were doing.

The cook was preparing a fire and, as he struck the first match, the bushmen yelled and bolted, Back they came after a while, keeping a scared eye on the cook, who struck another match, and away they went again.

This could have gone on indefinitely had not one bold gentleman stood his ground, watching the match flare and die out. We beckoned him over, showed him how to strike a match, put the box and a match in his hand, and let him go. He was a brave man for he stuck it out and actually made fire all by himself.

Soon, we were surrounded. They all wanted matches to make fire. We handed them a couple of boxes and they were as happy as kids. It was the biggest act of local development since somebody stuck a stick in the ground and it sprouted.

Later, for a test, I got our cook and a bushman together in camp on fire making. The cook was still striking matches to a bunch of sticks when the bushman's fire flared up. He had gathered the dry pith from paperbark trees and lit it from a looped length of lawyer cane against a piece of dry tinder, holding them with his big toe, and won easily.

The result of this was rather ridiculous for our carriers and police began a craze of making fire with lawyer cane, and the bushmen worried us silly for matches. We could have got rid of the annual production of any match factory with ease and finally had to keep permanent camp fires burning as we were running out of matches.

Less amusing were some of the incidents which followed during the next couple of days.

On the third day we had apparently entered different tribal land, for the country seemed deserted until we reached a patch of high grass during the morning. Then came the rustling and padding feet, which didn't worry us, but soon there came a barrage of rocks, yells, and peeping heads. After the first surprise our carriers began throwing the rocks back. We had to stop this and push ahead as fast as we could to get clear of the grasslands, otherwise it might have turned into something more lethal.

Once clear of the grass, things quietened down, and we moved without incident until after lunch-break when we came to a wide sago swamp. The leading police and carriers had taken a few steps into the muddy water when they screamed and fell. One held up his foot. There was a bamboo stake embedded in it and blood was turning the water a rusty brown. We hauled them out. Three carriers and two policemen were the sufferers, and their wounds were bleeding freely. Posting a semi-circle of armed police around us we dressed their wounds. Two of them had very nasty, jagged wounds and were litter patients. There was another hold-up while these were roughly made and the carriers' loads were redistributed.

George and I went ahead with our heavy-soled jungle boots, dragging the mud as we waded through, with the party in line following our steps'

Carrying the injured men we pushed on, hoping that soon a tree trunk, a creek, or some almost unobservable mark would be the boundary of these peoples' land.

We had gone for about a mile when, turning a corner, we came up against three armed men standing fair in the middle of the track. They had hunting spears, bows and arrows, and they looked as though they would certainly not move out of our way.

The police corporal, his rifle at the ready, moved forward and beckoned them aside. They ignored him. George moved up. They glowered at him and one half-raised his spear. Almost instinctively, George struck him right across the stomach and he went down. The corporal swung his rifle and caught another in the ribs, and the third man stepped backwards, tripped over a bush, and also went down.

With the police and ourselves standing over the men we ushered the carriers through. They needed no urging, but went for it and we had a bit of a job keeping up as we watched and hoped that no more obstreperous friends of the fallen were hiding in the bush. .

Ten minutes later we crossed a small creek, the boundary we had been expecting, and we hurried forward to make camp well beyond it, wondering if the mob who owned this piece of ground were also antagonistic.

"It's the pig," the police corporal told us that night, and we remembered that a small party had been through this way and had killed a bush pig which ran out in front of them. As everything that kicks, bites, and scratches in this land belongs to the nomads, the party's unwitting act of killing a lone pig had brought trouble upon us, the next people to come through.

The next morning dawned cold and when I opened my eyes I couldn't see the tent opening. As I got it into focus I found myself staring straight at a tall bushman standing silently at the end of the bunk. Another was standing at the end of George's bunk. Both had seven-foot black palm spears, and the pungent, sickening stench from their unwashed and pig-greased bodies filled the tent. My trusty .38 revolver was lying beneath my pillow. George's was on his pack on the ground beside him. He was still asleep.

The routine, of course, was to whip the gun out so quickly that they didn't have a chance to raise their spears. It happens in movie pictures but it didn't happen here, for my intruder and I just remained staring at each other, and neither of us moved.

From behind our tent the police guard was talking, and chattering was coming from the carrier lines, yet here were the people we were guarding against, standing right inside our tent. Nobody had heard or seen them and they could have been there all night for all we knew.

Watching his hand loosely holding the spear, I muttered between tight lips, "George, George, open your eyes."

He opened his eyes and was out of his bunk like a moon rocket but not fast enough to catch the bushmen. They turned and fled, straight through the carrier lines and into some bordering shrubbery. For one moment they stopped, turned and looked at us, then sped away like swift shadows.

The carriers were in an uproar and the police began shouting. We called the guard together and gave them a rough ten minutes. Double guards to stop intruders and they just walk in. If they had been our pals of the previous day the whole camp could have been wiped out, and that was the only consoling thought; that they were of another people, and were just inquisitive.

This was the fourth day, the track was comparatively easy, and after the night's experience we were moving on a strict routine that allowed no carrier to fall behind, nor permitted the line to straggle out. We wanted no lame ducks at the tail-end being taken away suddenly.

Out of a patch of thick timber we came to the foot of a small, steep knoll about 200 feet high. It was cleared of all undergrowth,

bare, with short grassy patches and rocks making it appear barren. On top was a large communal house with its occupiers outside busily engaged in their everyday tasks and quite unaware of our closeness.

The track led straight up towards it and we began to climb, reaching about half way, when there was a shout and the whole crowd rushed inside, barricading the small entrance hole at the end.

As we came abreast of it we could hear the cries and whimpers of women and children inside. A dog began howling and pigs grunting. From slits in the main walls arrow tips appeared and they covered every step that we took as we tramped past within a few feet of the house. We must have made lovely targets but we kept moving, without talking and without slackening pace until we went down on the other side and entered the cover of the timber again, and just kept going.

That evening we camped in a beautiful shady patch of light timber, an ideal spot for any picnic, with a creek of fresh cold water, and a few yards away a miniature waterfall draining into a perfectly round basin of hollowed rock.

We both stripped off and ran to the bank, preparing to jump in, when a policeman waved us back and pointed down. The surface of the rock pool water was broken by crocodile snouts, small, freshwater ones, but they still had their teeth.

We compromised. Selecting the low branch of a young sapling, and with a policeman standing on each side, rifles at the ready, we each swung out like Tarzan, dipping in and out as the branch bent. It wasn't much of a bath but we did get wet and remained physically complete.

The next afternoon we were very close to the river when about fifteen bushmen appeared. We halted as they raised their hands. Then they came towards us, laughing and yodelling, with hands outstretched to feel our clothes, stroke our boots, and make signs that they would carry the loads and the injured man who was still in the litter.

We followed them through the forest and across creeks until the thick blanket of jungle suddenly broke and there was a small clearing, the skeleton of a camp site with white-ant eaten timbers.

The bushmen began explaining by signs the coming of two men, one tall and one lying down. They had come from the river and they had left again, going down the river. Then we understood. This was one of Jack Hide's and Dave Lyall's camps, a memento of their last journey that led to the coast, six hundred miles away, and death.

Aerial view of Vanimo, West Sepik area

These logs from the Goldore Timber Lease at Vanimo are destined for Japan

We turned away and climbed a small, steady rise. Below us the Strickland River flowed swiftly, splashing against a rock-face eighty feet below us. Ahead there was a glorious view of mountains, gorges, and the river covered by a medley of forest and jungle.

This was good enough. This was to be the camp, and we set about preparing for the night, clearing a patch of timber and undergrowth, cutting poles, and setting up temporary quarters. Our new-found friends helped willingly and when the camp was ready, they just disappeared.

Just to remind us that we were merely puny humans around the place, a cyclonic storm came howling out of the mountains as the sun set, with the wind and rain whipping through our hastily built shelters, the lightning flashing, and the rumble of thunder shaking the earth.

There was no hope of cooking food, so we just crouched under our tent-flies and waited until it had passed. An hour later there was a bright moon and a sky full of stars and a camp of wet, weary, hungry and miserable men fit only to lie in wet blankets and sleep.

"We just made it in time," said George, as he blew out the hurricane lamp. We had. Just. But George still had to walk back over that track, and I thought that with any more tempests like the one which had greeted us, he'd be web-footed when he reached Kiunga.

George Christie stayed on the following day, not to rest but to work, for there was so much to do to make the camp habitable. It was only a clearing in the forest, the widest section being no more than a hundred feet, with no set shape, but stretching raggedly wherever the forest allowed. The lighter timber had been felled and the heavier remained.

On one side there was a perpendicular drop of eighty feet into the river and as you walked the narrow track, bordering the edge of this drop, that led between the huts, the police, and carriers' lines, the thought was always present that if an earth tremor or an exceptionally high flood came along, half of the camp would collapse.

The condition of the ground dictated the camp's position. It was just one of those abnormal humps in the land that seemed quite prevalent, a narrow upthrust which, in this case, the river had half washed away. Behind the camp was swamp, and on the other side of the river the land was barely three feet above water level and was always flooded when storms swept out of the north.

One could extend downhill on each side along the river bank if one was prepared to accept the possibility of floods and the constant threat of being swept away through the erratic nature of the river. I have seen whole sections of jungle sailing downstream and quite often there was, for days, a continuous procession of trees jammed tightly together; jostling, groaning, and breaking under the force of the floodwaters.

One can best describe the Strickland as a river which roars out of the mountains. Only in the backwaters has it a gentle flow. In the main channel it gallops out like a pack of wild horses, destructive, turbulent and crazy with its own strength.

It starts as small streams draining the folds of the Victor Emanuel Ranges to the west, the Central Range and McNicoll Mountains to the north and east, in very rough and broken country. It squeezes between the Blucher and Muller Ranges in a series of deep, precipitous gorges, and syphons itself through the Devil's Race—an aptly christened section—jumps several rapids, and then decides to act like a river.

From the rugged limestone country it drops sharply and with such a volume of water that the country below is swamped and flattened by detritus, so the river twists and turns and cuts its way through wherever it feels inclined. Only when it reaches hard rock-bottom mother country is it confined to a course, and over the centuries these sections have been eaten away into ravines, gorges, and nasty, narrow rock bars.

If its isolation can be overcome, there is tremendous potential in this land, the greatest of which would be hydro-electric power.

From our position high up on the river bank the view was an artist's dream. On clear days, and some of them were perfectly clear, for the atmosphere had been washed and cleaned of all impurities, one could look down a long stretch of foaming river and across to a wonderful panorama of the lower limestone mass leading steadily higher into the folds of the Muller and Blucher Ranges, and still further again to where the high peaks of the Victor Emanuel Mountains stood out like blue-grey etchings on a royal blue sky. The colours were so intense that all the ripples and folds in the land contrasted; the lights and the darks, the blues, greens, and greys, and the stark white blotches of barren limestone.

Most magnificent of all, and directly in front of the steps of my hut, looking straight up the river towards the rapids, was one inspiring, lonely mountain peak whose height must have been over 12,000 feet.

From about 1,000 feet below its peak a huge scar hung for almost one third of its height and each evening the setting sun would light this up like a long, shimmering silver spear. It glowed and glistened

103

far above the whole country as if a giant were holding a flaming sword. It became a perpetual riddle. Was it a waterfall, or a massive outcrop of white rock, or was it a huge seam of mineralization, of gold or of silver, for it changed from one to the other as the angle of the sun's rays shifted.

Too far away to determine even through binoculars, it became an object of fascination for the whole camp, with police and carriers gathered together to watch the sun's rays shifting across the mountain and trying to guess its origin and substance.

Once I pointed it out to a bushman who had come in with some food. It was at its best, glowing and pulsating, for it was one of our perfect evenings.

He looked at it and rapidly turned away, muttering a few words to himself, and walked behind one of the huts. Nothing that we could do would induce him to look at it again and we could obtain no idea of what this fiery sign in the sky meant to him.

For all its roughness and caprice it was a very beautiful country and retained this quality from the first flush of dawn, through the heat of day to the cool of evening. On the nights when the moon was full and the sky free from storms and loaded with thousands of glittering stars, it became soft, alluring, and very tempting, bringing an urge to go out and walk among its shadows and curving slopes; to ignore the harshness of rocks and tracks, the tired and torn feet, the cramped muscles and weary, exhausted bodies for those who responded to its enticements.

There was beauty and music everywhere; from the thousands of birds, the flowers and creepers in the forest, the steady rhythm of the river, the sharp contrasts of colours, and the enormous clouds of butterflies that would periodically descend on the camp, make a brief inspection of everything we had and then flutter off, over the jungle.

At night the cicadas took command, and this was not music but a strident, imperious throbbing that rose to a crescendo in an ear-piercing shriek. It battered the eardrums, set one's teeth on edge and alerted one's mind for that inevitable moment when the final shriek would stop instantly, and there would be nothing but complete silence for about one minute; then would begin the faint, steady throbbings of another wave. And so it went on, hour after hour, all through the night, a love call that was music to a cicada and hell to everything else, for the power and strength of this volume of noise from millions of small insects silenced the most raucous of night birds, and the incessant, brain-piercing din made normal conversation impossible.

104

They served one good purpose, for they told us when bushmen were hanging around the camp. At night I would stand with the police guard in the clearing and we would listen to the cicadas. At times their call would turn ragged and stop, not as a whole but piecemeal, and the policeman would point into the darkness and say, "Bushmen," and we knew that they were coming round, singly and silently, to squat for hours and watch the lights and movement of the camp.

Curiosity seemed to have impelled them, for they never disturbed us. We had our doubts, for the memory of the three strangers on the track was very vivid, and though we called to them at times they never responded. On moonlight nights one could sometimes pick out a silhouette or a black shape moving between the trees.

Once a policeman shone his torch into the forest. There was a scatter in the undergrowth, and silence, and as the torch went out, the thud of a stone in the camp. It paid to leave them alone.

Rations always remained a problem, for we could never build a sufficient reserve to ensure that the camp could live satisfactorily over a long period if we should be completely isolated. For the first few weeks we lived on what we had carried over from the Fly River, and portage, by human carriers, is never a humane, economic, or socially satisfactory method. Mathematically it doesn't work out. The more food you need, the more carriers you must have, and with more carriers you need more food to feed them, and from that point it starts enlarging and you never get to a basis where it becomes a simple, routine operation.

Except for those few we had met on our arrival, the bushmen had given us a wide berth, and for three weeks we were entirely on our own. They were probably watching but that didn't affect us.

Then unexpectedly one morning a bunch of about twenty came along, squatted down on the perimeter of the camp, and began a low chanting and whistling.

They held up pieces of meat and bunches of wild yams, so we beckoned them in, and they filed up to where the police and carriers were standing. Each man had his full accoutrement of weapons, and in their shy, nervous state, it would have taken only a small incident for them to have started using them.

Right at the start, for instance, one of our carriers reached out to touch the necklace of dog's teeth worn by one of our visitors. This was a definite breach of local etiquette, and the wild man, who was a very tall, brawny chap, stepped back, scowled, and began fixing his arrow guards. We pounced pretty sharply, pushing our carriers right back and marking a line on the ground over which they were told not to pass. We ignored the visitors and they stood somewhat uncertain of what was going on but knew that they were not involved.

Then, outside the police guard tent, I drew a large rectangle on the ground and had it framed with stones. Into this, and with the aid of the corporal, we induced our visitors to lay down their weapons and, for good measure and a panoply of authority, we posted a fully armed policeman to stand guard.

These few minutes were well spent for it became an accepted unwritten law that visitors should lay down their weapons on entering camp, and that none of our people should touch them, and this rule was never broken.

We never had trouble with the bushmen within the camp when they came as visitors, even when, on one occasion, no less than fourteen separate groups arrived, some of them undoubtedly hereditary enemies, for they were breathing fire and brimstone at each other all the time, from a safe distance of course, for their weapons were in the ring and the bonds of confidence remained.

One paramount characteristic of the bushmen was that they were perfectly behaved gentlemen when they came in peace. They never entered camp without stopping at the boundary, calling, and seeking permission. They never abused our hospitality by stealing, although they looked at everything in the place, including a pot of boiling stew in the kitchen one day. They were courteous and smiling and willingly tried to give explanations to our questions when they understood them. Once, when we were building a new hut, they came in and voluntarily thatched it for us and refused food or pay in return.

One chap indicated that he would like a tin of meat, so I gave it him. He tore the label off the tin, stuck it round his forehead and threw the unopened tin of meat into the bush. Understandably they wouldn't eat our food, even when they saw the police and carriers eating. It could have been poisoned for all they knew.

Their most practical value to us was as food suppliers, a service which, after we had secured their confidence, they maintained very regularly.

This meant the start of trading, an activity which, so far, they had had no experience of. Therefore they had to rely upon our own values. The corporal and I put our heads together and evolved a scale of exchange from a box of matches or a razor blade up to a full-sized steel axe.

Envious of our possession of steel tools, they all strove to obtain knives, tomahawks, and axes, and once they understood the rates of bartering, our food supplies took on a sharp upward curve, with everything from wild yams to huge bush porkers being brought in almost daily.

Most impressive one day was the arrival in camp of two sturdy men, each with half a carcase of pig drawn over his head and shoulders like a helmet, with the bodies of the carriers running in a mass of intestines, blood, and shreds of meat. They must have caught it on the way in, sawn it in half and stuffed it over their heads, for the carcase was still warm, and blood was flowing freely. Being covered in leeches and flies, as usual, it was quite a messy object to handle.

Shooting by the camp personnel was forbidden. We could not go beyond the camp boundaries except in large parties. To do so singly would have been to invite a clubbing or spearing, and we could not go shooting indiscriminately around the country. The dear little porker which the previous team had killed had given us enough headaches, so what a couple of full size bush sows would have brought upon us was frightening to imagine. We just couldn't afford to bring home that kind of bacon.

We found freshwater turtles breeding in the gravelly river banks, and their eggs helped out on the menu.

The carriers, all Goaribaries, spent Sunday, their rest day, working like Trojans felling trees in the near-by bush and cutting out the grubs and bees' honey nests inside. For the amount of food this supplied it was a very low paying job, but that was the way they wanted to spend their rest day.

The big fat wood grubs were quite good, dropped on a piece of hot iron and roasted until they resembled pork crackling, with a nutty taste, but there were never sufficient for a hearty meal.

There were sleek, long tree lizards inside the bush, a tasty and attractive morsel for any Goaribari, but they were not game to go in after them. There were other fast, sleek things inside and one armed stranger meeting another armed stranger is not likely to stop and ask questions.

Our worst pests were the leeches. They were there in millions, ranging from tiny things like threads of cotton up to fat, thick, ugly creatures as big as one's finger, all searching for blood to gorge on, silently creeping over you, filling themselves up and dropping off. They were dangerous, too, for they crawled into bunks and over sleepers, and if they were disturbed while feeding, the resultant sores could fester and become serious wounds.

Death adders were prevalent, lying on tracks and around the camp after heavy rain. By good fortune nobody was ever bitten, although many of the reptiles were killed, and many more seen.

Treatment for a bite from this snake would have been a razor slash, Condy's crystals, and a lot of hope. We had no other means.

Among the bushmen it was noticeable that elephantiasis was prevalent, many having it to an extreme degree, with ugly, swollen legs. Hernia, too, was common, probably attributable to their mode of dress, a pubic nut tied tightly by a fibre cord round their waists.

No women ever came our way. Once, purely by chance, while out walking on the uncontrolled side, a few of us stumbled upon a group of women busily making sago. We had heard the noise from ahead and had taken precautions by moving forward slowly, and it was well we did so for, from the top of a small rise, we could see the women working below in a swamp, while a bodyguard of ten fully armed warriors encircled them. They weren't taking any chances. Neither were we, so we crept backwards and went another way.

Now civilization has moved over the border into this uncontrolled sector with the establishment of a government patrol post at Nomad, on that river, a few miles north of the Rentoul River. Recent news is that there are a hundred children awaiting a school, and in 1968 an electoral team went round seeking names for the common roll. Such are the anomalies of modern democracy.

It seems inconceivable that in this land, which is barren socially, economically, and culturally, a government should endeavour to introduce democratic parliamentary principles before there is any economic justification.

From official reports of the area, the first duty of any government officer is to catch his man, and waving census forms or electoral cards wouldn't do much to help. They can run too fast.

And just to remind us that old times and old ways linger, the patrol officer stated that some of the bashful constituents stopped long enough to throw stones at the patrol.

They must be getting civilized. When we were there they threw stones while they were running, and we weren't preaching any gospel of political benevolence.

Some miles below our camp-site was the confluence of the Rentoul and Strickland Rivers. The Rentoul is quite a large, fast stream, coming directly out of the mountain barrier. Just how many miles below us the junction was I actually never knew as I only passed it once, while lying flat on a raft which was being swirled around in the currents of rapids.

On the Rentoul stood the village of Iungazim, the last settled village and the farthest inland of any on the Strickland. It may still be there for all I know, but the name has remained in my memory because of a curious story that one of my policemen told to me one night in camp.

This policeman hailed from the Middle Strickland River, from one of the lower, settled villages. He had been in the police force for quite a time and had served on many long patrols.

His own dialect, while similar in many ways to that of the people around us, was not the same, but he could, with patience, and the adequate use of his hands, lips, and eyebrows, make himself understood to the locals, an art which was to our mutual advantage.

We had been invaded by bushmen that day for some unknown reason. They crowded in and remained, leaving only during the evening. I had had a field day trying to pick up some of their words, a difficult task because one never knew if the answer was general or specific. For example, a tree may be but one of many kinds and their word could have meant "tree" or some particular type of tree. One had to chance that the word they gave was used generally.

That afternoon I had led one bushman to the river bank, and pointing down to a newly made dug-out canoe, asked him his word for it. "Montoro," he replied and repeated it several times. I checked with others and the reply was the same.

Now the *Montoro* during those years had been a regular Burns Philp vessel on the Australia-New Guinea run and was widely known. I doubted if its fame had reached the upper reaches of the uncontrolled areas, yet it seemed too great a coincidence that the word for a ship in their language should be the same as the name of an Australian vessel.

I checked with the police corporal and was surprised to hear that we had this Strickland River policeman in our camp, so he was brought along. The policeman told me that down at the village of Iungazim there lived a native who came from Hanuadada, near Port Moresby, and he had been there for many years. Originally, according to this story, he had been a crew member of the government vessel *Elevala* which had become stuck on a mudbank in the Elevala River for several months, long ago, and this man had deserted, gone bush, and had eventually finished up at Iungazim where he married and settled down.

The bushmen's term "montoro" for a canoe was, according to this policeman, the result of the Port Moresby man telling these people about the wonders of ships and describing the real *Montoro* to them.

Counting back I found that this happened twenty-four years

before we arrived. It was possible that this man was still alive. I asked the policeman to spread the word among his local friends to see if the man could be found, but nothing ever came of our inquiries.

The story fitted very neatly and the wandering seaman was a possible explanation. He must have been a brave man to leave the security of the ship to wander at large in bushman's country and finish up settling down with them. It was a little like Daniel in the lion's den, and he must have had as much faith as Daniel.

Work was interrupted one day by the arrival from Kiunga of a patrol officer, Jim Beharell, who brought his own police and carriers and a message for me to assist the patrol in getting up-river to a suitable site from whence an investigation could be made of one of the mountain peaks.

Jim told me that this mountain had been spotted from an aircraft some time before and his instructions had been only to go and find it, to pinpoint it on a map, and to return.

I took him to the edge of the river and showed him the skyline. "Its all yours, Jim. Take your pick." There were mountain peaks by the dozen.

He hadn't realized that we had so many mountains to spare. We could have supplied them wholesale. Beharell wasn't very happy at the prospect. He'd been walking for five days, now there were another fourteen in front of him, and five more to get back to Kiunga, a total of twenty-four days hiking around a country which few knew much about, trying to find a mountain once seen from the air.

For me it meant a few days' break from camp routine and we promptly began to get the canoes ready and loaded with provisions, equipment, and bedding.

From the moment we cast off next day the job became steady forced labour: pulling and tugging from root to root along the bank. The current was fierce, swirling under the banks and making it hard to get a good grip, but the paddlers held on, urging our canoes forward foot by foot.

My own canoe just missed capsizing right at the start, for as we rounded a small point below the camp, a crocodile, asleep beside it, awoke and shot off underneath us, lifting the canoe so that it heeled over, and shook with vibrations as we rattled across the bones of its back.

All day we kept this up, pulling, straining, and paddling fiercely when we were forced to leave the banks and take to a patch of water.

Once a paddler pointed across to the other bank and said, "oala,"

110

and I looked to the mudbank where a full size crocodile was sleeping.

"It is a white one," I told him, and he replied "Yes," quite normally, as though white crocodiles were common.

They are not common but there have been a number of instances where white crocodiles have been caught and photographed. They do exist and when you find a little one then there must be a mamma and papa somewhere, though whether they are of any value, I do not know.

Keith Tetley at Kikori has a photograph of two young crocodiles, one white, the other black, and Captain Alan Gran, a government trawler master, has a photograph of one he caught many years ago, a sixteen-foot white crocodile being hauled aboard while his ship was in the delta.

They rate with the five-toed pig that's known to inhabit this country, one of which I once saw at Kikori when the Resident Magistrate had it fenced in on the station. It tore the fence to pieces and escaped.

We camped one night and got under way again early the next morning, for this was to be a tough day of battling against a river that was becoming more and more violent.

We could hear the roar of rapids and noticed the increased current as we rounded the first bend. The white foaming crests and spume seemed enormous from our small vessel but the paddlers were unconcerned and pulled steadily along the bank right into a wall of foam so that we were all looking up at the rapids as they curled and fell.

We held our position for a brief moment and then, at a yell from the leader, all hands grabbed paddles and stroked madly, keeping the head of the canoe directly in line upstream. The water boiled and flooded over us, but the canoe rode steady as a cork and we slowly went diagonally across the river as the current carried us backwards.

Then slowly we had to paddle forward, bypassing the shoulders of the rock bar into calmer waters, and so on to the next stage of the river.

The experience is exciting and a bit frightening, for one faulty stroke and the canoe would be turned over, and when you pull on and on right into the teeth of the rapids, with the spray spilling over the bows, you begin to remember that a quiet life ashore isn't too bad, even if you have to walk.

There were more rapids and the process was repeated but it was not until eight o'clock that night, in a blinding rainstorm, that the leading paddler indicated a dim, muddy bank on our right as the destination.

We pulled in, scrambled up to the top, spent half an hour pitching a tentfly and making rough bunks, and then turned in, wet through, weary, and hungry. Looking for dry timber to light a fire on a dark night at the edge of the jungle in a tropical storm had no attractions.

There was a horrible stench hanging round and I mentioned this to Beharell, who answered that he didn't care what stank, he was tired and sleepy. All night this smell was wafted over by the wind as I slept and awoke fitfully and when daylight came I got out to investigate.

Behind a fringe of low bushes right next to our tent was a crude frame of saplings bound together with vines and supporting a platform of bark upon which rested the putrefying body of an old woman.

She had been placed sitting up, her knees brought up to her chin, and her hands placed round her legs. She was, or had been, entirely naked and the remnants of her possessions, a fibre plaited bag, a stone adze, some unrecognizable bits and pieces, and a few animal skins were draped around the platform.

Her head had fallen forward and was resting on her knees and from where I was standing beneath I could see the empty eye sockets staring out of a half-eaten face. The skeleton was beginning to show through patches of dried flesh and skin. Part of the body was bare to the bones, some sections had the semblance of form and shape, with the left breast and hip quite distinct.

Soon she would become a collection of dried bones to be wrapped in a new sheet of bark and taken to the communal charnel house, an eight-sided, kiosk type of building, very similar to the city tobacco kiosks, situated near the back entrance of the communal house which stood a few feet away.

At first we had not recognized the purpose of these octagonal buildings, for they were the only things that bore any signs of decoration in rough, ochre-daubed concentric circles. They are the best constructed of buildings, with finely woven cane walls sectioned into rectangular patterns, with one area open and used as a doorway, much like a service window.

I had discovered their use by the simple method of sticking my head through the window opening just above a musty heap of thigh bones, skulls, and odd ribs.

The communal house near by was empty and built to a standard, barn-like design on high, thin wooden piles. Its length was about forty-five feet and its width about half of that. A notched tree trunk served as a ladder and led to the circular hole used as the entrance.

There were two floors, the main one and another about two feet beneath, entered by another hole in the floor. The inside was dark and the air stale, for the only light came through the narrow apertures in the walls which were used as fighting positions if the house were attacked.

The remains of family fires near the sleeping areas, and the women's section at the far end, were just as if the residents had only recently got up and gone.

Holes had been made at the edges of the floor for the disposal of rubbish which falls directly down underneath the house and forms a compact heap of putrefying refuse that smells as strong as a compost heap. Perhaps this smell helps to keep mosquitoes away at night, for that could be the only possible reason for living in such an unhealthy and disgusting atmosphere. Of course, going out to carry the rubbish away would always be a danger, and it's far easier to drop rubbish down a hole than to carry it away.

In daylight we could assess where we were. The house occupied a very prominent position on the high river bank and commanded an excellent view of the river and of the country northwards towards the limestone ranges.

It was, in fact, on one of the foothills of those ranges, and from here the land rose quite impressively to a high, flat plateau which appeared to stretch interminably towards the east. Beyond, as a backdrop curtain, rose tier upon tier of similar plateaux discernible faintly through the blue mists of early morning. Close at hand the limestone shone ghostly white; cold, inhospitable and uninviting.

When I returned to the tent, Jim was having a drink of tea.

"Still a horrible stink round here," he remarked, and I suggested that he might like to look round the back of the bushes. He rose and wandered off, returning in less than a minute with a look of disgust on his face, emptied his tea on the ground and called to the police to get ready.

The patrol was ready and I moved off with them, for there was no hurry for me to get back to the camp. We went forward until we found a native pad leading down the slope and followed that for a mile, when Jim decided that it might be better to plot a course.

"This is going to be nice," he remarked after pencilling some figures. "It's somewhere over that way," and he indicated north-east, and then I told him of what I had seen on the skyline that morning, the tier upon tier of flat ranges that never seemed to end.

Still following the pad we walked steadily until we reached a gap in the forest on the crest of a rise.

Almost at our feet the country dropped down into a gorge and then rose abruptly into what was the first of the really steep climbs. Timber still covered the hills, but beyond, on hills on which the sun now shone, the country looked bare and hungry. The faint trace of a track wound round the slope but there was no smoke from fires, and it seemed that as far as we looked the world was desolate.

I left the patrol there and turned back, watching only until they disappeared below into the gloom of the gorge. After they had vanished, I stood alone looking into a silent, deserted country with the feeling that I was the only human on earth.

Yet I knew that there were other humans in there somewhere while beyond, in vast fertile valleys between the ranges, thousands of people lived under their own secluded tribal conditions, with a highly developed system of agriculture that nobody outside had even suspected existed until a year before.

It had taken us two days to drag ourselves up from the camp. It took only twenty minutes to return. Once we hit the main current we rode it like a surf board, and with only two paddlers, one at the bow, the other at the stern, we descended the rapids in grand style, with the paddlers just touching the tips of the waves, playing on the balance of their craft as a musician plays a harp. It was grand to be alive, and when we rounded the last bend a cheer came from the camp as we headed into the bank and a quiet haven.

By now, I guessed, the patrol would be starting to climb the first of those big hills, and I walked up to the hut to tune in on the coast. It was time for the afternoon call and they would know in Daru before Jim had been able to step the first mile.

The dead old woman was still in my mind. From her perch on top of the riverbank she must have seen quite a lot. She had probably seen Karius and Champion coming, back in 1927, and Hides and Lyall only a few months ago, apart from stray Malay bird shooters and other strange wanderers.

And she had probably gazed in superstitious awe as a plane droned high overhead, and trembled because she had no conception of what was coming into her restricted world. Perhaps one of them had been blamed for her death.

We are inclined to regard these people of the jungle as unsophisticated, and one finds the word being used loosely to define those who have no awareness of civilization, an interpretation which is incorrect, for in describing them as unsophisticated we are speaking the truth: that they are people who have not been spoilt or corrupted. The more primitive they are, the more unsophisticated they remain.

114

Indirectly we are pointing the bone at ourselves when we say that we are sophisticated, although we are inclined to regard ourselves as being the fount of wisdom—a misconception if ever there was one.

The artificialities of our lives find no place in theirs. They don't strive for personal wealth, and whatever power and prestige an individual obtains are garnered through the strength of his own personality and ability.

The way to leadership in the society of the jungle lies through a man's own merits, and once obtained he must hold it through his own efforts. High office in primitive society is no sinecure as it can be in ours. It is this failing that often makes the native people question our methods of creating leaders and causes them to wonder why a man who, outwardly, does the least amount of work, secures a high position and is obeyed.

It was noticeable among the bushmen who visited our camp that there were leaders among them. These were the men who, according to their thinking, faced the dangers of first approach, the ones who first stood in full view of an alien, white-skinned race, and for a few brief seconds, awaited their destiny, for good or for ill. The man who first faced the flaring match was one of them, as was he who stepped from the bushes surrounding our camp and made the first tentative gestures of friendship.

It is this personal characteristic that must be recognized in them, for if you ignore the leader and attempt overtures to the ordinary men, you will get nowhere. You cannot go to a junior assistant secretary in making an approach to the big man. You go to the top, and primitive though they may be, their friendly reaction is immediately apparent.

We found this to be true in dealing with them, for we soon found who were those in authority; those who, by gestures and words, were obeyed, and they were the men whom we first turned to in bartering our goods for their food.

It was not a difficult problem for there are many ways in which one can find out, by observation, and by the general manner of their approach.

Our easiest was the square drawn on the ground into which all visitors were required to lay down their arms. To relinquish his spears, bow and arrows in strange surroundings among a foreign people, without knowing whether they are trustworthy or not, must call for a tremendous decision from a wild bushman. Yet, after only a moment's pause, one man stepped forward and laid down his weapons. Then the others came in and did the same. The one who made the decision was the man we watched, and in many little, unobserved ways, we stressed our faith in him and influenced him to encourage his people in bringing food.

It was a wise investment, for except for one occasion when tribal fighting was taking place, our fresh food supplies of green vegetables and bush pig remained constant for the whole time I was there.

It was during this period of tribal trouble that they suddenly stopped coming in, and as we had no idea of any reason, our first thought was that the people, being nomadic, had moved to other areas.

For two weeks this silence continued but one morning a couple of young lads came running into the camp, gesticulating for us to watch them. The fact that two young boys had come in alone was surprising, for until then our visitors had always been staid old and middle-aged gentlemen, with never a sign of youths or women. In fact, no woman ever did come near the camp.

We gathered around the boys and watched as they performed a pantomime of hitting each other and falling, twisting, crying, and holding their heads and stomachs. It became easy to understand. There had been a tribal raid and it had been accompanied by the usual killing and wounding.

They pointed out over the trees, gave us all a cheery smile, and dashed off home through the jungle.

Next day the staid old gentlemen began arriving again carrying food and apparently not unduly upset at the massacre of the previous days. In their own quaint way they tried to apologize for leaving us unattended for so long. There were a few whom we had become accustomed to see who were not among this group and I wondered if they had become casualties.

One I missed was a nice old chap who seemed the living image of King George the Fifth, fine featured, with rather heavy eyes, and a beautiful closely trimmed beard. How he managed it I never found out, for he only had bamboo and stone knives to cut with, yet his beard had the appearance of a finely mown bowling green.

We had our troubles. The nightly storms gave us our most miserable hours, always commencing around sundown and continuing for an hour or two, to disappear as suddenly as they came, leaving the skies clear and full of stars.

They were vile, terrifying things, with lightning that hissed, deafening thunder claps that resounded for minutes among the gorges, and rain that almost beat the camp flat and sent torrents of water streaming through the huts and lines of tents. One would

116

have been foolish to attempt to walk in it, for if the wind did not sweep one over the bank of the river, the force of water would have stifled all breathing.

Somewhere in the mountain country there must be a high mineral content, for the origin of these nightly storms was a mystery. We could sit and watch them form in swirling, black masses, rising from gorges and whipping around peaks, and within what appeared a perfectly normal, clear evening. In ten minutes lightning would be flashing and thunder rolling, and the whine of the cyclone as it tore down the gorge, directly towards us, would be sufficient to send us inside to batten down. Then it would be on us, screaming, tearing, and deluging the whole countryside, a mad rampage of vicious elements which did their best to destroy us and then, suddenly, disappeared.

Is lightning generated through heat and the magnetism of metals? I have noticed, here and elsewhere, that mineral fields usually endure terrific electrical storms. It seems to be a phenomenon of mineral belts, that the metals in the earth subscribe to, and perhaps generate, atmospheric electricity. Is lightning a Geiger Counter of Nature?

This is a conundrum that physicists should be able to answer, and it may, for all I know, already form part of mineralogical research and exploration.

Other headaches were leeches, snakes, and shortages of food. The leeches we just could not beat, there were so many of them; the snakes we killed when we saw them, and that was quite often; and the shortages of food often resulted from weather conditions between our camp and the main base on the Fly River.

Once we had an attack on the camp by bushmen whose greed for steel tools overcame their fears and gave our complacency a rude jolt.

We had become accustomed to the fact that the bushmen clustered around the perimeter of the camp at night, and attributed it more to curiosity than any other reason. They had never entered camp in daylight without first awaiting our approval and we had had no night visitors. That they walked around at all during the night was a bit surprising in view of their natural fear of ghosts, goblins, and their bloodthirsty neighbours.

The attack came at dawn and caught the police night guard completely by surprise. It was the yelling from the carriers' lines and a shot from a rifle that awoke me, but by that time our ration store was ablaze and there were bushmen running right through the camp.

When I left my hut there was smoke billowing across the tents. About half a dozen bushmen were milling around the clearing as if undecided what to do next. In the reflection of the fire I saw them

117

run back towards the bush, and there was a second rifle shot, fortunately a high one for it ricocheted through the trees.

We had no hope of saving the store. The thatched roof, sago walls, and bush timber exploded in one burst of flame, and we stood and watched as our food supplies were destroyed. They had obviously intended burning down our tool hut, and had probably watched as we stored the axes and knives each evening, but in the excitement had picked the wrong hut.

Our only casualty was a carrier with a sprained ankle. He had pitched over a fallen tree trunk while running away, which was fortunate for him because if he had reached the jungle his head probably would have been bashed in. None of the bushmen were hurt and not one was captured.

There were a few arrows and a couple of spears left behind but no reports of arrows having been fired. They had probably been dropped during the mêlée and in the excitement of the chase.

Having our essential foods destroyed was serious for us as the main items of rice, tinned meat and fish, sugar, marmite, tea, dripping, and medicinal oils were not easy to replenish. They had to be carried over rough tracks by labourers from the headquarters camp, which under the best of conditions meant a five days' hike.

I called Kiunga as quickly as possible and told them of our plight. They promised immediate aid, and it speaks well of their efforts to say that within eight days a ration party came into camp.

There had been constant heavy storms, creeks were running bankers, and swamps had become dangerous and, in places, impassable. These inclement conditions had saved them from any antagonistic intentions of the local bushmen, but when the party staggered into camp they were in bad physical shape, nearly all of them suffering from weakness, sores, and cuts, and their planned return over the track was delayed for several days.

This, of course, reacted upon the supply situation, for their own travelling rations, which had been reduced to a minimum, soon ran out, and they were forced to draw upon supplies which they had carried for us. But that was the way it always went, a chain reaction of misfortune that kept up for weeks until the balance of our security was restored.

For a couple of days following the raid no visitors arrived and this made us wonder if our old pals down the road might have been the culprits. It proved to be an unjust thought, for on the third day a team of them came gaily into camp carrying provisions and acting in no way guiltily.

They stood looking at the remains of our burnt out hut and then, obviously full of information, they turned to the police and with the usual signs and shouts indicated that the raiders had come from the north and were strangers around these parts. The local lads knew that foreigners were around and had stayed at home, fully expecting that they would become the victims of a raid. As nothing had happened they decided that the alarm was false and had come along to see us.

They were most lacrymose over our loss, expressed their grief and concern, and were almost apologetic for the misbehaviour of the oafs from the mountains.

Better still, they returned later with piles of fresh vegetables and fresh pigmeat, which they gave to us for nothing. So we shook hands all round, declared a pact of mutual friendship, and away they went very happily.

Their fears of becoming victims were soon substantiated. That night, screams and yells came floating up the river in the still night air, and as we looked down to the dark borderland of forest, a red haze grew into a mighty glow in a pulsating reflection over the forest, and we could hear the crackling of burning houses.

It was the old, old story. The raiders had gone into hiding, moving slowly down-river through the jungle to prepare for their next attack. We could do nothing to help them, for we did not know the tracks through the swamps, and the carnage would have been over even if we had been able to find our way in the darkness.

Just before dawn the camp was awakened by four men, victims of the raid, who had escaped. They were in a sorry state, crying and groaning, and beseeching us to go with them back to their village.

We organized a party of armed police, and with them, I followed bush pads and trailed our guides back through the forest. After about three hours we came to the scene of the massacre.

There was nothing but the ashes of what had once been a big communal house. It was still smouldering, and there was the sickly smell of burnt flesh in the air. There were no sounds from inside the wreckage and I guessed that this had been the funeral pyre of the women and children. I doubt if any of them escaped. Three bodies were lying near the edge of the clearing. One still showed faint signs of life but they were all hacked and mutilated, and the one who still lived was beyond aid.

A dead dog, with its side ripped open, lay near the ashes. That, and the smoking heap were all that was left. Our four guides were sitting under some bushes, keening and wailing. One, I noticed, had blood seeping down his face from head wounds he himself had probably made in his agony. We signed for them to come with us but they took no notice, so we left them and the ashes of destruction and murder, and returned to camp.

This was something far beyond our province for we were not there as upholders of human rights. I thought how easily we might have been the victims of these marauders had their hit-and-run raid been better planned and more substantial.

I reported the incident to the coast, answered a few questions, and that, so far as I knew, was the end of it. From then on the camp was put under very close guard with armed police escorting work parties whenever they went into the bush.

For long afterwards we saw nobody. Our stock of provisions grew less and we lived on hornbill soup, an occasional goura pigeon, and some green stuff which the lads called "cabbage." It was good and sustaining but it became monotonous, for hornbills are not noted for their soft, succulent flesh. They haven't any.

A ration party had been sent out but it was forced back by bad weather and eventually reached the camp eleven days after making its third start. For once we had a feast, and gradually the camp came back to normal, but it took time and patience, and there were occasions when we couldn't look a hornbill in the face, while if anybody mentioned cabbage he was looked at with repulsion.

Visitors began to arrive again. They were a different crowd, and where they came from I never discovered, but they brought pig and vegetables. They were a nervous crowd, yodelling to let us know they were there, and then growing very quiet and well behaved, and exceptionally polite.

A number of them were afflicted with wounds, sores, and diseases. One had a gash on his shoulder which he had roughly covered with mud and leaves; many showed signs of yaws, and there was one character whose two legs were afflicted with elephantiasis and who could barely move.

The man with the wounded shoulder demonstrated that he had been cut down with a stone axe but he laughed over the incident and told us, in a volume of words that nobody understood, that he had speared and killed his attacker. He pantomimed the whole performance and seemed very proud of it.

So, over the weeks, the work went on, felling big trees to make river canoes, clearing the rubbish and fallen timber around, extending the camp boundaries, building new huts for extra accommodation for the time when the field party arrived, and making our stocks of food and tools doubly secure so that no other steel-hungry savages could come along and upset things.

Despite all our efforts, the camp still looked like something a cyclone had left behind. The giant tree trunks we had felled could not be moved and they were far too wet and green for burning. They criss-crossed our clearing and made walking difficult, but we could do nothing with them except at the expense of considerable time and labour, and there were more important things to do.

However, it was a habitable camp. The huts were strong and well built, thatched tightly to keep out the heavy rains. The police and labour lines were clean and orderly; food supplies were sufficient; communications good; and we were quite happily settled in the knowledge that whatever Nature had in store for us, we had only to sit down quietly and see it out. Let it rain, let it blow. We, at last, were secure.

Then the sickness came, and my memories of what went on during the days that followed became a hazy recollection of intermittent spasms of understanding.

It began as a headache and a slight fever, and on my morning radio call to the coast I gave the normal "all's well and nothing to report" and added, "I may not come on again this afternoon, Harry. I've got a touch of fever and I'll sweat it out."

These were not famous last words, but they nearly were, for I did not touch the radio again although it was only twelve feet from my bunk. By evening I was sick, by midnight I was sicker, and when morning came I couldn't get out of my bunk to operate the radio.

Three days later I was in such pain and sickness that morning, noon, and night were merely periods in which I came to between bouts of sweating and semi-consciousness. The rising surges of fever and the increasing ache across my kidneys, plus the fact that I was passing a dull, thick, reddish liquid, told me the truth. I had blackwater fever.

The corporal was running the camp. I called him in and told him to get one of the policemen to burn everything that belonged to me. He looked at me as though I was crazy. Maybe I was, but I knew that the mortality rate of blackwater victims was about eighty per cent, and that with good medical attention in a hospital. What happened when you were alone and 600 miles from medical aid didn't worry me just then because in my mind I was set to go the whole way, say in another seven or eight days at the most.

In my more lucid moments I lay looking over the wall of the hut towards the mountains beyond. It was a beautiful place, with big hills, deep gorges, forests, and the mighty river flowing just outside.

In the clear, bright sunshine it was magnificent, one of the finest scenes that human eyes could look upon, and a lovely place to die in, strange as the thought may seem.

Perhaps I became obsessed with the thought of dying—actually there was little else to ponder over—and as the illness grew worse I felt that I was more and more part of that vast landscape before me.

At one period I became part of a tremendous peace. I couldn't move, I couldn't talk, and I couldn't hear, but my eyesight became so intense that I could plainly see the trees on the mountain slopes miles away, not as a mass of dark green and brown, but as individual trees, their branches swaying in the wind.

The movement of the camp was all around me but I heard nothing. Two of the labourers were working just outside my hut, talking together and glancing back at me lying in the bunk. I heard nothing, although one was wielding an axe and the other using a shovel, but I knew what they were thinking about. One had sorrow on his mind because I was sick; the other didn't care a damn.

Far away, at the end of a gorge, a small creek was tumbling over rocks, and I watched it very intently for I had never seen it before, yet now it seemed that I was but a few feet from it.

Later, during my convalescence, I spoke of this period to the doctor. "You were well into the Valley that time," he told me, but all I know is that if this was approaching death, then it is a very pleasant experience. It was as if I could go happily into the mountains, the gorges, and the forest and be welcomed, without pain and without fear. I am still not a religious person, but I am still not afraid of death. To me it appears to be like birth, a transition from one stage to another without any personal awareness.

This was only a period—it may have been the climax—for my senses returned, and the pain and fever surged through my body. The little creek disappeared, the misty mountains and forest went back into the distance, I could hear the river, feel the breeze, move with agony, listen to the noises around me, and think how lovely it would have been to have stopped away out there where there was peace and contentment.

I tried to focus my eyes back on the mountainside, but everything was an indistinct blur, and I searched for the water tumbling over rocks without success, and then I slept.

It was early next morning when Bill Christie walked into camp at the head of a ration party. He gave one look at me and said, "You've had it, brother, you've had it," and sat twiddling the dials of the radio.

Bill was a cousin of George, the man who had accompanied me

on the first trip over. The ration party had been delayed a week because of unusually heavy going. If he had arrived on time, I would still be lying somewhere along the Strickland River, for he would have returned before my sickness struck.

It was past time for the regular morning radio sked and Bill turned the dials until he received a slow, long reception of dots and dashes. I knew them well, for they were almost on our own beam and interfered with our sending. They came from a government patrol somewhere in New Guinea being led by Black and Taylor, and I had often cursed this unknown operator who was obviously practising his morse code right on top of our own channel.

Bill called and called, and by sheer chance a voice came crackling back. Within thirty minutes our message had gone through Rabaul to Moresby and on to Daru; the air was open and the doctor was giving directions. And I had been looking at those dials just out of my reach for five days, only twelve feet from help.

Bill was an energetic chap. That evening a raft was built in the camp. It was tied to the small landing at the foot of the slope that led to the river, ready for me to be loaded on at dawn, and speed away downstream to meet a vessel with the doctor aboard.

Two policemen came and slept beside my bunk that night so that I could call for Bill if I needed him, but they slept so soundly that when I did call out to them sometime during the night they didn't move.

Just before dawn the lightning flashed and the thunder rolled, and out of the mountains came one of the usual howling, cyclonic storms, with rain and wind that swept through the hut unrestrained. Perhaps the mountain gods were angry at losing me and were saying so in the most unpleasant way.

I was still awake when the sun rose and Bill came in to tell me that the raft had been swept away. There would be another day to wait.

They found the raft that afternoon, dragged it back and repaired it, and when darkness came I wondered whether we would have a repeat performance by the elements, but the night was calm and clear, with a sky full of stars and a chilly breeze from the mountains to cool my body.

One of the rules governing the treatment of this particular sickness is that the patient must not be moved. It was about to be broken in a very violent way, for Bill had the camp astir as soon as the first rays of light seeped through the forest, and soon I was being hoisted on a makeshift stretcher down the slippery clay bank to the raft, for a journey of hours that carried us over snags, shallows, rapids, and through whirlpools, until there was a hail from the crew, a steadying of our momentum, and the doctor drew alongside in a Higgins swamp craft.

Then another mad dash, at high speed, to the big river boat lying off Lake Murray; a rough, hard trip as the high-powered craft crashed its way down-river. I was thankful when it was all over and I could lie and watch the scenery from the comfort of a stretcher on the upper after-deck as we sailed steadily for Daru.

It had been a horrible experience, and many more months were to pass before I was fit again. Nevertheless, I have always retained a feeling of sorrow at being forced to leave the big river and the solitude and grandeur that one finds only in out of the way places. Somewhere up there, on one of the high spots, is a tree with my initials carved into its trunk. It would be nice to go back and find it, though of course I never will.

Weeks later, while sitting resting in the hotel in Port Moresby, a hand dropped on my shoulder and a voice said, "Congratulations. Welcome as a new member of our club."

I looked up to see Charles Karius, and to my question he answered, "The Feet-First Club. The only qualification is that you must have been taken out of the uncontrolled area feet first." So we had a drink on it.

4 | journey into fear

THERE APPEARS TO BE little logical reason why Vanimo should have become the administrative headquarters of a district, or even a township of any importance. It lacks the requisites of a main centre and possesses only one obvious advantage which, without the other elements, brings small importance.

Perhaps it was established on one fact—the ever-present ghost of white prestige, an uncontrollable malady which still exists, and is used to advantage on this northern coast, for Indonesia's big town of Sukarnapura lies only forty miles westwards, and the border of West Irian is barely twenty miles away.

This factor of prestige with respect to Vanimo was openly announced on an A.B.C. radio broadcast recently as being one of the reasons. The town was also described as a sentinel on the Indonesian border.

Perhaps this is more ludicrous than the first, for it glosses over the fact that a company of Pacific Islands troops was stationed there long before a District Commissioner moved in, and that as defence is the armed forces' concern, there is no good reason for the Administration to adopt the warrior's stance.

And now that the menace of infiltrating refugees has been removed—if that is considered a fact—there is still less reason for Vanimo's pre-eminence.

It is a town of contradictions—a controlling centre for over 87,000 people, of whom only 4,000 live within the sub-district, the remainder being scattered over a radius of more than one hundred miles. This makes central administration more difficult and expensive.

From Vanimo's backdoor to the border there is a quarantine strip, twenty miles wide and 350 miles long, stretching from the

Bismarck Sea to the Torres Straits, within which no development takes place, and government suzerainty is restricted to the overlordship of native villagers. Except for the operations of a timber company on a very small lease, the country remains idle.

Even local government council work, the first step towards self-government, remains at bedrock and once over the big hills which overshadow the town, the people's understanding is limited to what they can eat.

Total lack of development, with no incentives towards their own improvement, has kept them very close to the nomadic level and generally unconcerned with the functions of government, until they do something wrong.

Lack of centralization is another handicap. If government is to be an effective force then it must operate among the people. To do this, Vanimo officials must spend a proportion of their time flying to reach the outside populations and potential areas of development. Remote control has never been successful except in the duplication of official personnel.

Land is not available. The township sits on a peninsula that lies like a big blob in the ocean. Just beyond the narrow neck is the airstrip and the town's boundary. A strip of land along the coastline provides a foothold for the local people, but elsewhere there are mountains, heavily timbered and difficult of access.

The one advantage, an excellent harbour, has limited use without more road communications. Only the timber company has made any real attempt at road construction, with fifteen miles of good highway into their lease, and were it not for this, Vanimo would be restricted to its two main streets and a few side paths.

By any standards it must be an expensive baby to maintain. Shipping costs are high; cargo availability limited; general movement is by aircraft, mostly in single-engined Cessnas; the cost of living is high; production of primary products negligible—only twenty tons of copra were produced during 1967-68—and coffee, cocoa, and other cash crops are non-existent. The powers that be also have an inordinate confidence in the local timber industry which has yet to be substantiated.

Timber is the West Sepik's main asset and possesses the potential of a main Territory industry. Stands exist for hundreds of square miles, and as one flies over the inland areas, to Pagi, Imonda, Amanab, and as far as Green River, beneath the wings is one continuous carpet of forest trees.

Eastwards of the township is a timber area, said to be around 500,000 acres, that has been purchased from its native owners for

126

government leasing to outside, foreign investment interests. It remains idle because it is too vast for any one company to operate; it is unsuitable for sub-division and would require a consortium of industrial giants, with millions behind them, to make a success of the venture.

There is also talk in Vanimo that the Administration's conditions of timber leasing are not favourable for investment. Late in 1968 the Wewak Chamber of Commerce trenchantly stated, "The Forestry Department persists in the belief that it has unlimited areas of high class forest land—which it hasn't . . ." and went on to point out that the Territory's forest lands would not exceed 4,000 super feet, per acre, of saleable wood, whereas the average in the South Pacific Basin is in excess of 14,000 super feet per acre.

This is a hard business professional assessment and may be the reason why foreign investment shies off Vanimo and other areas. Timber leases are just not attractive enough and capital can be employed more profitably elsewhere.

This may be a very critical assessment of a struggling township, but any centre such as this is planned to be will require millions of dollars of public funds to build and maintain it, and the conception of an ivory-towered, isolated centre of government, with its many dependent departmental annexes, each costing a mint of money, is not pleasant to contemplate.

One could understand this situation if Vanimo were the only available location, but this is not the case. Aitape, several miles down the coast, which was runner-up in the headquarters stakes, would have been a far more practical choice, for here are all the essentials of an expanding control centre except a shipping harbour.

Development here is also more rapid than in any other area; there is a steady increase in primary products; a rise in domestic income; a potential of mineral wealth; a stable and increasing population; and Aitape is the centre of West Sepik activities.

Perhaps, sometime in the future, the Administration may be forced by circumstances to transfer its headquarters to Aitape. If that should happen, district development will receive a shot in the arm and the imbalance of costs must level out. However, while pressed pants and a well knotted tie prevail, such a move seems remote.

But this is a story of Vanimo. I have been there a number of times, but only two of my journeys, one in 1965 and the other in 1968, remain in the records as memories of value. On both I gained experience, and witnessed happenings about which I had heard but never seen, and both trips left a dry, nasty taste in my mouth.

The reason governing my hurried departure from Madang during the latter part of 1965 was a Sunday evening news broadcast from Sydney which stated that Indonesian troops had entered the New Guinea border village of Sekotchiau, some thirty miles from Vanimo, and had abducted the village policeman.

This was startling enough, but the message added that the army at Vanimo was standing by because of the situation. The implications were obvious, for those were the dark days of suspicion when President Sukarno's every word was being weighed with caution and a $16 million airfield at Wewak was being constructed to take the latest types of warplanes, and anxiety among the people of New Guinea was very real.

By morning I was on a plane bound for Vanimo and when I stepped out on the small airfield and parked my bag near the cargo shed, near a signpost which bore one finger pointing towards Canberra and another towards the nearest maternity ward, my first impressions were ones of suspicion and hostility.

It is an old Territory custom for strangers to be greeted by locals and made to feel welcome. I knew nobody around, but although I was the subject of covert glances and whispered remarks, nobody inquired who I was or what I wanted. The usual types were there, government men, business people, a couple of army chaps, and a cluster of those who had come to see who had arrived, but it was not until the cargo had been cleared and the strip was nearly empty that the man who appeared busiest of all, Gordon Campbell, came over, introduced himself, and told me that he could put me up at his guest house.

Over a drink in the dining-room he told me that I was going to find it hard to get information in this town, and to my question as to whether he knew what my job was, he replied, "Everybody knows. Nobody reaches here without warning and I knew from remarks on the airstrip that you were from the paper."

I guessed that the good old James Bond business was in operation. For long I had known that six intelligence services work in the Territory: one each for the armed services, the Australian Security Intelligence Service, whose phone number is in the book for anybody to ring, and the Special Branch of the police force.

The sixth is an amorphous variety, the dandy of the lot, unknown and unrealized by most citizens, in which everybody within the Administration participates. This is a do-it-yourself—every man his own James Bond—affair and as few of its operators have had specialized training in intelligence and security duties it can prove a nasty weapon, as well as being subject to discriminatory practices.

128

In my line of business I have met it often and in various ways, and the best that one can say about it is that it has become an official mania. On this trip I was to meet it in its most virulent form but I didn't know this as I sat talking in the guest house.

Gordon Campbell's remark more or less confirmed what I had suspected, that air travellers' names and business affairs are sent ahead to their destination. This is logical enough in Vanimo, where suspicion and intrigue rule, although it may not apply to other services except in special circumstances.

I was to meet it again within a very short time. I had showered, dressed, and had dinner, and walked across in the darkness to the picture show at the near-by army camp. Sitting alone in the darkness of the back row, a shadow came up alongside and a voice whispered a name and "I'm with the army here. Would you come to my office at nine in the morning?" and evaporated again into the gloom. So, within an hour or so of landing, I was a marked man and I hadn't even opened my mouth except to eat.

At eight the next morning I walked up the slope to the sub-district office and found that I was expected, for without any introductions I was ushered into the inside office.

The officer in charge advised me that he was only acting temporarily as the officer I wanted was out on patrol. He could not give me any information. He didn't know if the patrol was going out to Sekotchiau, and as for the radio news broadcast, he was surprised to hear of it. My questions were answered very politely but without much substance.

I could not get on a government chartered plane to Pagi because none were going there, and when I explained that I had been told of four planes waiting take-off, he said that there was no cargo.

Again I interrupted to tell him that the airport agent was worried about the amount of cargo ready to go, and that a fellow passenger of mine, on the plane the day before, was standing with a ticket for Pagi in his fist and wondering what all the delay was about.

"Very well," he said, "we will radio the District Commissioner at Wewak for permission," and with that I walked out and headed across the town to the army camp.

The army officer was a pleasant type, and he made no bones about my arriving at an inopportune moment. Of course he knew all about me and what I wanted. "I can't give you very much," he began, "because the army is not at all concerned over the matter. Our point of view is that it is an Administration problem and one that does not affect us."

He admitted that he had nearly fallen out of his chair when he heard the announcement that the troops were standing by, and pointing out to the parade ground, he said, "There's the army, working, playing, resting, and receiving instruction, with not a care in the world. Does that look as though they were on the alert?"

I told him that I had got little encouragement from the district office and he cocked one eyebrow and remarked, "You didn't expect to, did you?" and chuckled as if the idea were very amusing.

Then he got down to serious discussion. "I don't know who gave out that report but it is a pure lie. What I do know is that a village policeman has been reported missing, and it is the government's job to take it from there. If Indonesian troops had been mixed up in the affair, I would have known about it first. We have our own patrols out on regular duties, and to the best of my knowledge, no Indonesian soldier has crossed the border." He pulled a map from a drawer and spread it across his desk. "Take a look at this and I'll explain how things are."

For over half an hour we studied that map, the officer explaining in some detail the soldiers' activities along the border. It was a military chart with all the information marked in red. "You should know what these symbols mean," he said, "and make your own appreciation," and went on to give me a general outline of the country and the people, plus a lot of information which would have to remain confidential.

He made no assumptions on what might have happened and admitted frankly that he didn't know. His whole conversation showed not the slightest trace of concern, but the story he wove was sufficient to give me a basis for the article I was shortly to write, and the items he missed out were the clues for a few more questions to other sources. "Whatever you write be sure to say that the army is not mixed up in it," he enjoined as he folded the map and put it away.

As I thanked him and prepared to leave he gave me a big grin. "One final word. If I were you I wouldn't try walking out to the village. It's thirty miles of tough going and I can assure you that you'd never reach it. We'd send a party out to bring you back."

So he must have read my thoughts, for I had intended to walk out, and why did he expect me to make my own appreciation from the map? Once, long before, I had been put through the army mill where they teach you that kind of work. Maybe he knew all about that, too? The place was becoming interesting.

According to my notes, next day was "D" Day, for the official I wanted was back and not looking too companionable as I entered his office.

130

"What the hell do you want?" he greeted me in a voice that could have been better used on the ghostly Indonesian troops, if there were any. I said my piece and added a request that I be allowed to fly out to the village but I found very quickly that I was right off the beam. "It's you newspapermen who have caused this," he snapped, "sending alarm stories to the radio. It wouldn't have happened but for you people."

Gently I reminded him that I was the only newsman around and I had known nothing until I heard it over the air. Did he think that I caused the upset? This brought on another diatribe against newspapers and reporters which stopped only when I interrupted to ask if he knew just who actually lived in the area, mentioning that I knew of one sawmiller and two patrol officers. Maybe one of those had sent it?"

This was not very diplomatic, and he took the bait at once. "Don't you accuse our officers of giving out information," he shouted, "and don't think you can go out there to question them. I'll order them not to speak to you. You can't get any information from my men, and if you try sending radios I'll have them stopped. You'll get nothing here."

I stared at him pretty hard, wondering just how much bluff was in the threat to stop my messages. For a moment I had a mind to challenge him and see what the consequences would be, but in the mood he was in it would have been stupid to irritate him further. The matter could keep until my office had been advised and they could handle it in Port Moresby.

I decided to try another tack, to steer away from contentious remarks, for a slanging match could have started at any moment.

"What did you find when you got to the village?" I asked.

"Nothing."

"Is it correct that you took twenty armed police with you?"

Again he jumped up. "I'm telling you nothing. Do you think I want to face Indonesian rifles when I go back in there?"

He didn't take kindly to my remark, "Don't be stupid," and for a while we merely glared at each other.

Once more I tried to explain that if he would give me a straight-forward statement, without revealing any secrets, I would be satisfied, but he brushed the suggestion aside.

"You'll get nothing. You're wasting your time."

I left him with the feeling that there was far more belligerency in the district office than could be found along the whole of the Indonesian border, and it had all been so unnecessary.

I had expected some opposition from army sources with compensating co-operation from the Administration, but it had been the other way round, and reviewing the performance in the district office, it occurred to me that the matter was more concerned with the reputation of government officials than any possible Indonesian infiltration, which I knew had not occurred.

It's a good idea, if you cannot find the reasons for a certain action, to discover who is most concerned and how it affects them. I knew this answer but there were still a few questions I had to ask. The matter had shifted from the plane of international affairs to the personal level and smacked strongly of sensitivity, which is a shallow human emotion and can seldom be suppressed, and it is so easy to ask questions.

I wandered down to the police compound, talking to odd ones and finding out which of them had been on patrol. Fortunately, some were Papuans and they spoke Motu, a handy language to know in New Guinea where ears are always listening.

We had some conversation and then I went on to where some West Irian refugees were working and did a bit more talking. Soon the blank spaces were filled in and I needed no official release to write my story.

The facts were that the village policeman had left for his garden one morning, and without telling anybody else, had suddenly decided to walk into Sukarnapura to visit his brother whom he had not seen for a long time. When the old man didn't come home the old woman became worried and rushed into the patrol post to report her spouse missing.

And that was all. The old boy came back some days later, very weary and wondering what all the fuss was about. Nobody had seen any Indonesians near the village. There were no rifles to point at the official breast, and he had spoken the truth when he said that he found nothing in the village. They had all gone back to their gardens.

Somebody had obviously played a silly hoax but whether he was ever found I do not know. Or else there was a saboteur with ideas of testing the efficiency of the border patrols, a neat way of finding out where the weak spots were.

You can take your choice, for the grass fire alarm which upset the dignity of Vanimo scarcely ruffled Port Moresby. My editor went round to check the story I had written and was told the whole affair without embellishment, and it bore out what I had sent in. It was a stupefying example of intrigue, suspicion, evasion, and James Bondism at its worst in a small town notorious for its ultra-security consciousness and the magnifying of insignificant incidents.

Father Leo of the Pes Mission, Aitape; with some of the men whom he has taught to work with cane

Men of the Pes Mission with examples of cane furniture

From other sources I heard later that the townsfolk had been alerted against giving me any information, a senseless move when you have a native population available for questioning. Their accounts may be exaggerated but some facts always tally, and sometimes they have a clearer idea of what's going on than many Europeans.

And now to 1968.

For over three years I had been following closely the fortunes and misfortunes of the refugees from West Irian and during that period I had built up a hefty file of information and records, some of which had originated in Sukarnapura.

They covered a variety of subjects ranging over the political, military, and social affairs of the West Papuans under Indonesian control. They told tales of heroism, endurance, privations, brutalities, and armed resistance but in the main they dealt with the domestic and national problems of those unfortunates who had fled their homes and families to take refuge in Papua-New Guinea.

In addition, I had established a line of communication from where I was stationed in Madang, through the Sepik and on to Sukarnapura, thanks to those whose confidence I had cultivated and to many informants whom I never met.

Fortunately I was in the position of being able to give facts and figures, whatever I wrote, for I had access to documents that described in detail the events I recorded. Names had often to be avoided for the obvious reason that retaliation could fall upon the people concerned.

The official reaction to refugees crossing the border was not one of enthusiastic welcome for it was an insoluble headache, an act of human resistance for which the Administration was unprepared, and a situation with ramifications extending far and wide. Consequently there were times when publicity was played down; figures were changed and facts were either distorted or denied, and there were also occasions when my material was quietly suppressed.

All this was beyond my control and affected me little for I had the satisfaction of knowing the correctness of what I wrote and that my stories were receiving official attention.

This alone was proof of their effectiveness and adherence to the key aim of publicising a situation which was rapidly being transformed into a matter of national and international importance.

With 1968 drawing to a close and the time for the "act of free choice," or plebiscite, as it is generally known, coming around,

Weaving cane blinds at the Pes Mission cane factory

I had noticed that the tempo of the organizations controlling the underground freedom movement within West Irian had quickened. Determination became the dominant feature among the plethora of words that streamed from their headquarters; the accent on dialectics had been subdued, and the flowery phrases and exhortations had diminished.

Indications of positive action became evident and it occurred to me that another trip to Vanimo and beyond might prove interesting. I sent out feelers for an interview with some of the refugee leaders to obtain their comments on the coming election.

The idea was welcomed and the wheels began turning to get me into their camps. With their campaign in full swing at the United Nations, an increase in publicity was much desired. They would receive me, safeguard my journey, give me what information they could, and ensure my return.

It was a matter of six weeks of preparation before I left for Vanimo, and with memories of my 1965 visit still very vivid, I was determined not to be nailed down again in the main street, nor fobbed off, nor threatened or hindered.

This was to be a one-man mission and when I landed at Vanimo I kept a very still tongue. The atmosphere had changed considerably, for the town was growing up and it had been gazetted as a district headquarters. There were no whispers in the dark nor hints of intrigue, although I was well aware that my arrival had been noted by the authorities.

I met a few of those I'd known before, parried a few hints, dodged all awkward questions, joined in some heavy humour, and within a couple of days received instructions on the continuation of my journey.

The call came at half-past two one dark night when I was awakened and taken to a beach where two small craft were waiting, one to take me, and the other as a guide and to carry provisions. We were off almost at once westwards towards the patrol post of Wutung and the West Irian border where a rendezvous had been arranged.

By dawn we had reached the spot, a quiet, steeply sloping beach beneath a cluster of coconut palms, and we idled until lights flashing from the shore gave the signal to come in. We rode the breakers of a dangerous looking surf, grounded on the beach, and I was hurriedly dumped together with some stores. Five men awaited to guide me to the camp which, I was advised, was less than an hour's walk through the forest.

We sat until the sun was up, and then, leaving the foreshore, plunged into the forest and followed a small native pad. There had been no introductions, but the leader of the party spoke Pidgin, and keeping close to me, he explained the preparations that had been made for my visit.

Somewhere to our right was the government patrol station, and we bore deeper into the bush, still following pads that wound through undulating country. My companion explained that it was necessary to travel unobserved, as the refugees had been forbidden to move around freely, and if villagers or policemen saw our party, an alarm would be raised and we would probably be taken into the government station.

This constant evidence of fear was surprising, and during the days which followed it became manifest in many ways in speech and actions. During the journey we stopped and hid in the undergrowth on an average of once every ten minutes, and our passage was like an advance echelon of invading troops, with scouts out ahead as we stealthily stepped forward.

The sounds of childrens' laughter, or women's voices, were sufficient to send us scuttling into the jungle, and when we broke through the borderline of a newly planted garden area and disturbed some women at work, our passage became a panic as we clawed our way back through the scrub into thicker jungle country. Vicious barbed lianas tore our clothes and bare arms, and faint, almost hairlike tendrils, armed with spikes like fish-bones, wrapped round our legs while our feet stumbled and tripped over a multitude of roots, creepers, and ground shrubs, and still we went on with the frightened shouts of the women ringing through the jungle. Sore, breathless and scratched, we laid down beneath some bushes until the cries died away and silence was restored.

I had never seen fear expressed like this, yet I was to discover that it was the most elemental force which ruled the whole community. Fear was the underlay of every normal human function, in eating, sleeping, walking, talking and in every human action.

It was reflected in the children whose shouts and laughter would be suddenly stilled by a call from a hut and they would run inside to hide and peep and whisper to each other, their wide open eyes showing panic and their parted lips ready to scream. One could see it in the mothers as they came out of their houses, paused uncertainly and glanced round as if an enemy were in ambush. One could see it in the men, in their tightened lips, sharp penetrating looks, and during the sudden moments of silence in conversations.

It lay on us very heavily, travelling the tracks, for we had entered a country of steep, rocky hills and deep gullies. There were still

135

scouts ahead, and hand signals and whispers and pauses to listen for the faintest of sounds in the thick, silent forestlands.

Once we stopped while the five men held a whispered conference, and the leader came back and told me that two men were to go ahead to find a track.

It was then that I knew we were lost, a suspicion that had been growing over the past hour, for our course had been most erratic. We had followed gullies, climbed hills, and doubled back on our tracks, seeking whatever appeared to be the easiest paths.

"We have never been here before," my companion remarked, "and we do not know this country." I looked for the sun but it was somewhere high overhead and hidden by the forest. We could take no bearings from that for another hour or so and we already had been travelling for over four hours since leaving the beach.

The shape and size of the country around us indicated that we were well into the foothills of the coastal ranges. They rise to between 2,500 and 4,000 feet and we had no way of telling how far we were in among them.

We crossed numerous creeks but they were dry and for the whole day we saw no water. Some were filled with huge, water-worn boulders that had been swept down from the mountains in the wet season. One or two showed crystallization and shone brilliantly, and there were traces of mica and black sands.

We pushed on until well into the afternoon when two more of the party left us with the intention of finding camp and returning with water. This left the leader and myself following slowly behind, for by now we were both sore and weary and my feet and legs were swelling.

The tracks of the other men were soon lost and the two of us moved forward to the edge of a gully, twenty feet deep, its sides showing compact, red clay. Here we rested for a while, clambered up the far bank, and pushed through more thickets of jungle. Then we struck a clearly defined pad with the footprints of women and children clearly marked. It bore to our right and we followed it between bush country that turned into high grassland.

From ahead there came the chattering of women and shouts of children and again we crouched in the bush. My companion went forward through the scrub and returned soon to tell me that there was a large waterhole just ahead of us and that the women and children were washing and that we should wait until they had gone.

"I know where we are now," he said. "We shall be in camp in half an hour."

136

He had said the same thing ten hours before and I hoped that this time he was right, for in an hour or so it would be dark and I had no liking to camp unprotected in this country all night without even a fire to cheer us up.

We sat there a long time. The evening shadows were darkening the land when we heard the last of the women leave, and we were about to move when an old man came singing down the track, stripped off his clothes and waded into the pool for his evening wash. We sat watching him through the leaves, hoping that the growing darkness would hasten his ablutions but he was a meticulous old gentleman, scrubbing himself a number of times very carefully and then attending to his grey, crinkly hair with a long, wooden comb. Even when he had finished and waded out he sat alone looking at the water while his body dried.

At last he left, singing quietly to himself, and we hastened over the creek into an abandoned banana patch and up the hillside on a twisting track that in fifteen minutes landed us at the campsite.

There was just enough light left to see. The clouds were coming over and a light sprinkle of rain began to fall. By the time I was in the hut and lying flat on the floor, the clouds burst and a deluge was upon us. We had just made it in time, for this preliminary burst was the forerunner of high winds and driving rain that continued all night, with the spray driving through the open walls of the partially completed hut making us wet, cold, and miserable. We were too exhausted to care, and after one of the women had come in with a billycan full of hot coffee and we had drunk it with a couple of dry biscuits to eat, we rolled up in our blankets to go to sleep, oblivious of wind, water, and the mosquitoes.

I remember my friend the leader saying to me, "Tonight you are safe. We have three guards posted in the camp all night," and the thought went through my mind, "What the hell. This is a free country, isn't it?"

It is a question that has been in my mind ever since.

A few words on the background of the West Irian refugees are required to give the context of their problems and situation. No people leave their families and homeland to seek sanctuary elsewhere without cogent and compelling reasons, and some of these men, women, and children had been exiles for from two to three years.

Many had left fathers, mothers, wives, and children behind and most of them had received no information concerning their relatives since. One of the men had left with his wife and seven children, fleeing before armed brutality that would have brought death to himself and possibly to his family. For a year they had lived in the jungle like wild animals, under flimsy shelters, scratching the ground for food. Then his wife had fallen ill, and in the absence of any medical assistance, had died. The man had returned to Sukarnapura at night with his seven children and had left them with friends. Then he had fled again and had crossed the border and was now in this camp.

He had heard, through underground channels, that there had been police and army raids, his friends had fled somewhere, taking the children, and then he had heard nothing else.

This was only one of the stories that those in the camp could tell. They varied only in the intensity of the threats, brutalities, and sufferings and the degree of hopelessness that lay behind their words. Democracy, to them, was something that was the prerogative of Papua-New Guinea, and when trouble struck it was to this country that they fled. Since their arrival they have discovered that there are also degrees of democracy, and the only words they have heard so far have been, "Go back to Sukarnapura."

If "humanitarianism" is a word in the vocabulary of this government then it must be on the prohibited list. There can be no other explanation for the treatment that these people have received. Their big "crime" is that they have been promised freedom and independence and these promises have been repudiated, and because they have raised up their voices in protest, armed force has been used to subdue them.

What began as a series of minor incidents in 1963 has now developed into a huge national crusade which has not yet reached its peak. From it has grown the Freedom Movement of West New Guinea, the parent body of thirteen underground organizations pledged to fight for independence. Their aim is to consolidate the people's right to self-determination by all measures; political, social, economic, and by force if necessary.

They are determinedly anti-communist and anti-Indonesian, claiming that as a race they are Papuans, not Indonesians, and demanding their own country and their own government, as promised by the Dutch Government prior to 1962.

For this they have been executed, imprisoned without trial, beaten, and chased into exile under threats of retaliation and death for any who share their views.

When one remembers the horrors of the Second World War it seems incredible that such things should still exist a quarter of a century later. The world now celebrates Human Rights Day, as part of the Four Freedoms. Such an event is a mockery to people

138

such as these, whose human rights are the last on the list after political expediency and manoeuvring.

One of these organizations, and the one in which I was directly interested, is the Komando Pembebasan Papua Barat—Angkatan '69—the Liberation Command of West Papua—1969 Forces.

This was the organization whose fortunes and misfortunes I had been following for three years. Its duties are to man the border zones of West Irian and New Guinea. It is an integral part of the whole Freedom Movement whose controlling voice is that of Nicolas Jouwe and his administrative headquarters in Holland, where he has been in exile since Indonesian control.

Jouwe was the number one choice for president of any Republic of West Papua that might have been proclaimed if the plebiscite in 1969 had gone in their favour. It is possible that he may form a government-in-exile now that the elections have gone against them.

The strength of the whole movement is conjectural, for it has support overseas as well as throughout West Irian where 700,000 people live.

The K.P.P.B. claims 5,000 members scattered from Japan down to New Guinea and West Irian. This figure may be low and may only indicate its active members. As any guerrilla leader knows, one trained man can influence many others, and with hidden activists and a population which is sympathetic to the organization's aims, the figure could be five times as much.

Take this as an average and multiply it by thirteen and you have a potential force which is quite impressive in numbers. Add to it the determination of its members to fight to the death and it could become very effective.

Determination, however, will not win wars, or ballot boxes, against the greatest armed power in South-East Asia, and the quality of the insurgents' military hardware is so nebulous as to be almost negligible.

"We will fight with the weapons of our forefathers if we have to," one of the camp's leaders told me. This is a noble sentiment and I, for one, sincerely hope that they will not do so, but it does indicate the spirit of determination which fills these people.

When I asked one of the women what she would do if it came to actual warfare, she replied, "I will do what our men tell me. We will all do the same."

Two of the thirteen organizations have been fighting units for a long time, waging war against Indonesian forces. It is claimed that in one engagement they destroyed 1,500 Indonesian troops.

In 1966 I was given a view of the battle order of one of these

139

organizations. This was at the time of actual field operations and it was signed by the Movement's Commander-in-Chief. It showed an impressive understanding of military dispositions, and indicated that there existed a quality of military strategy among the leaders of this force. It may well be that there is a core of trained militarists in the movement whose predominance is now coming into focus.

The martial aspect is only of recent origin, for the movement is primarily political and was centred for a long time on the guarantee of an "act of free choice" as detailed in the Bunker Plan that gave control to Indonesia.

Their own idealistic approach to political salvation showed all the elements of theoretical political idealism and naivety. This was an understandable characteristic, for under the Dutch Government their advance towards self-government and its responsibilities had been sincere and thorough.

A New Guinea Council had been formed in Hollandia, as it was then, with sixteen out of its twenty-eight members elected by the people from among their own kind. This had been regarded as the instrument to lead the people into independence by 1970 and consisted of men of high quality.

The standards of West New Guinea native leadership were, and are, far higher than those achieved in Papua-New Guinea. They do not consist of a revolutionary rabble but are men of education, many of them holding Dutch university degrees.

In this camp was one Bachelor of Science, one Bachelor of Arts, a cultural lecturer and ex-New Guinea Council member, two ex-parliamentarians, teachers with high qualifications, missionaries, police officials, a law student, and a young woman who had been an official in Indonesian national welfare work. There was a fully qualified nurse, a radio expert, and tradesmen in many branches.

Altogether, in four border camps, there were 148 people with seventy-six men, eighteen women, and fifty-four children, and their numbers are being augmented at the rate of thirty or more new refugees each week.

My companion, the one who kept by my side during the whole of the visit, had a Dutch university degree and had travelled widely. His wife was a qualified nurse and their three children were all under the age of six.

He had returned to Sukarnapura from overseas and had been promptly arrested as intellectually dangerous. Kept in gaol for a while, he was then released and told that he was on no account to associate with those who advocated independence. For him this was an impossibility. He was West Papuan, as were his family, friends, and fellow students. He had no Indonesian contacts for he had been abroad at the time of the change-over of government.

Soon there came a whisper that he was to be arrested again and sent to Jakarta. As this is regarded by the West Papuans as tantamount to a death sentence, he fled with his wife and family into Papua-New Guinea. Here he met the treatment that most others have, and was ordered to go back to Sukarnapura, so he took refuge in the camp and has become their most intellectual leader and a determined fighter for freedom.

"I am confident we are going to win the plebiscite," he told me, with a confidence which, to a stranger viewing their difficulties, seemed hard to justify. "Our organization is ready and so are the others, and we have the fullest support of our people."

His words were another indication that they had started to throw off political theory and to aim for practical results. Trained as they have been, with full confidence in their Dutch tutors, they have a childlike faith in the fulfilment of promises, so that when repudiation came after the Indonesians gained control, it was hard for them to readjust their minds to the fact that solemn assurances of national independence were being broken.

In the beginning they carried on a battle of polemics, arguing from all angles that such promises could not be broken, quoting authorities from past history with a variety of cultural, social, and economic ties, to support their discussions.

They could be regarded as quiescent insurgents, intellectuals who were content to fight their battles within the boundaries of proclamations and political theses and not to plunge into the dangerous depths of open revolt. Honest in purpose, they either did not know, or disregarded, two facts; that domestic politics are dirty and international politics often far more filthy, and when they pitted their idealism and belief in the inherent goodness of Man against the pragmatic realism of Indonesia, it was an uneven contest.

Time has brought too many disappointments, and their search for refuge and understanding has failed. The transformation from passive protest to active assault is almost inevitable.

It is this ingredient of political participation that has affected the Administration's attitude towards them. There is an attitude that if assistance is given to political refugees still plotting against their established government, international relations may be jeopardized.

If this is so, then it shows a terrible weakness in the character of the government, and an inconsistency in its pleadings for the victims of Biafra while, at the same time, it is prepared to push similar victims, on its own soil, over the cliff.

141

"Go back to Sukarnapura," with its death, beatings, and brutality, is no substitute for humanitarianism, a quality of mercy that costs little to dispense—but which may have to be backed by manoeuvring in the arena of international politics.

The hut to which I was assigned was a new one on the edge of the camp-site clearing. It had been only partly completed. Half of the roof was still unthatched and the wall partitions were missing, as was a section of the flooring.

They apologized for its defects, explaining that the village people around had forbidden them to use local bush building materials and that now it was necessary to travel a long distance to cut timber and sago for their requirements.

"There was a time when the people gladly helped us, but now they don't. Somebody has turned them against us," they said. They pointed to the ridge, three hundred yards away, which was Indonesian territory. "We get most of our supplies from over there. It is a hard job climbing the mountain and it takes much longer to do the work. We are safe enough, for no Indonesian soldiers ever come there, and we have our own people watching."

Beyond the ridge and down in a valley I learned that an Indonesian army patrol post of one lieutenant and six soldiers was permanently stationed on border guard. Their duties covered the border areas and a strip of coast, giving them an almost impossible job of maintaining a watch for refugees coming through. It would need a couple of battalions to do the work properly in this heavy, rough country of jungle and mountains, and with the local village populations friendly towards the exiles, there was no hope of seven men stopping the travellers.

That would not prevent the soldiers from lining the ridge and watching the camp and I pointed this out to them, but they shrugged it off. "They probably do if they feel that way inclined, but we have our own watchers, too."

On my first morning in camp the noise of an axe and the sound of men's voices had woken me at four o'clock. It was still dark, still raining, and when I looked out of the doorway, a white, opaque curtain of cloud hung over the camp.

I remembered that they had told me, "We start work at four o'clock each morning," but it was too wet, cold, and dark to take any interest in what they were doing and I curled up in the damp blankets until dawn came.

When the light was stronger a gong rang. I climbed down from the hut and felt my way over the rubble to where, in a cleared patch, the men were erecting a tall, thin pole. As I stood watching, others came from their huts across the gorge and through the forest and soon there were almost thirty men, women, and children huddling under the shelter of the hut.

The camp commandant came over to me. "You have arrived just in time," he said with a grin. "Today is the second anniversary of the forming of our organization, the K.P.P.B., and this is the first time we have raised our national flag."

The men formed in two ranks, with the women and children fanned out in a semi-circle. The old, grey-haired chap, who was in command of the whole organization, stepped forward and gave an address. He was followed by my companion, the second-in-command, and a third man came next, reading a long list of names, the names of their companions who had died or had been executed.

Then a colour party of three men stepped to the pole, unfurled a flag, and with the parade at attention, hoisted it to the mast-head. It was a large, new ensign, a white star on a red background with thirteen blue and white stripes. It fluttered in silence for a while, the wind stretching it to its full glory, then the whole assembly started singing the first verse of their national anthem. A prayer from one of the members ended the ceremony and the parade broke up, gathering in groups to talk together.

It had been quite impressive; the short speeches, the flag-raising, and that final burst of song in the midst of this isolated pocket in the mountains. In a moment of kindness the sun had shone faintly, giving me a few photographs, and a touch of pleasure to the assembled people. It was as if Nature had paused in respect for a few minutes. Then the clouds swept down again and a drizzle of rain commenced, and soon the clearing was deserted, with only the flag flying high.

To celebrate the occasion the day had been declared a holiday from work and I had the opportunity of meeting and talking to the people. Even within the camp there was not the freedom of movement and association that one might expect, for fear was still the predominant note.

"You must keep inside," they pleaded. "The village people pass this camp on their way to their gardens and if they see a white man here they will run back to the station and the police will come."

So I kept within shelter, screened from view by one of the outside walls, while the people came, singly and in small groups, and spoke of their lives, their troubles, and their hopes, and the children gathered round waiting for me to take their photos.

They were very quiet and subdued, a little timid, but straight-forward, and the stories they told were without embellishment and without rancour, although outbursts of anger would have been fully justified. One woman, who spoke very reasonable English, talked on behalf of her friends, softly and gently, with spasms of silence, and sentences left unfinished, for there were some things they didn't want to talk about.

One tired man with his wife and three little girls came in and sat down on the floor. He said that his age was forty but he looked much older. He was the father of six girls, the eldest nineteen, some of whom had received their schooling in Sukarnapura before he had been forced to flee two years previously.

"They took me from my work and put me in gaol three times," he said. "The first time was for ten months. They told me that I had been talking too much to the people about independence, but I was never tried in court. After they released me the third time I could get no work, and one of the policemen who had been a friend to me said that they were going to arrest me again and take me to Jakarta."

He stopped to see if I understood. "Jakarta means death," he exclaimed. "When they send you there you never come back and nobody sees you any more." Again he paused to recover his breath and then continued, "We ran away before they could find us and walked all the way down here through the bush. That was nearly two years ago, and I went into Vanimo and asked if I could stay with my wife and children, but they said, 'No. Go back,' so we came out here in the bush and the village councillor gave us a house to live in, some food, and told me that I could build a house for us on this ground.

"He and his people helped us a lot at first and we tried twice again to get political asylum. Each time they said 'No.' Then I went to the station and asked if my children could go to the school. There is a school on the coast at Wutung, but when I went down to the patrol post and asked the kiap if my children could go to it, he said that they could not and that no children from this camp could go to school.

"I do not think it is the fault of this patrol officer because he is a nice man and he has treated us as well as he can, but he is under orders from others on top, and these are the people who are stopping our children."

His words died away and the voice of a young woman took up the thread. "This is one of the unkindest acts of all," she said quietly. "To deny the children their rights of education is wrong. They label everything about us as political yet children are not political, and most of the mothers here have nothing to do with politics. In your

Bible they say something about the sins of the fathers falling upon the children. Is that what your government acts by? Do they think that we want our children to grow up uneducated, unable to read, or think, or live decent lives?"

My hut companion turned to me, "She's right," he said. "I have three children and there is no schooling for them, yet I am a university graduate and I have always expected that my children will be as well, or better, educated than I."

The young woman interrupted. "We do try and do something ourselves, you know. We have made simple reading books in the camp, and the women take the children and teach them as much as they can. The men have made them some toys to play with, and we have a strict programme of children's schooling in the camp, which we are trying to keep up. It is a very hard job and it falls far short of proper schooling, but we do our best."

I took stock of this girl. They told me she was only twenty-two years old and had worked officially as a welfare officer in West Irian and had held a responsible job. She spoke clear, carefully enunciated English. It was not good, extensive English, but it was understandable, and I knew that she spoke other languages, including Malay and Dutch.

She was the best dressed and smartest woman in the camp, a cheerful girl with a good-natured grin. Her dress had been tailored with care, and the shoes she wore were of good quality. I knew that she had put these on because of today's ceremony and because there was a stranger in the camp, and I knew that when she returned to her hut she would change into old working clothes and go out into the garden.

But here she stood apart, neat, confident, and friendly, wearing her hair in a high bunch at the back after the style of Javanese women I had seen. It had been well groomed and it suited her rather round face with its broad eyes.

Later I was to ask her why she had thrown in her lot with the refugees, and had she been in danger?

"My brother was a member of the Movement," she told me, "and they left us alone for a long time, until one night our house was raided by soldiers. They said that they were looking for my brother. We were all taken outside and questioned, and then three of the soldiers took me away into the bush."

She stopped and looked appealingly at me. I understood and didn't ask her any more, but after a while she continued, "From that moment I hated them and I was determined that I would fight them, so I ran away and went to some of my friends who looked after me and then helped me to come here. I will fight, too, if we have to when the trouble comes."

"You couldn't live in the jungle and carry a rifle," I said.

"Perhaps not, but I can cook and look after the sick and do all that is required to look after our men. I'm not afraid of the jungle and I'm not afraid now of the Indonesian soldiers and it doesn't need a strong man to press the trigger of a gun. I'll do that if I have to."

Her face had hardened and her eyes were showing anger, but after a few moments she had relapsed into the quiet, smiling girl again and she said, "I can tell you a lot of nasty things, and so can all these people."

I watched as she got up and walked away, trim, neat, and attractive and an excellent wife for any young man, if she ever returned to her own station in life.

The bareness of this camp was oppressive. Meal hours were twice a day, at 10 a.m. and 4 p.m., if there was sufficient food. Medical supplies consisted of a small roll of adhesive tape and some iodine. No quinine for fevers, no bandages for cuts and sores, no drugs to ease pain, no common remedies for common ailments.

This was the first camp I had ever visited where there was no sick line. Those who were sick laid down and slept until the sickness wore off, or they died, or as happened occasionally, the camp took courage and appealed to the Administration to assist. This last was an uncertainty, for some who had been sent on to Vanimo had been turned back.

"If you have a little sick you can go to Wutung patrol post. If you have a big sick then go back to Sukarnapura," was the message they alleged they had been given by the Administration authorities.

"Tell the Australian authorities that we will build a school and build a hospital and staff it with our own people if they will provide school materials and medicine and drugs," was one of the pleas I heard.

I told the authorities that when I returned, but by then it was too late.

There was an old chap sitting close to me who hadn't spoken and seemed to be lost in his own thoughts. I turned to him and asked, "How many times did they put you in gaol?" He answered in Indonesian and we had to call upon the interpreter.

"None," he said, and slowly pulled off his shirt. Across his back were four white weals and another showed on the right side of his neck. "They came to my house and began beating me up," he explained. "These marks are knife wounds and I nearly died from

146

them. My friends nursed me and brought me down here. I don't know why they did this for I am an old man. Maybe it is because I am a West Papuan."

They all had stories of horror, brutality, and endurance and they all knew that if they went back to their homes again and were caught, it could mean death.

One young man had been twice across the border, had been forcibly returned the first time, and had survived. His account is illustrative of the silent struggle which is being waged between the refugees and the Administration.

I had heard reports of this long before but never the complete story, and here was one of the actual participants to tell it. This was his tale:

"On 4 January 1963 I was one of a party of forty-four men who fled from Sukarnapura because soldiers and police were trying to arrest us as members of the West New Guinea Freedom Movement.

"After several days in the bush we eventually arrived at Vanimo and asked the authorities for political asylum. This was refused but we were kept in a group for three weeks until the District Commissioner at Wewak came to see us and question us.

"Our group consisted of teachers from colleges and law students, with some from other professions. I was a student then.

"Telegrams were sent to the official Australian representative at Hollandia who also flew to Vanimo and questioned us. He said that Indonesian soldiers were worrying him about our departure and wanted to know where we were. He said that we must go back because he was having trouble over us.

"One of the things he said was, 'I can't sleep at night because of the soldiers coming to me all the time.'

"He then flew back to Hollandia and the next day an Administration vessel came into Vanimo and we were all put aboard. With us was the District Commissioner from Wewak, an A.D.C. from Vanimo, and four armed policemen.

"When we were at sea we were told that the Australian Government had ordered the ship to go direct to Hollandia, or Sukarnapura as it is now called, but all of us objected and asked if we could be put ashore at the Tami River, a few miles inside the West Irian border.

"They agreed to do this and we were all put ashore on the beach and given supplies of tinned meat, rice, and fish and told to return to Sukarnapura. Then the boat sailed back to Vanimo.

"We all walked back to Sukarnapura and the Indonesian police immediately arrested the lot of us and put us in gaol. When they questioned me I told them that I was not running away from the

Indonesians but from the Dutch and that I had been afraid of them. They believed me and let me out and I went back to the university to study.

"But in May 1963, the soldiers came looking for me again. I was warned by a friend so I ran away and walked down to the border by myself. I have been living in the bush and in this camp ever since. I will not ask the Administration to help me again because they will send me back on another boat."

By all humanitarian standards these people should be assisted, whether Indonesia likes it or not.

"If you had been treated like we have been, wouldn't you run away to another country?" I was asked. I began to think about our own Papuan and New Guinean people who have been promised ultimate self-government and are being trained for independence.

If these people were told by the race of people responsible for guiding them that all promises of freedom were henceforth to be repudiated, wouldn't they want to fight, and wouldn't the Australian Government (as an outsider) offer to help them?

I have seen a letter written to the Minister for External Territories asking that a section of land be set aside for the West Irian refugees upon which they could settle and secure work.

I have also seen his reply in which he states that the Australian Government does not want minority groups in the Territory and that its aim is for the integration of the refugees into the community.

If that is the aim then why were forty people, from Vanimo and Wewak, suddenly flown direct to Manus Island and herded into a police compound; and the refugees in the border camps chased back over the line by armed police, and some of their houses burnt down?

Those at Vanimo and Wewak had jobs, settled homes, and their children were at school. At Manus Island they are issued with rations on a labourer's scale, have no work or income and, at the last report, are busily building homes for themselves from native bush materials. This is a remarkable interpretation of the declared policy of integration.

One of my questions to them was, "Did you talk to the United Nations Visiting Mission who came here at the beginning of 1968?"

They smiled rather sardonically and answered, "The United Nations team came to Wutung and inspected the border marking post on the beach. Then they went back to Vanimo and Wewak. We did not know they were here and they probably did not know about us. Nobody told us anything but heard about their visit from a passing native policeman six weeks after they had left. No government officer told us anything."

Paul Lapun (left) Member for South Bougainville in the House of Assembly, with a village leader at Rorovana, Bougainville

Villagers meet to discuss the CRA land dispute with Paul Lapun at the Meeting House, Rorovana

I doubt whether the United Nations know that yet. I travelled for a while with the Visiting Mission and they were a body of men who were really on the ball. Had they known at the time, I am certain that a meeting with the refugees would have taken place.

This is one of the nastier aspects of the whole problem. Nobody with official authority had ever been to the camp; officially, nobody cared; nobody wanted to know just what was happening; nobody wanted questions asked; nobody wanted any responsibility in the matter; and nobody had any humanitarian feelings.

One final and important question they did put to me. "Can you get your House of Assembly members to ask for an open inquiry into our conditions so that our problems and situation can become public?"

I wrote this question into a story that was published, and I also lobbied any elected members I could find. The question was raised in the House by two members, one of whom asked that the Administration act sympathetically towards these people. The answer to that came in a charge that the members were insulting the name of New Guinea! What a magnificent example of political quibbling.

Of course the subject died, as it had to, for by then all those refugees who had been granted permissive residence had been promptly shifted over to Manus Island, far away in the big ocean, and the other unfortunates had been chased back into their own country by a hundred policemen.

All this happened before any publication of the situation had been made in the papers. With no problem left to solve there was no need for an inquiry, and besides, there had been a newspaperman on the scene to see and hear for himself, and you know how welcome newsmen are.

This was the domestic and social situation as I saw it and there was sufficient material to write about it for hours. It is still going on, as I know from reports which are still coming through, and a position is developing which will take far more than a hundred policemen to settle. I fully expect that there will be guerilla warfare on the border of West Irian and Papua-New Guinea, for events are shaping that can lead to no other result.

I doubted that these people would win their plebiscite, for the forces against them are too strong, but I do know that they will fight, and they're not bluffing over that. Unarmed, underfed, and the underdogs in an internecine conflict, their national spirit and determination will not be subdued too easily, and if aid is available to them from outside then trouble will eventuate in capital letters.

There is a second, and more serious aspect to this coming conflict,

A nightmare section of steep grades on the road from Kieta to Paguna, Bougainville and it will overshadow anything that happens within West Irian. I can only repeat what I was told. It is for the powerful ones in the land to judge and assess, and what is written here they already know.

It was the last day of my visit and it dawned brightly with clear, blue skies and an invigorating, cool air. The mountains hemming in the small camp-site were standing clear-cut as if painted by an artist.

In the sharp, early light of dawn the scene appeared to have little relation to a centre of intrigue, suffering, and despair, for there were the songs of the birds, the sound of an axe in the forest, the blue smoke of morning fires, and the cadence of women's voices from across the gully.

One could easily mistake it for a pioneer bush settlement where peace and labour prevailed and the future looked bright with development, but it was only a passing impression, for twenty yards away a man was busily tapping on a typewriter beneath a lean-to of sago leaves that represented the office.

More letters, more proclamations, and more reports were being churned out and these bore no relationship to our rustic surroundings.

Everyday I had noticed this young man at his perpetual task of typing, with the leaders almost at his elbow, passing papers and advising while he tapped the keys. His endurance must have been amazing for his hours were long, from dawn until very late at night, always typing, and the echo of it could be heard in the continuous stream of staccato taps throughout the whole camp.

The machine, from what I could see, was their one main piece of equipment. It bore the markings, "K.P.P.B.69" and had obviously been carefully carried through the bush sometime previously. Without it, the momentum of this particular organization would have been greatly impaired for it served as their voice, transformed into reams of flimsy papers that were distributed far and wide through the whole movement, keeping each organization in touch with the others.

The appreciation of how vital this one piece of equipment was came to me as I watched this man, day after day. The simple typewriter was one of the main organs of the movement. Destroy it and each organization would be floundering within itself, groping for communication, planning according to its own limited capabilities, without central direction or control over matters that could mean life or death for thousands of people.

True, all this paperwork had to travel by couriers to destinations in other parts, and that took time, but were everything to be hand-written the task would become impossible.

Of secondary importance was the camp radio set, tuned in each evening to Sukarnapura and Jakarta to pick up Indonesian broadcasts, and I strongly suspect, an occasional message to those who were planning revolt, for these people were thorough and their intelligence services were superbly organized.

One could hardly expect them to ignore the advantages of a friendly announcer including messages during his schedules, for I had already been told how the agents of the Freedom Movement were installed in all stratas of official Indonesian fields, from the President's office to the remote rural district army and police headquarters.

After a cup of morning coffee my companion, the intelligence chief, came and advised me that arrangements had been completed for me to begin my homeward trip that evening.

"We will see you safely back at Vanimo," he said, "and this afternoon we shall hold a small conference which we would like you to attend."

At two o'clock that afternoon the tall, grey-haired, rather emaciated commander of the organization walked into my hut accompanied by Marten, my companion of the last few days and nights.

He spoke a few words to those who were sitting in the hut and they all rose and left the three of us alone.

Unfortunately the commander knew no English or Pidgin, but Marten spoke four languages, including English, and he acted as interpreter as well as prompter to his superior officer.

For a while they spoke together, and then Marten turned to me and said, "We have some information which we wish you to pass on to responsible Australian officials and high officers of the army. Can you do this?"

It was a request that I was not prepared for, as I had no immediate contacts with high officials, either governmental or military, and I could only assure them that whatever information they gave me would be sent forward to the best of my ability.

I suggested that if it were of a confidential and important nature they would do better to present it to the local District Commissioner at Vanimo who had the authority to push such matters through official channels.

This they were vehemently against. "We do not trust your Administration," they told me. "In the past we have made tentative approaches to the Administration for them to hear what we have to

151

say but we have been brushed aside. We have absolutely no status in the Administration's eyes and they just won't listen. I am sure that they do not realize that we have information of value to them and you can hardly expect us to reveal what we know without a certain amount of friendly consideration. This we cannot get so we have lost faith in them."

The old man spoke very passionately for a while. "He says," interpreted Marten, "that this information is far beyond our own troubles and is of national importance to Papua-New Guinea and to Australia. It must reach the Australian Government."

After another talk together, Marten opened out with a long explanation of the merits of their intelligence systems, many points of which I already had proof.

"Our people are everywhere," he said, "in the villages, the towns, police, army, and government headquarters. We have our own men in contact with the President's Executive Council and we know of every plan and order that goes through. We know what the future Indonesian policy is and how it will operate, and we are not exaggerating when we say that we have documents to prove all we tell you."

A lot of this I knew to be true, for I had seen similar documents in the past and some must have been of great national importance.

"This is what we have to tell you, and this is what we want made known," he went on. "The long range policy of Indonesia is to take over Papua and New Guinea and may, from what we know at present, also include parts of Australia. In the schools of West Irian, your Territory is shown as East Irian, and the children are taught that it is fundamentally part of Indonesia. We know also that any move of conquest by the Indonesian Government will be supported by the Indonesian Communists and the two will work together.

"Action on this cannot start before the plebiscite in 1969 because Jakarta must first of all subdue our country and we are determined to fight. But we are weak and will be the buffer. Once West Irian has been consolidated then it will be Papua-New Guinea's turn. We know this is to happen because we have documentary proof."

"When is this planned to happen?" I asked.

He shrugged. "We don't know. We know that we are in immediate danger and we know that you people will be next. It is inevitable and it will be in co-operation with the Communists."

An improbability struck me at once. "But the Indonesian Government is suppressing Communism," I told them. "From what we hear there have been from 200,000 to 300,000 people killed, and action against Communism is still going on."

152

He agreed that there had been a campaign and admitted that the figure of about one quarter of a million casualties might be correct. "Don't forget," he said, "that most of those killed were village people, many of whom were not Communists and had little to do with Communism. Some of the leaders were killed but the organization survives and is still strong, as you will have learnt from recent outbreaks."

"The Indonesian Communists are primarily nationalists," he continued, "and that means that in any attempt at conquest they will join in because it will be ultimately to their advantage. Later, when they are strong enough, they will challenge the Indonesian Government again, and what it has obtained they will take. They are wise enough to subjugate their own political desires for the sake of broader gains, and they will co-operate, no matter who their partners may be."

I had to admit the logic of their argument but I wondered if in the idealism of their cause they were becoming blind to realities. The one weakness in their political behaviour is that they believe in honesty of purpose, and for that they have suffered. They believe that the United Nations can ensure a free and open plebiscite because the agreement says "an act of free choice," a phrase that can be interpreted in many ways.

I have little personal doubt that Indonesia intends to remain master of West Irian and I know that these dreams of including "East Irian" in their Republic were once very real.

Do these dreams still exist? There are reasons to believe that they do, despite the foreign aid that is pouring into Indonesia now and the new international face she is showing to the world.

Assuming that Indonesia might, and could, take over Papua-New Guinea, would it create more than a diplomatic flurry among the nations?

As the best equipped, militarily, in South-East Asia she could accomplish a take-over with little trouble, and as we have already experienced during the Second World War, Papua-New Guinea is expendable. There could be another "Brisbane Line" theory, which by inference might indicate that Northern Australia is also expendable.

It seems very doubtful that America, after her Vietnam experience, would again commit large forces within the Asian region, and an expansionist policy in Indonesia, prodded by internal Communist ambitions, fits well into the overall pattern of insurrection that prevails from Korea, through Vietnam, Thailand, Laos and down through the archipelago of South-East Asia.

That it will happen is probable, although it may take five, ten, or even more years to become manifest. The hidden menace is not Indonesia but the Communist kernel within, and it would be foolish to say that it can't happen here.

The old man began speaking again. "We expect Australia to appreciate what we have to say and to be willing to assist us when our time comes," he said. "Tell them what we have told you and tell them that we are prepared to meet Australian leaders and give them all the information we possess."

The conversation drifted off onto their own affairs, to plans for the formation of their own government, and for long we talked of this, asking questions, and reasoning together.

They gave me a tentative list of their ministerial office holders in a government to be created and asked that I refrain from publishing it until the whole Freedom Movement had met and agreed upon the names. This I still have, awaiting the word for its release.

One could not ignore the implications of what they had told me, and as I packed my gear ready for the hike through the jungle to the coast later that night, I wondered just what reaction this news would have on those responsible for the country's safety, for I was determined that I would make every effort to pass this information on. It was the least that I could do in repayment for their confidence.

As an epilogue to this conference I can say that the information was passed on to both the Administration and the Australian authorities. By good fortune I met a high ranking military officer and placed the subject in his hands.

Later I received an acknowledgment from military headquarters that the information had been received, and although not a word came from the Administration, I know that they were very promptly advised.

At sundown, over one hundred men, women, and children gathered in the camp outside the hut to say goodbye. This was the end of a wonderful few days of friendliness and confidence, and I felt rather helpless in that all I could return were my thanks and a promise to try, within the scope of my professional duties, to let the outside world understand something of their problems, hardships, and hopes.

I realized the futility of expecting too much, for I have had a full share of experience in the pragmatism of government, in its ability to dissemble and its complacence in re-orienting facts to suit its own fixed desires.

I knew that this was not a popular subject in official minds; that

154

the problem had been swept under the carpet for many years; that it had been subject to distortion and evasion and that any words of mine would be rendered as harmless as possible.

The first casualty of political expediency is humanitarianism, for facts must be rendered expedient to the tin God of Public Relations, and the human element often becomes the least important factor.

I knew that I was the first European person to come to these people and live with them, to try, in some small way, to understand their points of view. They had been consistently shunned by everybody; made outcasts of society, avoided like lepers, and treated like jackals.

Their greatest offence was that they wanted national freedom and the fulfilment of promises made to them years before, and they were prepared to fight, and die, for that objective.

They had travelled the same road as the people of Papua and New Guinea are now travelling and I often wondered how the people of this Territory would be regarded if promises made to them were repudiated and they decided to fight for their enforcement. There is little doubt that they, too, would be shunned and driven into the wilderness as offerings on the altar of political expediency just as these refugees from West Irian have been.

And when I finally shook hands with them all, with firm grips from the men, a few quiet words from the women, and the shy, timorous smiles from the children, the full force of this tragic waste of human talent became very apparent.

In this group were men and women of high professional abilities trying to live normal, family lives and hoping that somewhere in the world, sometime in the future, their children would receive their rights and be trained as future citizens.

These people had been refused their place in their own country, and they had been refused any rights in Papua-New Guinea. Now they were between the devil and the deep sea. They could go back to Sukarnapura and be shot and imprisoned, or stay here and rot in the jungle. They also had the choice of suicidal warfare, and this is the one they had chosen.

Yet every one of them could be assimilated into modern society, with work, homes, and family security, and become a credit to the country which adopted them.

If positive efforts were made towards this end there would be no more talk of insurrection and sacrifice, for no man wants to see his womenfolk and children starved and mangled to death.

I did not know then that a call, made some weeks later by members of the House of Assembly in Port Moresby, for a more humanitarian attitude towards these unfortunates would be arbitrarily silenced as "an insult to New Guinea."

Accompanied by about a dozen men, we shouldered our packs and we plunged into the forest, towards a track that led through a belt of jungle down towards the coast. For almost an hour we stumbled along the track in deep darkness, each man holding the hand of the man in front and guided by one of the leaders who must have had eyes like a cat.

For me it was quite an agonizing journey, for my feet and legs were still swollen and infected from leech bites, and this was the first time I had worn shoes for a week. The rest had brought signs of improvement but now, stumbling blindly through the night and tripping over rocks and roots wiped out the recuperative gains and added fresh sores and cuts.

We came to the edge of a small coconut plantation adjacent to the patrol post at Wutung, and through the trees could see the lights and hear voices from the station. Suddenly we became mixed with a group of station hands, and when we had got clear of them, turned sharply again into the jungle beyond the border of trees and hurried forward towards the west.

"They will go back and tell the police about us," a man whispered, and again that element of fear arose among my companions. We pushed on blindly until screened from all possible search parties. Then we stopped for a rest and a whispered conversation about the canoe that was waiting somewhere for me to board.

Time and direction seemed to have been abandoned and I guessed that we were, by now, well inside the West Irian border. To our right I could hear the ocean rollers crashing over the reefs but all else was stillness and I was sincerely hoping that my departure from the camp would not take another tortuous ten hours similar to that experienced in reaching it.

Two men moved off to scout the beach and locate the canoe and we crouched down in the undergrowth cooling off from our exertions. There was no speaking or smoking as we sat silently in the darkness with only the mosquitoes which came to plague us. Soon one of the men returned and we started again, heading towards the beach and stopping in a fringe of light trees bordering a wide strip of sand.

From our left a canoe appeared, being pulled through the shallows by two men. It was a simple dug-out type with one outrigger and a small platform amidships, and its appearance belied its ability to take us back across the twenty-odd miles of open sea, to Vanimo.

156

There were a few hasty farewells, my gear was taken, and I followed to the canoe, splashing through the warm, salt water and clambering aboard. Out in the ocean the breakers were catching the first beams of moonlight, the sky was clear, and the water smooth and oily. As they pushed us from the beach the last words I heard were, "Selamat tinggal"—"Goodbye," and then we felt the first swell of the rollers. I glanced behind but the beach was deserted. From somewhere under the trees they were watching.

There were three paddlers and myself and we stroked steadily towards the first line of foaming breakers. Between us and them was a comparatively quiet stretch of water and confidence overcame caution for we had barely gone thirty yards when suddenly the canoe veered broadside to the swell, tipped dangerously, and began to spin. Though paddling fiercely we were carried westwards, still out of control and still spinning, for we had caught a fast tidal rip that treated all our efforts with violent disdain.

The bright clusters of lights from Sukarnapura seemed very close. I could distinguish them along the foreshore and rising up into the hill behind the town, while a wide, red background glow reflected across the water and upon us.

Back we went to the beach out of the rip and straightened up. This time the four of us waded and swam the canoe forward, pushing against the rip diagonally until we were clear of it, then clambering aboard and paddling straight ahead for the breakers.

Our luck was out, for two huge combers roared down, swamped the canoe, and sent us back to the beach again.

A torch flashed from somewhere along the shore and we dropped into the water, holding the canoe steady with our hands, ready to let it go and dash for the scrub if the stranger turned out to be a patrolling guard. Nobody came and nobody called, so slowly we waded eastwards along the shore line back towards Wutung, clambering aboard again at a deserted patch and paddling slowly and silently towards a line of fires that marked the station.

The smell of sandalwood smoke came to us like heavy incense as we moved forward, and soon we could see small groups of people sitting, and hear their talk. Warily we paddled forward waiting for an inevitable hail from those near us. I pulled a blanket over my head to hide the whiteness of my face for the moon had risen and the night was soft and bright. They disregarded us, probably thinking that we were fishermen. A dog barked and a woman's voice silenced it, so we sailed on close inshore until, a mile further on, we came to a narrow entrance through the reefs.

One hour and a quarter after boarding the canoe we were in the open sea, and once behind the headland that juts out from Wutung station, we set our course direct for Vanimo, twenty miles away, happy at getting free from the troubles that had hindered us and glad that the night was clear and bright and the sea smooth with only the faintest of rolling swells.

A land breeze sprang up and chilled us, for we were all soaking wet, but the steady rhythm and exertion of paddling soon warmed us as we passed down the long, dark, silent coastline without one glimmer of a light for mile after mile towards the stubby, peaked patch of land far off on the horizon.

Behind, the lights of Sukarnapura were getting dimmer, and out here we had the freedom of the sea—it felt like the freedom of the world.

At three the next morning, eight hours after leaving Wutung, we rode the breakers into the flats of Vanimo. As our canoe grounded, a rain squall hit us, and we waded ashore and sat under the trees until dawn.

We had completed a trip that many West Irian refugees had done before us. For them it has become an occupational hazard. There are police, soldiers, shore patrols, and an occasional cruising launch to stop the flow of exiles. We had been more fortunate than many of those before us for our passage had only been hindered by the elements. If there had been immediate dangers then we had missed them.

The risks were now in the realm of past possibilities and I could imagine the furore which would have followed the capture of a foreign newsman and three refugees on the border beachhead if we had been unfortunate enough to have met a patrol.

Viewed retrospectively, the trip had been worth it. I had completed what I had set out to do and had obtained the information I sought. The crippling pains of infection were small in comparison with the accomplishment, thanks wholly to the aid and assistance which these people had given me.

We sat until the morning light threw the first glow of dawn over the station and then rose and went our ways, the paddlers to some friends of theirs in town and I myself to a small cottage near the airfield which I had been kindly allowed to use.

Physically I was thankful the trip was over for my clothes were salt-encrusted, my body chafed and weary, and my feet and legs throbbing with pain. The salt water had washed the plaster covering from my wounds and the walk from the beach, through the still sleeping town, along crushed coral roads had been quite painful.

All I wanted was a hot wash, some tea to drink, and a long sleep. Fortunately I was on my own and I doubted whether anybody would be interested enough to disturb me.

The authorities knew that I was back for I had passed police night patrols on my way to the house and the fact would be reported and noted.

I stayed on in Vanimo for a week after my return, most of the time nursing my injured feet and legs and gathering together my notes for stories that had to be written. I answered questions from many people, hiding nothing of what I had seen and experienced, and there were long sessions at the District Headquarters talking over the situation. I told them bluntly that within the next twelve months they could expect an outbreak of guerilla warfare and that this would increase the flow of refugees. To my surprise I found that nobody at headquarters knew where the main camp was actually situated, whether it was in the Territory of Papua-New Guinea or in West Irian. This confirmed what the refugees had told me, "Nobody has ever visited us."

Whether this lack of knowledge was real or part of the general smoke-screen it was hard to tell, for there were people in town who knew where the camps were, and there had been individual refugees coming in to Vanimo for hospital treatment or other matters.

The exhibition of such complete ignorance of these people seemed to border on the ridiculous, for there was no good reason why the location of the camps should be kept so secret. It was general knowledge everywhere except in the district headquarters, an attitude which I strongly refused to accept but which is typical of the intrigue and secrecy that is a predominant feature of the Administration's attitude in its border areas.

There had been some concern, I was given to understand, when my sudden departure from Vanimo had been discovered, and I learned, about two weeks later and in another place, that radio messages had been flying all over the district seeking news of my whereabouts. Ostensibly this had been centred upon my own welfare. Had I drowned or had I gone bush and got lost? One remarkable fact was that in all the calls outside my name was never mentioned. Patrol officers were questioned, "Have you seen a strange man about? Another kind of a man near your station?" and the confusion that this started among junior officers who had never met me, and had no idea of what type of man was wanted, can be imagined.

"If you come back again come and see us. We'll help you,"

they told me. But the memory of my first visit to Vanimo was still fresh, and besides, I knew well enough that official aid given to a wandering reporter on matters that were best kept quiet could boomerang against any unfortunate official who stepped out of line. It was better to go it alone and not put any sympathetic official into a false position.

In all my talks I carefully avoided any reference to what the refugees had told me of future Indonesian plans. There were other channels open for passing on this information, and they could be used to greater advantage. The Administration would hear in good time but the information was of too great a significance to spread abroad. If there were to be questions on this matter then let them be asked elsewhere. On the truth or otherwise of this subject I could not talk. Let others, with greater knowledge and resources, gather the scraps and fit them into the overall picture. That is why the intelligence game is no longer a one-man show, and district headquarters are only clearing houses.

So I went my way for another two weeks, to Aitape, Angoram, Ambunti, Maprik and Wewak in a wide circle, gathering what news was available and collecting notes for later stories.

At the Wewak hotel, where I stayed one day, I was called out to meet a visitor. He was a West Irian with an offer to act as courier for me to and from Sukarnapura, bringing me news of the latest developments. All he wanted was permanent employment at regular wages. I turned him down on the grounds that this would be a matter for my newspaper to decide, and after he left I wondered how he had discovered that I was in Wewak and where I had been in my wanderings.

There was a second visitor, too, a high government officer who called me over and remarked, "You've been stirring things up on the border, I believe," and laughed. I was left reflecting that it doesn't take long for news to circulate, and that apart from the wires humming there must have been somebody around who was still interested in my movements.

And so to Madang, to start on the heap of accumulated work. If I had held any expectations of breaking some startling news they were futile, for within twenty-four hours of my arrival the radio announced that all the West Irian refugees in Vanimo and Wewak had been airlifted direct over to Manus Island and that police patrols had been sent to the border areas to order the inmates of the camps back over the West Irian side.

This was the government's answer after three years of procrastination, and it was executed so rapidly that it tended to reduce

160

the impact of the stories which subsequently appeared, thus subduing unfavourable reactions to the plight of refugees.

There were reports and denials, and later confirmations, that huts in the camps had been burnt down. Even in this there were contradictory reasons and when questions were asked in the House of Assembly they were parried. The situation of a government which shelters refugees known to be planning insurrection in their own land is not an enviable one but the situation had existed for a long time and had been known, as documents and official announcements proved. Why then this sudden spurt of action? Was it to circumvent any possibility of a call for an inquiry, so that if a call came, a clean pair of hands could be shown and a *fait accompli* presented to demonstrate that no problem existed?

Those most affected were the men and women and children who had settled in Vanimo and Wewak, where they had jobs, homes, and schooling. To be unceremoniously bundled aboard a plane and deposited in a ninety feet by forty feet police barracks in Manus, without work, privacy, or income, was hardly an act of humanitarianism.

I have seen letters from some of them in which they say that they have been told to build their own native material houses on a selected piece of land; that they are on government rations; that their standards of living have dropped to that of mendicants on government aid, and that their children are the greatest sufferers for their home lives have been disrupted, and without work or wages the parents cannot provide the extras that children need, nor can they provide clothes for themselves or their families.

An official announcement was later made that any employer seeking help could apply to the Administration for the employment of these people anywhere except in the border areas, but who among the employing class would be prepared to risk the engagement of people of whom he knew nothing, with the added responsibility of being liable for their families? So the onus is on the employers and the refugees to solve a situation which neither one nor the other has brought about.

Even viewing the move from political aspects, it has served no good purpose for the lines of communication are still open, the planning still goes on, and it does nothing to remove the spectre of insurrection after 1969.

Forty people isolated on a small island will not remove the threat of armed action while many hundreds roam the bush with a determination to resist, and this is the matter that should be given attention for it is real and growing more serious.

161

journey into depression

HAVE YOU EVER SEEN a prosperous town being steadily pulled to a halt and then begin slowly to wither? Have you ever seen residents of long standing, with families and property, meet in the shadow of doubt and in fear of their whole life's work crumbling about them? Have you been in a place where the native population is listless, drifting and caring not whether it works or not in a country where unemployment should be classed as a crime? And it all started so differently, with a wave of optimism that was going to carry everybody on to the sandy beach of security.

Take a map of New Guinea. Draw connecting lines linking Lae with Madang, Madang with Mount Hagen, and Mount Hagen back to Lae, and you have a triangle that could rightly be called the Heartland of the Territory.

According to the 1966 census, 850,000 native people and 10,000 foreign nationals are directly affected within this space which has an area of 37,000 square miles. It includes four districts—Morobe, Madang, the Eastern and Western Highlands—and if you go beyond these boundaries, among the perimeter populations, the influence of this main pivot can affect a total of well over the million mark, one-half of the Territory's population.

Around the edges are the Chimbu District with 180,000 people, the highest concentration of population in any one district, and the Southern Highlands with more than half of its 184,000 inhabitants in its northern sector, and 50,000 in the Northern District.

All these are affected to some considerable extent by the four main areas, as is the concentrated government and commercial centre of Port Moresby.

Look for a while at the advantages which are contained in this comparatively small block.

162

In coffee alone, the Highlands' districts have five-sixths of the Territory's acreage; they produce 100% of the pyrethrum and passion fruit industries; 100% of plywood and veneer manufacturing; and an unchallenged lead in the newly established, highly capitalized, tea industry.

Madang produces the largest amount of copra on the New Guinea mainland and its cacao harvests are creating another industry of considerable strength.

Large cacao interests are also established in the Morobe District which carries 75% of the Territory's cattle population—another 16% are in the Madang District—and the town of Lae is rapidly rising as the industrial and manufacturing centre of Papua-New Guinea.

Valuable timber potential exists in all of the areas—in the Ramu Valley, the Jimi River, and the pine forests of Bulolo. Mineral deposits are unknown but they are being investigated. There is talk that the Finisterre Ranges, a 12,000-foot rugged mountain chain that spreads across the eastern flank of Madang and northern Morobe, may contain big deposits of iron ore.

There is plenty of water and arable land by the thousands of acres with the country rising from 10 feet above sea level on the coast to 12,000 feet inland, with Mount Wilhelm, around 15,000 feet, as king of the lot.

There is a main highway of over 300 miles linking Lae with Mount Hagen, and feeder roads that go on to Wabag, Wapenamanda, and beyond, as well as a network plunging down into the Southern Highlands.

Another road is pushing its way up the Ramu Valley from the Markham to within 40 miles of Madang, and on the coast there are plans and work going ahead on a road westwards towards the Ramu River estuary, 150 miles from Madang.

The airlines have a network concentrated on the four main centres and the Overseas Telecommunications System has a base at Madang and is in contact with the whole world.

The best of harbours and facilities, second only to Port Moresby, are at Madang, and these are capable of coping with any expansion within the foreseeable future.

Lae and Mount Hagen are less than one hour's flight from Madang; Goroka is thirty-five minutes from Madang and forty-five minutes from both Lae and Mount Hagen. You can do the whole round trip by DC3, with stopovers in Mount Hagen and Goroka, in less than three hours, and faster than that if you connect with the Fokker Friendship service at Goroka.

163

With these advantages optimism in the future of this Heartland seems justified, for the four districts have the fundamental basis of country whose viability still rests upon its agricultural potential.

Outwardly, as you wing over its plains, valleys, and mountains, it presents a picture of confidence and security. To any student of national economic and social development the future looks bright.

Even to the uninitiated it must seem that with concentrated attention towards the further development of natural resources, social advances, encouragement of primary and secondary industrial expansion, and the maintenance of essential communications and services, an axis that will lead to ultimate national viability is assured.

One of the important influencing factors has been the remarkable natural growth in this area since 1946, a form of internal combustion that has pushed expansion ahead, far beyond any expectations.

The exploratory years of the 1930s confirmed the enormous reservoir of human and natural resources that were available for development. If the war years had not intervened, the economic growth of this region would have been far more outstanding. As it was, with revitalization awaiting the ending of armed conflict, the advances made over the past twenty-five years have produced an example of human endeavour that stands as high as any throughout the civilized world.

Against modern competitive demands, New Guinea contains an inordinately high proportion of "waste," in humanity, land, and resources. Not all the scientific accomplishments of our civilization can overcome these disabilities.

The people are extremely primitive, the terrain is rugged and in places impenetrable, there are uneconomic residues of resources, and there is an overall pattern of impregnability which defies conquest.

Man has got to the moon, but in New Guinea it is beyond human capability to bring the most meagre of civilized benefits to people less than 80 miles from a main urban centre; aircraft skim the Territory at 300 miles an hour, over sections that, if you were walking, one mile of progress, or less, would be a hard day's work; elsewhere in the world, billions of dollars are spent on destructive warfare, yet fertile land and potential mineral wealth lie untouched here because of the uneconomic costs of their development.

In this world where everything must be justified as a monetary investment, New Guinea is a long way down the list.

When the impediments are considered, the economic rise of the Highlands' area has been remarkable. The Highlander has been one of the last to come within the orbit of civilization, yet he has progressed at a far greater pace than many of his more sophisticated brethren on the coast who have had almost a century of settlement and guidance.

A combination of things brought this transformation about: the Highlanders' own characteristics of initiative and adaptability; the broader, more co-operative outlook of the foreigners who settled in the country; the trump card of an agricultural potential—high grade coffee—that was not available in other parts of the country; and a general pattern of incentive plus initiative which has been the dominating feature for all concerned, both white and black.

It is no exaggeration to say that nowhere else in the Territory can be found such high co-ordination of purpose and principle between the two races as is evident in the Highlands.

The Highlander is no mere hewer of wood and carrier of water, content to come at the flick of a finger, or go at the wave of a hand. He is a determined, highly principled man, anxious for advice and instruction, fully prepared to serve his apprenticeship, capable of assimilating the basic requirements of a strange industry, a man possessing trust and confidence in those who have knowledge and who never shirks an opportunity to launch out on his own in competition with others and in work that calls for hard labour.

It is to the credit of the early white settlers that these qualities were recognized and understood, for this has resulted in the blending of two entirely opposite social groups in a mosaic of co-operation and the evil of most developing countries—the pattern of conquest —has been avoided.

The Highlander is a businessman, a hard-headed pragmatic gentleman who can see where the advantages lie and he will work to achieve them. He recognizes the rewards and power of private endeavour, he appreciates good management, and many of his compatriots are men of substance and wealth in material assets, in plantations, vehicles, and healthy bank accounts.

One hears little talk of self-government or independence among the Highlanders. There is no yearning for emancipation and a far from intensive interest in political ideas that come wafting down the valleys from outside. He has an ambition for economic security and this pushes abstract theories of political freedom to one side.

There will be time enough later to study such things, and as many predict—quite rightly—when the Highlanders plunge into the political arena, only then will the shape of any future independent government become visible, for they will be the ones who will hold the purse strings and the power that goes with it.

Half a million Highlanders, welded together in the school of practical experience and knowing what they want, will be a force to reckon with, and those who oppose them will probably be defeated.

For two decades after the war the Heartland of New Guinea boomed and every component part felt its effects. Goroka was first thrust ahead by the expansion of the coffee industry under leadership which pushed development in land, roads, and settlement. The momentum extended to the Western Highlands, bringing a phenomenal expansion to Mount Hagen and a growth that soon created its own internal problems. Services could not cope with demands; supplies were always short; road communications poor, and although the airlines increased their services the pressures remained constant.

For a while Mount Hagen had all the appearances of a frontier mining centre which, in some respects, it still maintains. But the boom had substance; it was no pot of gold at the foot of a rainbow but was made of solid earth and vigorous people.

Madang, an hour away by plane, became the natural port of entry and the outlet for the Highlands' trade and produce.

Here were all the facilities, the port installations, the nearest and most direct route to the coast, an excellent airport little affected by the vagaries of weather and a natural partner in any scheme for the Highlands' development.

Madang became the second most important air freight terminal in the southern hemisphere; its shipping tonnage climbed steadily to make it third among Territory ports, and like its neighbour, it reflected a healthy growth.

With Goroka, Mount Hagen, and Madang, the initial triangle of progress was formed, unaffected by outside pressures from other parts.

Lae, at this period, was outside the direct circumference of this inland development although it had a share of the opportunities in the small percentage of trade which struggled along the rough, semi-constructed Highlands' Highway where maintenance, expenses, and the irregular availability of the route created some prohibitive barriers.

The perversities of war, which had left Madang a heap of rubble and had clamped down on the Highlands' development, bestowed upon Lae a residue of service roads and airstrips that brought rehabilitation to the area far more quickly than elsewhere.

Recovery at Lae was comparatively rapid. Bulolo and Wau were back into harness; the Markham Valley was being resettled, and by 1965, the main highway from Lae had climbed to the top of the Kassam Pass and was pushing towards Kainantu in a fever of reconstruction.

Next came the link of fifty-one miles to Goroka, completed in 1967, and now the road is being further consolidated towards Mount Hagen and over the treacherous Daulo Pass country, a bugbear of loose clay and landslides for many years.

While this work was progressing, Lae was being built up as the Territory's second most important centre, with an emphasis on industrial and commercial development.

The opening of the Highlands' Highway changed the original picture of the existing Heartland, which was no longer confined to the other three centres. With it came changes in transport, airline services, shipping and commercial endeavour, for freight by road was considerably cheaper than freight by air, and the sea route was not as long as that to Madang.

The effects of this were felt by Madang. Within months air freight dropped alarmingly; shipping went into a decline with some vessels taken off the Madang run; and normal export and wholesale business of commercial concerns fell to depressing figures.

For twenty years there had been a call for a road linking Madang with the Highlands. At first the terminal was to be at Goroka, but as Mount Hagen moved into prominence the site was changed to that town.

The advantages were very obvious. It meant a shorter, more direct route of half the distance from Lae to Hagen; a passage to open up inland country that, to date, remains remote and undeveloped; access into areas of commercial timber; the encouragement of population movements under schemes of closer settlement; an incentive towards the establishment of industries; and, above all, the assurance of Madang's development into an important centre.

The consolidation of the Highlands' Highway was recognized as a death blow to Madang's hopes, and resulted in a renewed combined drive, by civic leaders of Madang and Mount Hagen, to force a definite decision on the construction of a road between the two towns.

In 1965/66, a private contracting firm was commissioned to make feasibility surveys of four selected routes with estimated costs ranging from $16 million to $24 million.

Optimism remained high and pressure continued but fickle Administration policy could not be conquered so easily. Without decrying the need for such a main link, officialdom produced an ace from its sleeve in the form of a proposal to extend the Markham

Valley road over into the Ramu, through Gusap, Dumpu, and on to the patrol post of Usino with a very indefinite suggestion that this would, in time, link up with Madang, forty-two miles further on.

Here, they said, is a road to Mount Hagen. This was fundamentally true, although the road wandered over most of New Guinea to get there, and was still of secondary importance to the existing Lae route.

There was very little likelihood that drivers of heavy vehicles, after battling through all weathers across the roof of New Guinea, would decline to use the 100-mile straight stretch into Lae in preference to another long and wearisome journey over a second-class road to get to Madang, even if the link went through.

There was also little possibility that commercial firms representing Highlands' interests, having once established themselves in Lae, would then duplicate their formations in Madang on the off-chance of collecting the crumbs of trade which fell from Lae's table.

It is doubtful if Madang will ever be linked with the Ramu road. There have been four proposals for roads from the Gogol River to Usino, none of which has been surveyed to any degree, none of which has been costed, and none of which has been shown to be practicable.

The House of Assembly Public Works committee stated that the Ramu road will be constructed at district level, for about $250,000, and will take three years to complete, so Madang looks like having no access into the Ramu for some considerable time . . . if ever.

Perhaps there are plans for digging a deep sea channel into the village of Usino, a suggestion that would be well in keeping with a lot of policy plans that flourish and then change.

Two schools of opinion have arisen—the official one backed by a few private interests supporting the Ramu plan, and that of the diehards still demanding a direct route. They serve to illustrate not only the slavish and servile obedience of district officials to the dictates of headquarters even when they are contrary to majority opinion, but also the antagonisms and schisms that so easily appear in a small town community where unity of purpose is a delicate product.

Fortunately for the Administration, a United Nations Transportation investigation team was due in the Territory to study the needs of the country's communications, so the problem has been handed over to them. The subject is now back in the official folio. Whatever the recommendation may be, the Madang-Mount Hagen Highway looks like remaining a pipe dream.

However, as the serviceability of the Highlands' Highway is limited by astronomical maintenance costs, and the impetus of development inside the Highlands cannot be stopped, the proposition of a direct route to the coast is not yet a dead duck, and there may come a time when the government will have to re-align its thinking and act hurriedly to put a road in before the Highlands wither up as Madang is doing now.

But go to Madang, and you will be told officially that development is going on and the tales of depression are simply not true. There are new sealed roads, new bridges, a new settlement area, a new post office, a $1.5 million wharf complex, the promise of a new district headquarters, a road leading seventeen miles out to the Gogol River which has a new and expensive bridge, an area of plantation country taken over for an extended airstrip with other land purchased for closer settlement.

Admittedly this is development, but it is non-productive development.

The roads are in the town area and necessary anyway; the new settlement area contains fifty-two new administration houses partly occupied by government personnel; the new post office, "to meet Madang's expanding economy," is half its originally planned size and is the only project of community benefit. The expensive wharf installations are only working at about 30% of their capacity and there are likely to be restrictions on the new administrative centre if more key government personnel are transferred without replacements being made.

The Gogol River has been bridged, but if you walk over it you will fall forty feet into the bush because there is no continuation of the road and the intervening land on each side of the seventeen miles of new roadway from Madang is not being developed, while the timber lease on the other side of the Gogol has been hawked around without drawing any takers.

Lastly, the plantation country purchased for new settlement areas has been leased back to the private company for a further three years.

Somehow, progress in Madang seems to be a rather doubtful quantity.

I spoke to a manager of one of the commercial firms about the depression and he remarked, "There's no depression here. We are enjoying increased business every month because every new arrival in the town means another $200 spent in the stores each month."

Where do the $200 for each new person come from—productive labour or government salaries? Does this $200 *per capita* per month really represent $200 of material development in Madang? I doubt it. More likely it is a transitory gain from a floating population that, sometime or other, will cease.

Yet retail trading by big firms seems to be satisfactory, for expansions are being carried out by other companies with some renovations to premises, and there are few, if any, murmurs of recession.

This is in conflict with facts and figures submitted by the Madang Chamber of Commerce in a presentation to the Administrator. The delegation, representatives of the Chamber and of private enterprise, stated that they were concerned over the business recession, evident since 1966, and that this had grown to alarming proportions. They charged that the Administration should promote economic confidence and ensure planned development. They maintained this was not being done in Madang, and that there is no confidence among the people.

"We are not prepared to see years of effort and considerable investment in the Territory wasted because of continued vacillation by the Administration," the statement said, and here are some of the facts they presented.

In shipping, there were 61,227 tons of general cargo and 24,529 tons of bulk fuel passing through the port in 1965/66. By 1967/68, these figures had dropped to 48,163 tons and 16,500 tons respectively.

In air cargo the loss was more serious, with 49,842,841 pounds for 1965/66, and only 20,421,731 pounds for 1967/68, a drop of 29,000,000 pounds which is greater than the total increase for the current year, a percentage loss of 60% and equal to what was carried during the whole period 1966/67.

The Chamber submitted a list of seven commercial undertakings which had closed down, and added that the only private medical practitioner in the town had also left. Among the seven commercial firms were three Chinese businessmen.

Real estate values had declined, and in a town where accommodation had always been an acute problem, one investment of $135,000 in flats was lying idle, with business blocks unsaleable at reduced valuations.

There had been a decline in the income of the native labour force and an upward trend in unemployment. Business firms had reduced staffs, hotel accommodation demands had decreased and travellers representing large companies were bypassing the town as the available business did not cover their expenses.

The statement added that two of the town's building contractors

170

were leaving the district, one of whom had been in business for fifteen years.

Within the government itself, six senior Administration officers had been transferred and there had been no replacements. They included a Deputy District Commissioner, two District Officers, two Lands Titles Commissioners and a Regional Local Government Officer. The Lands Department office had been closed and the Sub-Treasury staff reduced.

The delegation said that the General Hospital, built at considerable expense, was not being fully utilized. One complete hospital wing was used as staff quarters and the main operating theatre, fully equipped and air conditioned, was being used as an office.

The post office, costing $116,000, and designed to cater for all Highlands mail as well as coastal services, had suffered staff reductions now the Highlands mail had been re-routed through Lae.

It asked if these buildings were to become national monuments or whether they were to be used to the full.

The delegation told the Administrator that capital expenditure must be fully warranted and fully utilized, that this had not been the case, and that if the programme had been undertaken by private enterprise, only a foolhardy Board of Directors would have authorized such expenditure under such circumstances.

While the Minister for External Territories had stated that there had been no development on the new Madang-Mawan road, the delegation pointed out that there had been no alienation of land in the Madang district for agricultural purposes and that out of 3,061 blocks made available for settlement, only two had been allocated to the Madang District.

Finally they presented another appeal for the construction of a direct road to the Highlands with revised figures of expenditure which, they stated, "may show a completely new aspect to the economics of the road."

It is doubtful if anything progressive will come of this appeal. There have been so many, but the attrition continues and Madang, at the present time, lives mainly upon the income from government monies in wages, contracts, and so on.

This keeps the town's domestic economy moving, but it has a limited scope.

Go beyond the boundaries, into the Ramu, up in the mountains and along the coast. The district is dead. There are plans and schemes and talk, but one has to search, and usually in vain, for signs of real progressive development.

When the word development is mentioned, one is shown new

houses for administration staff, or patches of roadwork miles from anywhere as sops to local pride, or areas of forestland sitting idle and awaiting private investment to come in.

Once before, the then Assistant Administrator for Economic Affairs, the late Mr F. Henderson, stated, "The centre of development has shifted from the New Guinea mainland to Bougainville." This was at the time that Conzinc Riotinto were negotiating the copper leases on that island.

This has meant the abandonment of all important, industrial and social advancement in northern New Guinea in favour of solitary spearthrusts on a fragile basis to collect handouts from foreign investment. This prohibits solid, permanent, and widespread development and is an abnegation of multitudinous promises of building a secure economic foundation for future self-government.

The most noticeable advance has been in the greater consolidation of the expatriate public service, with increases in numbers, diversity of positions, salary ranges and benefits; an expanding burden that the economic ill-health of the country and the people just cannot afford to carry, and entirely contradictory to the dictum that the local people must, in future, live within the country's economic standards.

The evils of this system are very plain; dissension within the local public service, frustration at the local government and village levels, and a cost of living that is discriminatory against the average native worker.

The first casualty is Madang. Under this mediocre type of leadership, there could be others.

All one needs these days to encourage interest is to wave a flashy mineral sample over your head and you will be besieged by officials with plans, projects and grand statements. The old ideas of leading the people, of keeping promises, of faithfulness of purpose, and dedication to the job are fast disappearing.

The leaders are too busy trying to become politicians to worry overmuch about such ideas. The qualification of "talking in millions of dollars and to hell with the public," has become quite a factor in public affairs as a glance through Hansards will show.

When a private citizen has, on an average, four of five native people coming along each day asking for work—most of them sincere and prepared to work at anything that will bring a modicum of wages—in a township that can only be classed as small, and in a country that could, and should, have twice as much work available for the population it holds, it makes one question the sincerity of official statements on native development.

172

There is money enough—the Australian taxpayers provide most of it—but there is also a hungry bureaucratic machine, and after that's been satiated little remains for substantial native participation in development.

Anyone who may be around Madang way sometime should take a good look at it. Nature has been kind, for it is an attractive place, but don't be smothered by the hibiscus and frangipanni and the beautiful views of mountains and valleys. The real view is away down underneath, in the villages, among the unemployed, the low-wage earners, among the women and children and those who have been sitting for years wondering if white colonization is as good as it says it is.

"Come and stay with us. We will give you land and build you a house if you will stop here and show us what to do." I've had this said to me within sixty miles of Madang, and that is not an isolated example.

There are a lot of places like Madang in the Territory; some have been even less fortunate.

journey into fantasy | 6

ONE CANNOT MOVE around this country very far without, in some way, coming into contact with what is known as cargo cultism. The term can be used in a general sense because some primitive beliefs, based upon traditional thought and action, produce a cultism full of native religious significance and are not inspired by cargo materialism.

However, whatever the basis of these beliefs may be, materialistic or otherwise, they exert an overriding influence on native thought during the transition of the people from primitiveness towards comparatively elementary standards of civilized conduct. It is a phenomenon that is not exclusive to Papua and New Guinea but it is exhibited to a remarkable degree in many places in this country and shows all the signs of being a complex problem in the field of social development.

It is natural for human beings to be superstitious, and while it is easy to deride and condemn the features of cultism among primitive native peoples, it must be remembered that we, within our own highly developed society, have certain set beliefs that possess no fundamental basis of truth. We also indulge in extraordinary political and religious presumptions which, their exponents claim, are cure-all remedies for society's ills, and we also have that adventurous streak of hoping to make money from situations whose main ingredients are volubility and gullibility.

Primitive cultism is, for many native people, a definite way of life which controls their emotions, their behaviour, their attitudes towards others, and their acknowledgment of authority as it exists within their own society. When it emerges from beyond this limited periphery and meets the conditions and demands of modern society, it becomes basically a challenge from the inferior to the

174

superior, the dispossessed against the possessors, the restrained against the privileged, and the rule of the individual against the rule of common law. Because of a transformation of ideas to meet new circumstances, it creates conflicts and becomes a menace.

In the fields of anthropology and associated sciences, cargo cultism has become a subject of scholarly research, but to the outsider without this kind of professional background it can remain only a subject of interest and general conjecture based upon individual observation and experience. However, there are elements which appear good to an observer and are worthy of sympathetic support, but it must be admitted that these are few and are greatly outweighed by constituents which are bad and obnoxious, and it is these contradictions which have made cargo cultism the danger it presents to modern administration.

Professor Peter Lawrence, of Queensland University, in the introduction to his work, *Road Belong Cargo*, states, "New Guinea cargo cult has attracted a great deal of attention since the last war," a sentence which could indicate that there has been a change of substance, or attitude, in cargo cultism, and that war acted as a catalyst in transforming primitive ideas, which existed long before 1939, by creating new horizons, new ambitions, and giving it a more substantial form of materialism. This cannot be denied, for cultism has developed as an economic factor which may or may not have political undertones, a factor which existed long before, as the word "cargo" indicates, and though perhaps not realized then, has since been accentuated to a tremendous degree from the effects of the last war.

With the rise and encouragement of political awareness, this new attribute has been blended into the pattern, so that today we find movements seeking not only material gain and wealth, but power and prestige as a further means towards the attainment of their desires. Under western democratic processes now being introduced into political life it is within the realm of possibility that a substantial cult movement could obtain a degree of political power and cause disruption. Doubtless, if such a situation did arise, the movement would be proscribed as subversive, for that would be the only remedy for maintaining sound and responsible government.

Fortunately this remains a supposition and a remote possibility, although the indications of such a situation did arise during the 1968 elections but failed mainly because of its own lack of substance in leadership and intention, and the poor comprehension of its supporters.

Of more interest is the groundwork of this cultism, the primitive

175

bases which formulate the ideas and act as an incentive to action.

On one occasion a United Nations representative, a district official and I secured horses and rode out of Alexishafen, fifteen miles from Madang, into the foothills for a few miles to where a village straddled a long, sharp mountain ridge. Our journey had been prompted by the district official's description of cargo cultism being practised in this village. To the United Nations man, who was an excellent horseman, it was a refreshing exercise and outing; for the district official, a routine trip; while for myself it became a journey marred by some apprehension and physical discomfort, for I had not ridden a horse for over thirty years and by mischance had secured a spirited nag which required more than my involuntary cussing to stop his capering.

The route took us through a winding plantation road, over spurs of limestone, and up into steep, pudgy, glutinous red clay country until, after about one hour's climbing, we reached the village. It was spread out in three individual sections, the first one a staunch Catholic community, the second, a couldn't-care-less group, and the third, the abode of the cultists which, generally considered, was a satisfying mixture for any inquiring visitor.

There were rows of old, drab looking houses perched wherever space would allow, in some instances apparently defying gravity as they teetered over the edge of a gorge. The crest of the ridge had been flattened to resemble some form of a main square and at the end of this stood one solitary building, the only one with any claims to pretentiousness, for it was comparatively newly built of woven walls of plaited sago, thatched with palm fronds, and surrounded by a thin, straggling line of flowering shrubs.

Despite the apparent poverty and depression of the people there was a feeling of freedom up here on the long finger of the mountain with the drapery of forest and jungle falling away on each side into darkened gullies. The air was fresh, the sun bright, birds were singing and Nature was at its best, while far below, undulating waves of jungle spread out into wide valleys, with a magnificent panorama of the coastal belt, the plantation country, the small settlements, and the ocean dotted with islands beyond.

In this small paradise only Man seemed vile, for the people who came slowly out of their ramshackle houses were prematurely old and weary, with dull skins and wrinkled faces. Many were suffering from the loathsome ringworm disease of grilly, or sipoma, brought about by continued association with dirt. They bore the hopeless look of forgotten people on their faces. As we dismounted, an old man came forward to greet us. Around his neck he had a small key suspended from a dirty string, and after a few words with the district official, he turned and opened the wooden door of the building. He was, we discovered later, the keeper of the treasure within and the guardian of this temple of irresponsible hope.

Coming from the bright sunlight it took a few minutes to become accustomed to the dimness of the interior where light filtered through the cracks in the walls, for there were no windows. Beyond a passage we turned into an inside room furnished with rough, timbered shelves. On these stood rows and rows of four gallon empty benzine drums, old enamel basins, and rusty tins of many sizes. A carved head of wood gazed down from one wall, some dried flowers drooped out of a beer bottle, a sheet of tapa cloth with painted symbols hung from the rafters, while necklaces of dog's teeth, the tusks of a boar, a string of cowrie shells, the trappings of a dance leader, and an empty string bag belonging to some woman added to the decorations. Over all was the fetid stench of mustiness and decay.

There were a few coins in every empty drum and tin and they rattled as we lifted and shook them. Our guide bent down and dug from the ground some more coins, which he quickly reburied. There were other coins in a small porcelain dish, and a child's sand bucket in a corner contained a couple of Australian shilling pieces.

There was little else to see and we walked out and went across to a bush shelter under which some men had gathered. "Tell us about this," we asked them and one old fellow cleared his throat and croaked out his story.

"During the time of the war my father was told by a soldier that if money was planted in the ground it would grow, just like a seed, and become a big tree with money as its fruit.

"We all heard about this and we talked about it round our fires at night. Some believed it and others didn't, but as my father had told me I believed it was true although we never tried it. We kept this story in our mind for a long time and one day a young man who had been a mission teacher and could read and write came to this village and told us the story again and showed us a paper with a picture of money growing on a tree. He said that white men believed that money grew. He had heard them praying for it and when they put money into a bank, and it stayed there for a long time, there was always more than they put in.

"He said that white men buy slips of paper with numbers on them and these sometimes bring a lot of money back and he told us that if we have patience and lead good lives, he could make money grow for us.

"He told us to collect some money and some tins and when he came back he would show us what to do, so we collected $800 and all the empty tins, and when he returned he put some money in the tins, locked them in that house, prayed over them, and then told us that in eight years he would come back and open the tins and we would all have plenty of money. Then he went away."

"What happened to the remainder of the $800?" we asked him, and were told that the enterprising young man had taken that with him. He had not returned yet but they were sure he would do so.

We began to explain how foolish they had been, but a chap in the back row reached into a small fibre bag and pulled out a tattered piece of paper. "Look at this," he exclaimed. "This is in your own language and it tells you that money will grow like a tree." The scrap of paper was a torn sheet from an American magazine with an advertisement for an investment firm. "Watch your money grow," it proclaimed, and under the heading was a picture of a large tree blossoming with green dollar notes, some of which had fallen to the ground, which a man with a haversack was busily picking up.

They waited for us to deny it, fully prepared to pounce on any explanation we might attempt. We tried, but it was hopeless. They were deaf to what we were saying and their eyes were still on that dirty piece of paper. It was in our language, and all they wanted was for us to admit that this was true.

"We have never tried this before," the spokesman began, "and we don't know whether it is good or bad, so we can only try. It is our own money and we can do as we wish with it. Have you ever tried it?"

We had to admit that we had not, a damnable indictment of our own apparent prevarication. Their eyes spoke volumes and said plainly that they would do things their way while we could do things our way, so why come and try and stop them? It was impossible to shake them, so we returned to our horses and as we mounted could hear them chattering among themselves on the weird ways of the white man who had never tried to grow money and was trying to keep the secret of making wealth to himself.

They were far from amused at our visit and our attempts to convert them to more orthodox ways of investment, and they watched, as we rode down the slope, with rather supercilious grins on their faces at our ignorance of how to make money the easy way. Their complete faith in their glib-tongued compatriot was astounding, and I often wonder if they are still waiting for eight years to pass, and what their reactions will be when they do get round to opening those tins.

More amazing still was an erratic method of making money which came to light during a Supreme Court case which I attended. The offender here, a middle-aged man, had previously been a member of the police force but had lost this position because of a desire to dabble in the occult.

One would have expected that having been trained as a law enforcement officer, although a lowly one, his attitudes towards cargo cultism would have been self-suppressed, but this had not happened and he found himself in the dock charged with desecration of a grave as well as certain other acts.

The trouble started while he was on leave in his village and was speaking to a friend whose brother had recently died.

"Don't worry, my friend," he told the sorrowing man. "Your brother is dead but his spirit will help you to find much money and I will show you how it can be done."

He secured a photograph of the dead man, talked some ready listeners into assisting him, collected picks and shovels, and with the dead man's brother, moved out to the graveyard. Here he squatted beside the man's grave, set the photograph on the ground beside it, and instructed the willing helpers to dig down to the body while he said a few words to help them in their labour.

Earth was being thrown far and wide when along came the village councillor and a bunch of people who were not at all impressed at having their graveyard violated, and showed no enthusiasm or faith in producing gold from dead bodies.

Despite the fact that the promoter assured everybody that the spirit of the dead man had entered his body and that soon he would go down and pass up lots of money, the councillor grabbed him, marched him off to the nearest patrol officer, and ordered that the grave be filled in again. Yet there were many who still believed that money was lying at the bottom of that grave and that the councillor had spoilt what might have been a very profitable afternoon.

Although these are examples of cultism in its crudest form, they do reveal the materialistic objective behind such actions, ideas which bear no relation to any traditional religious meanings. These particular cases were ones of greed, cunning, and criminality as well as being demoralizing to those who participated, and perhaps could be considered as outside the sphere of cargo cultism in its most centralized and developed form. They are, however, typical of things that do happen among some of the more primitive and superstitious people, the majority of whom have experienced government control and mission influences but who, through their sheer inability or unwillingness to move beyond the restricting bounds of their village

179

and tribal environments, are prepared to listen to any scheme that promises easy wealth, like a carrot dangled before them.

The law moves in and punishes, but this results in nothing more than a temporary halt and provides no positive remedy, for the circumstances which promote such devious thinking remain. Apart from the factor of personal greed, the fundamental trend is for economic amelioration, and until some form of physical development, however slight, is introduced, the ways of those with weird ideas are going to prevail. The problem calls for money, a positive developmental approach, and firm direction. Commodities which are always in short supply are invariably used only where profitable returns can be guaranteed within the foreseeable future.

One big trouble with these artful gentlemen whose minds are obsessed with impossible feats of procreation of wealth and an alchemist's dreams of the Midas touch is that from some dim unresolved point of origin, tales have drifted down that white men possess the secrets of making money grow and of creating goods to any specification required, by some esoteric means which the white man jealously guards, so it is fair enough to try anything once and if you do this often enough then you must hit the jackpot sometime.

Which is a line of thought often followed by some of our own more enlightened brethren, so who can blame the illiterate bushman?

However, when cargo cultism sheds its image of the miraculous and becomes a down-to-earth, day-by-day way of life adjusted to the social and psychological circumstances of the people, it presents a proposition which no government can afford to ignore.

There existed in the Madang District, and still does to a limited degree, a cult structure known under the general name of the "Yali Movement." This, as Professor Lawrence points out, was a loose term, but descriptive enough, for it lacked a true organizational structure, and there were many amorphous factors which contributed to its birth, the main one possibly being the amazing personality of the man to whom it was attributed, Yali Singina.

This man became more than a mere figurehead, and irrespective of the rights and wrongs which occurred over the years, it was this natural, undefined characteristic of leadership which pushed him to the top and has held him there as a person of veneration to the hard core of his disciples.

Since 1945 he has run through a whole gamut of nomenclature as a leader, a wastrel, a Messiah, a criminal, an upholder of native culture, a despoiler of women, a subversive influence, an inspiring force—you name it and he's been called it sometime or other—yet,

A typical Local Government Council house, used for village discussions, has super-seded the old Dubu

for close on a quarter of a century, he has maintained a varying degree of prestige, and authority, as a native leader.

I know of only one man, John Guise, who has a comparable record, although the two men are entirely opposed in thought and principle, and ability. But both, by virtue of their personalities, have held dominant positions in native society over a long period, which is remarkable because native fidelity to a cause can be very ephemeral.

The changes of direction and development within Yali's movement have been many. It had originated as a pagan revival, changed into a cargo cult, created general uneasiness, usurped the legitimate processes of law and entered the political arena, while Yali, himself, during the 1950s, served five years of imprisonment. But, although he has been discredited many times, he has not been altogether discarded and within the confines of his own small area he is still a highly respected patriarch.

He is getting on in years now, and age has taken its toll, but he is still a pleasant, well-spoken person, quiet in manner, with a benevolent lord-of-the-manor attitude towards his own people.

I came to know him well both before and during the election campaign of 1967-68 when, at his own invitation, I went to the Rai Coast area and stayed at his village for about one week. I had also attended some of his meetings in Madang and elsewhere, and although he had been out of circulation for quite a long while, the fact that Yali was speaking was sufficient to attract large attendances.

He could not be classed as a good candidate for the House of Assembly. His main theme was his historical past, as one of the local lads, his war record, and the fact that he was an acknowledged leader among the people. Of policy and platform he had none; except for generalizations there was nothing to appeal to the more understanding voter. However, as most of his audiences were composed of village people and plantation workers, this lack of an aggressive approach did little harm except to give, at some places, an erroneous impression of his progress.

His main opponent was a Papuan, formerly employed as a government clerk in the sub-district office at Saidor, the home area of Yali. This man, John Poe, was much younger, was well-educated, spoke English, Pidgin, Motu, and his own languages, was a churchman, had an impressive personality, and was a typical product of modern administration.

The contest between these two candidates—there was a third who had but slight effect—promised to become an indication of the relative substance of present day administration against the doubtful quality of superstition and the old way of life.

People of Dopima No. 3 Village

Patrol Officer at Dopima No. 3 Village, talking to villagers

Coconut plantation, Aramia Village

A bush grave in Aramia country

The electorate consisted of voters who were mainly illiterate and full of primitive native conservatism, and it was a matter of interest to see just how staunchly they supported one of their own local men, who, despite his shortcomings, had been prominent among them for many years, against an educated, government-trained, foreign native man from Papua.

There was a possibility that in spite of Poe's abilities and local experience he could be rejected by a New Guinea rural electorate mainly on the grounds that he was a Papuan. The result was in favour of the Papuan by quite a large margin, and the effect of this setback upon Yali was rather disastrous.

This had been the second loss he had suffered at elections, and although he had at one time been president of the local government council, and was still an elected councillor, the fact that he was spurned by his own people was rather hard for him to take. Lack of ability to contest an election was possibly the main cause, but there had been signs for some considerable time that the more intelligent and critical members of the local council were against him.

I remember attending one meeting a year before where Yali was openly charged with having collected council taxes without authority. There was some doubt about the truth of this charge but it stemmed from the fact that many councillors had been told by their people that their allegiance was still with Yali and that they had contributed to his movement and would not pay council tax. Irritations such as this did little to help him during the election and there could have been a strong local movement among the council to ensure that he did not get elected.

During his campaign I flew out to the Rai Coast, and by truck and bush track eventually reached Yabalol, his own village. This village is in an extremely attractive situation. One reaches it along a coast road after leaving Saidor main station, and skirting the foothills of the Finisterre Ranges, one comes to the seaboard village of Galek. From here the track branches in towards the hills in a comfortable hour's walk through grasslands and along the banks of the turbulent Yunge River as it cascades from the mountains. There is a dash of magnificent forest and river scenery as the track gradually rises by a short, but stiff, climb into Yabalol. It lies in one of the most secluded and charming of settings at the end of a huge valley with the surrounding range rising steeply like the sides of a basin.

Almost directly above, after an exhausting 1,000 feet climb, is Yali's birthplace, the old village of Sor, now only a collection of two or three houses. I must admit that I reached only to where the curved top of the hill gave me a distant view of the few houses, for the climb, perpendicular in parts, was more than I had expected, and my guide, a local lad, galloped up like an antelope. Coming down was almost as bad, for it seemed that one slight slip could send one crashing down through the grass roofs of Yabalol, so steep did it appear.

Yabalol consists of two rows of houses built on stony ground among outcrops of rocks and screened by flowering trees and shrubs, giving an impression that considerable attention has been spent in decorating a somewhat bare site.

On a slight elevation at one end, and overlooking the village, is Yali's house, a long, roomy affair bearing indications of plantation style. It has one central passage leading into a series of fifteen rooms. These serve as self-contained flats, for his wives and their individual attendants—he had five wives when I was there, and introduced me to another young woman who could have been his sixth—in addition to his own private quarters, storerooms, and kitchens. His own section contains a living room, bedroom, office, and spare room with a private stairway leading out of the back of the house.

"This is mine," he told me. "Nobody uses it without my permission."

He is very proud of this house which, as his personal staff increased, has been enlarged by extra wings. He showed me around each flat, introducing me to his wives, some of whom I had met previously, and pointed proudly to the heaps of garden produce in the storerooms. "You see," he said. "We have plenty to eat. Nobody goes hungry in this village." I could well believe it, for there were stacks of yams, bananas, taro, coconuts, and other foods; sufficient, it seemed, to feed many people for several months.

I had been intrigued by his office, for I knew that he could neither read nor write, and here were books and stacks of papers, a table, pens and pencils, and all the appearances of a businessman's den. He told me that he had a secretary to do his work, although I never met the lady or gentleman, and it seemed more likely that this was pure window-dressing—a front to impress those around him that he, as leader, must have the same retinue—an office staff—as a district official. To see this dim and very untidy room, the table, the scattered heaps of papers, and the bundles of books preserved as a false symbol of prestige was a pathetic reminder of the futility of this man's life and spoke louder than the servile crowds of illiterate villagers who followed his every step.

One feature of the building was a small basement room. "That is the room for women when they get sick," he advised me. "They are not allowed in the big house."

My own camp was in the rest-house at the far end of the village. It was a bare, very dilapidated building, infested by white ants, and ready to collapse at any moment. I tested the main supports and found them as thin as paper, with the main beam supporting the roof a mass of white ants' nests.

Yali sent along his special chair, a wooden one with arms in which he had been hailed as "king" many years before at the height of his popularity, a folding table, and one of his numerous relatives, a very young lad, to cook for me.

Almost opposite, and slightly below, was a small, native-material building which was used as the Catholic church by an occasional visiting native catechist.

Yali and his followers are pagans but those who wished to attend church could do so and I noticed that some of those who ambled along on Sunday were also high priests of the tambaran house, the home of the cult, standing a few hundred feet away in the centre of the village.

Yali's association with the missions has varied from hostility to partial co-operation but at this time he impressed upon me that he had ruled that every child of school age must attend the Catholic school in another village some distance away. It is possible that the government and the missions had insisted that every child attend school and he was complying with instructions which he could not ignore.

I noticed that his Number Two Wife was wearing a thin chain with a cross around her neck, and when I spoke to her about it she told me that she had bought it at a Chinese store as an ornament. I asked if she was a Catholic and she looked at the cross for a moment and then tore it from her neck and threw it into the bush. "I am not a Christian," she barked and walked away.

It did not take long for me to realize that the standards of behaviour in Yabalol had a background of military discipline, stemming, of course, from Yali's presence. Each morning one of his wives would line up the women and young girls and lead them off into the hills for the day's work of garden-making. Those who remained had other tasks, cleaning, wood-gathering, child-minding, and washing.

Each morning also, at six, the men and boys would parade and be allotted their daily duties. About a mile away was Yali's plantation of coconuts and coffee and here a regular labour line worked under the command of one of Yali's lieutenants, as on a plantation and had their own houses nearby.

All around the hills and down the valley were large patches of garden, each one, I was told, belonging to Yali, and this personal

184

ownership included everything: the houses, the tools, the food, and the men, women, and children. "They are all my people and they do as I tell them," he said to me one evening when I questioned him on the work and behaviour of the many young men and girls around. "Inside this village they must behave themselves. If they don't then I send them back to their own places."

Surprisingly I found this to be very true, for Yabalol proved to be the best-behaved village I have seen. The disputes, shouting, and general noise that afflict most villages were absent here. Hardly anybody raised his voice, and when darkness came there was very little talking, for the village went to sleep early. I was never troubled by the pests of yelping and scavenging dogs, so common in most villages. Neither did the inhabitants hang around begging for tobacco and other items as most do. Occasionally one or two would come along and talk, but they always waited outside for permission to enter and their conversation was usually centred on Yali, his kindness to them, and his power.

Part of his system was voluntary aid from families in other villages, and quite a number of men, with their wives and children, came for periods of several months to work for Yali. Each family was given a house and food and allocated their daily duties. He told me that he paid them, but to what extent I have no knowledge, although when I left and offered the young lad who had worked for me some money, Yali quickly intervened and forbade the boy to accept any payment.

"You do not pay for anything when you stay in my village," he told me, and all the lad would accept was the remainder of my rations, some tobacco, and matches. He refused to take any other gift or payment.

Yali's income is drawn from the subscriptions of the faithful and these must be quite considerable, for I have seen collections from meetings almost fill the calico money bags which his retinue carried around, and he has been known to pay large sums of money in cash for articles purchased, and in travelling expenses for himself and those with him.

His own sense of responsibility towards his people is great. He provides all that they need and will help them if they are in trouble. This attitude extends to guests, for while I was with him he sent fresh vegetables and fruit to me each morning, and beyond some tobacco, would take nothing in return.

Each evening he would walk the village talking to everybody while the children hung on to his hands and arms and followed wherever he went. This action was quite natural and seemed to be part of his creed that he should speak to everybody at least once a day. He dresses well and is always clean with newly-laundered shorts, shirt, and stockings, and this standard of cleanliness is reflected by the others when they have finished their day's labours.

Yali's reputation with women and girls has not always been an honourable one, and there was a time when women were brought to him so that they could have children by him and thus inherit some of his qualities. I have heard more than one woman say, "Yali's baby" as she holds up her child, but against this there are reports that he is impotent and that he has never fathered a child.

At Yabalol there were no indications of moral misbehaviour. I mentioned this specifically to him for there were quite a number of young, attractive girls and young men. "There is nothing like that here," he said. "Most of these girls are already engaged to boys, and for those who wish to make trouble they can go somewhere else. Besides, while the girls are here they belong to me and I look after them." It is this absolute dictatorial control over everything that is a marked feature of the village. It is not altogether apparent, but it always intrudes, and even when he is away the rigid standards of control apply, their functioning being supervised by his wives.

It is a community which lives within itself, being as self-supporting as possible, under the command of one man who rules by the yard-stick of tradition. His outlook is definitely despotic, his manner that of a feudal baron, and his word is absolute; the patriarch of a people who accept this situation and have contributed to what he is, and accept the teachings of his movement.

This invariably brings clashes with established authority. He has been accused of working labour for no recompense, has been charged that he personally disrupts the work of the council, that he sends for his sympathizers from other areas and directs their activities and that he resents the intrusion of governmental authority. Yet for all this, people still follow him, listen to his words, work for him without complaint, and contribute to his maintenance.

His recent defeat in the elections has lost him quite a lot of support and there have been whispers that those who pressed his campaign are becoming ambitious themselves and that he is being relegated to the position of a Grand Old Man who is being treated with respect and consideration during his remaining years.

This is also true, but it is doubtful if there is anybody who can take his place when he dies, and it is quite likely that the whole movement will collapse and quietly fold up when he goes, for not one of the younger leaders has the personality of the old man.

The passage of time appears to be the only solution to the problem of Yali and his beliefs, for the days of primitive Messiahs are over, and if ever another arises he is quite likely to be armed with a university degree, a revolutionary fervour, and a vision of the future totally divorced from the traditions of the past.

When they first came along and told me that the Kabu ceremony would be staged each night I was not greatly excited or interested. I have had enough experience of trying to sleep in a village resthouse while drums thump, feet stamp, and voices yell intermittently until after dawn, and there are few areas where I would be willing to sacrifice a night's sleep just to stand around and watch them.

I appreciate the fact that they are an expression of the people, are a subject of interest for tourists and for scientific study and research in certain fields, but for me, half-an-hour of a native ceremony is more than sufficient, and the prospect of another disturbed night was not an enjoyable one.

Actually the ceremony to be conducted was only a small part of the Kabu, the latter stages of certain rites that had gone on for a considerable time and were due shortly to be completed.

Yali, at this time, had left the village for a couple of days to stir up enthusiasm among the electors, and most of my evenings were being spent in correlating notes and trying to read by the flickering light of a small hurricane lamp.

Somewhere between eight and nine the first sounds of the ceremony began, not with the resonant sounds of drums and high-pitched voices, as I had expected, but with very faint murmurs of wind instruments floating across the valley and echoing from the hillsides. Outside, the night was black, the air calm and warm, the skies clear and the stars mustered in thousands, and as I looked out over the village only a few isolated pinpoints of light shone in the darkness.

By this time the music was increasing in sound and tempo, the notes rising and falling in regular rhythm with the notes of the sacred gourds, a long, trumpet-like instrument, sounding clearly above the lighter notes of the accompanying instruments. As the melody gained strength, the dull, steady boom from slit gongs joined in, not as a harsh cacophony of noise but in gentle, rhythmic beats attuned to the pitch of the wind instruments and giving life and force to the cadence that was growing stronger every minute.

Soon the full power of the music burst into the night, the notes from the gourds rose higher, and the beating of the gongs, an insistent staccato drumming growing faster and faster, became a crescendo of sound that resembled the running of a thousand feet through the narrow valley.

Then it stopped abruptly and in the silence of the village you could

187

still hear the echoes haunting the hills and spreading down the valley towards the distant ocean. As the echoes died away, it was as if the village had died, for complete silence reigned for several minutes. Nothing stirred, there were no whispering voices, not even the breath of a breeze, until softly, and almost imperceptibly, the trumpets again took up the refrain in flute-like notes that rose and fell like waves on the ocean, to be joined by the gongs in repeating the build-up of rolling sound that finished in another climax of wild melody.

Then, as if on cue, the timing changed, and the insistent notes of the gongs were muffled into gentle finger-beats as the sacred flutes took the lead in a slower, steadier rhythm. From out of the darkness came the voices of women singing barely an octave above the music, in a beautiful accompaniment of clear chanting of songs of love and messages to their spirits. It was native singing at its best— light, harmonious, and refreshing with none of the raucousness that one customarily hears, but a tuneful blending with the music throbbing out into the night.

I put away my book, took a chair outside and sat alone in the darkness, enraptured by the seductiveness of the music, the singing, the night air, and the dark mountains. It was as if we were in another world, one of tradition, faith, and the beauty of human expression, fortified by the hills which surrounded us.

Somewhere among the dark blanket of trees the women were sitting singly and in groups taking their appointed part in the ceremony of music rising from the darkened cult house down below; the blackness of night became a spontaneous partner in the ceremony, emphasizing the impressiveness of the occasion.

In the brightness of day, with the sun, the birds, the trees, and the flowers, it would not have been half so majestic. The impresario of this rite, whoever he may have been in the long ago dreamtime of tradition, had kept very close to Nature, using the darkness to hide the rough edges of reality, and as a means of creating spiritual, hypnotic faith.

It was hard to associate all this with the rawness of cargo cultism, the suspicions, the jealousies, and the antagonisms of minds seeking solutions in a strange, new way of life. No wonder these people of simple understanding were still bound under the spells of the past and could readily accept the many wild interpretations and prophesies for the future which pass from one to the other through the villages.

This is the fundamentally beautiful part of their lives and when cultism dies, as it must eventually, it is the music of the gourds, the beat of the gongs, and the soft, pleasant songs of the women which must be preserved.

I sat there for several hours until the chill of night sent me inside to sleep, a transition that was easily accomplished to the muffled sounds of music, and an hour before dawn, the flutes and the gongs gently woke me and I stepped outside to watch the mountains and valleys take shape in the morning light, and to see the streamers of blue smoke eddying from the houses as the village prepared for another day.

Then the sun came over the end of the valley and the music stopped, and there were light and heat, movement and noise, and the bands of young men and women trooping off into the hills to labour.

journey into contradiction

7

I HAD FLOWN FROM Madang to Goroka to cover the official opening of a new regional hospital by the Minister for External Territories, Mr C. E. Barnes, when instructions came for me to proceed to Port Moresby.

"I want you to go across to Bougainville and find out what's happening there," my Managing Editor, Douglas Lockwood, said as he greeted me at the airport. "A nasty situation appears to be building up and there could be trouble. Have a word with all those involved, the Administration, Conzinc Riotinto of Australia, the planters, and the people in the villages."

Actually I knew little about Bougainville. I had never been there and it was well out of my province, for my interests had long been centred on the West Irian border and the trouble brewing there.

Superficially I knew that Conzinc Riotinto were about to mine for copper, that large overseas capital was involved, that the Administration was in it up to its eyebrows, and that it was the largest industrial undertaking ever to come to the Territory.

My information had been gleaned from newspapers, radio, and Hansard parliamentary reports, and none of these had given any hint that trouble might be an ingredient, although the House of Assembly debates had raised a few points that needed clarification.

The infusion of about five hundred million dollars worth of industrial development into the country's economy was the most welcome news for the last fifty years, and apart from some initial struggle in parliament over mineral royalties, there appeared no good reason why the project should not get under way as quickly as possible.

It is true that the House of Assembly members had been given a

190

period of three months in which to study and debate the proposition, but the agreement had obviously been drawn up by highly skilled Government and Corporation lawyers, and from what I had read in the Hansard reports, there appeared to have been a tremendous amount of necessary information that had not been presented or discussed. The impression I had was that the Bill had been jockeyed through without much fear of obstruction.

This, again, reflected the limitations of most of the elected members, many of whom, I have no doubt, had no clear idea of the tremendous importance of this legislation to the people, and no concept of the impression that one of the most highly industrialized corporations in the world would make upon their country.

Twenty-four hours later, after buffeting through strong winds and heavy rainstorms sweeping across central New Britain, we came out over Rabaul Harbour into a beautiful tropical evening of flecked skies, clear air, an ocean of royal blue, and the land beneath our wings one mass of contrasting colours as we swept down alongside the snouts of volcanoes to touch down on Lakunai airport.

Side effects from the Bougainville copper project were already evident in Rabaul, for the solitary airline flying between Rabaul and Kieta was having difficulties coping with extra passengers and freight, and of my own direct booking through to Kieta, they knew nothing. I was advised that the next available seat would in thirty-six hours' time.

The delay gave me the opportunity to scout around for some local opinion and background on the Bougainville situation, and thanks to our Rabaul representative, Dick Pearson, I was soon put in touch with some responsible people on the subject.

One week before, the Administration had served notice on the part-owner of Arawa Plantation, near Kieta, Mr R. (Kip) McKillop, that his property would be taken over as part of a new town site to serve C.R.A. operations.

Arawa was a 1,000-acre holding of coconuts and cocoa, 730 acres of which were held under freehold title. The plantation had an estimated overall value of $1 million, and its annual production of copra and cocoa was said to be worth $500,000. It was rated as one of the finest, most highly-developed properties in the Territory, the result of seventeen years of solid work by Kip McKillop, an ex-serviceman who was dedicated to his holding.

Apart from his plantation work he had also achieved the distinction of possessing the finest collection of orchids in the world, and had established, financially and materially with two other partners, a Plant Biological Research station on the property for the purpose of developing better-producing tree and fruit crops, many of which were growing to perfection on his land.

Married, with five children, Mr McKillop was the one planter who didn't want to sell out. Arawa was his life's work, and he had made the Territory his permanent home.

The monetary worth of his plantation was a secondary consideration. More important was the work he had done for his neighbours, the native farmers encircling Arawa whom he had materially assisted, over the years, towards becoming independent producers of cash crops with steadily progressing annual incomes.

The Administration had decided that Arawa was to go, and with it, a further 650 acres of native farmlands surrounding the area, most of which Kip McKillop had helped into productivity.

The official notice served on Mr McKillop was a "Notice to Treat," one of those quaint legal documents that puts the owner in a position of being forced to forfeit his land, whether he wishes to sell or not, giving him no right to decline, and the very doubtful privilege of stating his sale price.

This, according to all official statements, was generally included in the phrase "being of benefit to the Territory," a statement that all subsequent attempts have failed to elucidate.

Repercussions in Rabaul were considerable, the strongest coming from the New Guinea Planters' Association whose secretary, Mr Cyril Holland, told me, "We feel that the public and Mr McKillop have been left in the dark by the Administration, for the decision was made before anybody was told. It is obvious that the Administration does not see fit to advise affected persons. We certainly support Mr McKillop and the native growers in this matter."

He said that the Association was upset at the weak handling of land matters by the Administration since the war and considered that the taking over of Arawa Plantation was the first attempt to soften the blow to native landholders who would later be affected.

"If this action goes through, then the native smallholders who have worked hard will be sacrificed while others who have done nothing will be allowed to sit idle," he said. "This situation should never have arisen for it will alienate native workers."

He described the action as criminal and said that it was not made by C.R.A., as the company had submitted two other areas as possible sites for a town, both of which had been rejected by the Administration.

A representative of the United Political Society, an organization whose membership consists mainly of native people, publicly criticized the Administration and commented, "The whole matter should have been put through the House of Assembly. What is the House for? This clumsy treatment is a repetition of colonialism."

In general there was public alarm and disapproval of the Government's action, with some of the bitterest remarks I have ever heard. "The Administration has acted like a bull in a chinashop"; "It has failed to do its homework"; "If it can bungle then it will, and it has in this case"; and, "They knew this had to happen two years ago. Why did they spring it so suddenly like this?"

Perhaps the choicest remark came from a clergyman with whom I dined on Bougainville a week later and who dryly remarked, "The only difference between rape and seduction is a matter of salesmanship."

One man with whom I spoke, a planter and a leader in civic affairs, took a sympathetic view of the Administration's position. "It is unfortunate that somebody will have to be hurt," he said, "but that is the position." He added that if the plantation was valued so highly, and production had been so satisfactory, then the owner would have nothing to grieve about.

Of all the criticism, none was levelled at the company, and all who spoke praised the fact that the wealth from copper would be a shot in the arm for the Territory. Indeed, many took pains to explain that their criticism was directed solely at the manner in which the Administration had handled the situation, some going so far as to label it clumsy, incompetent, self-interested, and cunning.

A few individuals expressed a fear for the future, pointing out that this was a precedent that once established would be used again under other circumstances. In Bougainville I was to find a lot of these sentiments, and others, expressed more openly and harshly and, on occasions, supplemented with threats of open defiance.

We winged out of Rabaul in an old DC3 across the southern tip of New Ireland and the wide expanse of ocean. We landed, for half-an-hour, at Buka, and then went on down the centre of Bougainville Island, riding high over a thickening turbulence of boiling cumulus which was churning over many square miles of country surrounding smoking Mount Bagana, in the Crown Prince Range, a 6,500-foot volcano whose peak stood clear and solitary above the swirling masses of cloud.

On the western coastline the air cleared, and we came down on Aropa airstrip in brilliant sunshine and moist heat, rumbling over the rough, short landing ground that serves Kieta, some miles away.

It was a typical New Guinea bush-type of road, made of clay and pounded stone, that led into the township, hugged the waterfront and was barely wide enough in places for two vehicles to pass. Graders and bulldozers were gouging out a new highway and gangs were working on bridges and culverts.

At the hotel there was a bustle of movement; the lounge was crowded by people and baggage and the bar resounded with the noises of many customers and groups of vehicles huddling together in the small area outside. "We have about 300 transients passing through here each week," the manager told me when I commented on the overflow. He explained that plans recently approved for extensions would be put into action as quickly as possible.

Quite a lot of those crowding around were bound for the Panguna mine at the C.R.A. operations site away up in the hills behind and were waiting for one of the two couriers who travel continually up and down the steep, twisting mountain road.

My arrival at Kieta was not exactly opportune for I soon discovered that my priority list of those to be interviewed consisted of people who were all absent. Mr McKillop was bound for a meeting in Rabaul, although I did have two minutes with him on the airstrip as he boarded the plane which had brought me; the management of Bougainville Copper, at Panguna, were in Port Moresby; the District Commissioner was on leave, and the Deputy District Commissioner was also at a conference elsewhere, but I was introduced to Mrs McKillop, an exceedingly friendly and charming woman, who promptly took me in tow and invited me to lunch at Arawa.

In spite of the strain the McKillops were under, Mrs McKillop was bright, buoyant and, perhaps, the most optimistic person of all those whom I had met so far. She made little reference to the threat of the take-over. "Kip will tell you all about it," she said. "Personally, I've hardly given it a thought and I certainly haven't started packing up. We're busy people here and there's always so much to do. Somehow I feel that we shall be here a while longer although the notice expires on 21 May." She was referring to the Notice to Treat, the sixty days in which to state the conditions of sale.

Once she referred rather sadly to the subject. "It came so suddenly, and it was the last thing we expected. I don't know how I can explain this to the children at school in Australia. You just can't pack up a property of this size, bundle all your belongings together, finalize the thousand things that have to be done, and clear out in two months. It's ridiculous," she exclaimed.

She spoke of future labour contracts with many to whom they were already committed; of the cost of repatriating present workmen, some of whom had only arrived a short time before; the disruption to the harvesting of crops, market commitments, and the many minor business complications involved.

"They don't realize all this," she said, "nor do they appear to appreciate the work that Kip has put into this place and the way he has helped the people here. He is not a well man, either, and has been sick for a long time. This business on his mind doesn't help."

For her there had been no change of routine but a lot of extra work. She rose at four o'clock each day, supervised the early morning plantation demands, taking her younger children into school, shopping, checking stores, managing the home and conducting her husband's business while he was away, all at a fast, lively pace and with an inexhaustible fund of good humour and bright conversation.

A couple of days later Kip McKillop returned and I was able to get down to some active work with him, in the office, around the plantation, and on trips outside to villages and people.

The strongest characteristic of McKillop is his determination. This is evident in everything he says, in his actions and if one needs more proof, in the material results of his seventeen years of hard work, for these are all around, at Arawa, out in the foothills, in every village, in Kieta and wherever one travels, for he is respected by all as a man with strict humanitarian principles.

It was tragic to see the underhandedness of purpose operating against him, for the signs of initial shock at the demands made upon him were still evident, as if the subterfuges of government power and authority were nothing more than an ugly dream that would go away after a period of logical reasoning.

The mental burden that this man was carrying must have been tremendous, but not once, during the many days that I was with him, did he discuss the money angle or the probability that his whole life's ambition of settling down to enjoy the fruits of his labour was likely to be torn apart within weeks.

One might have expected personal bitterness and regret at the position he had been placed in, but these were never voiced, and whatever his private thoughts may have been, outwardly he remained dispassionately cool, arguing logically against the circumstances that were daily being stacked against him.

I heard the story of how he had first received the news and it was far from pleasant.

A few weeks previously, the Administrator and his party had made an official visit to Bougainville and had been welcomed as distinguished guests at Arawa. During the visit, there had been a suggestion of looking at the orchid collection. The Administrator, with Mr McKillop, stepped out of the house, while two native officials in the party also followed them outside.

Whether this was intended as a private moment for the Administrator to talk with Mr McKillop is not known, but a heavy shower of rain sent the party back inside the house, where they waited for a while, and then the official party left. Nothing about any future take-over had been mentioned.

One week later, a senior officer from Konedobu arrived at Arawa bearing a letter from the Administrator saying that the official had to discuss certain local native problems with Mr McKillop. During this talk, he told Kip McKillop that the property was to be taken over for a C.R.A. townsite and that a notice would be served.

The notice arrived three weeks later.

As far as McKillop was concerned the fiat came out of the blue. As he told me, "There hadn't been the slightest indication of this before," and there appeared to be no moral justification for suddenly placing a man in this position with only sixty days ahead to pack up and get out.

The notice was dated 21 March, and became effective on 21 May, and the same conditions applied, at the time, to the additional 650 acres of native landholdings nearby.

It cannot be argued that such an important decision was made within a space of two or three weeks or, if it was, then it was a closely confined secret among a very restricted group of senior officials.

It was pointed out to me by several people in Rabaul and Bougainville that the Administration had acted shrewdly, for there could be no doubt of protests once the matter became public, and the timing of the notice period was set between two sittings of the House of Assembly, which met in March and again in June.

If no postponement were granted, then any appeal to Members of the House would have been valueless as the matter would have been finalized before it could have been aired, although once it was announced, there emerged a public demand for a conference between all affected persons to sort out the position and to consider alternatives to what had been plainly revealed as an official muddle.

At the end of March, Mr McKillop journeyed to Port Moresby to interview the Administrator and heads of government. The Administrator was away in the Highlands at the time, but Mr McKillop did have several talks with departmental chiefs. The outcome of these talks can be assessed from a report which he submitted to the New Guinea Planters' Association in Rabaul, on 2 April.

Canoe and paddlers, Balimo

Old houses at Dopima No. 3 Village

Two Kieta lads with ceremonial initiation head-dress

People of Aramia Village

In Port Moresby he had met the Treasurer and Acting Assistant Administrator, Mr A. Newman, the Director of Lands, Mr D. Groves, and the then Director of District Administration, Mr T. Ellis. Later, he interviewed the Administrator.

All agreed on the points raised by McKillop, but none accepted them.

No explanation beyond, "in the best interests of the Territory" could be obtained, and no reasons for the resumption were offered.

The decision for resumption rested solely with the District Administration, acting upon reports of its field staff, the competency of both being questioned by McKillop in view of their lack of experience at Bougainville, the opposition of the Bougainville District Advisory Council—which voted seven to two against the resumption—and the support of this resolution by all native members. But all this had been ignored.

The company's choice of two other sites, made by their own professional people after eighteen months' investigation, was rejected by the Administration. McKillop was advised that "the Administration did not accept the proposition that the company were competent to decide what was suitable land for the purposes of a township to serve the mining project"—surely one of the most inept claims made by any government.

After considerable discussion, the Directors referred McKillop to the Administrator as "he would be the one to give the real reasons justifying the decision," but when the Administrator was interviewed, he stated that the decision was taken on the advice of the Directors and that their advice would be followed in the future.

McKillop's conclusion was that the responsibility lay entirely with District Administration and that political effect had been the guiding feature, "regardless of suitability and destruction of present economic development."

Furthermore, the District Administration clearly stated that it had no present plans for resumption of other native land for the resettlement of those who would be displaced, although an area had been bought from the Catholic Mission and there were hopes of acquiring more from a near-by plantation and other native land in another area.

The report stated that the ultimate Administration plan called for the resettlement of displaced people on land alienated from native tenure amounting to approximately 4,500 acres, with most of it to be on freehold property under European ownership.

McKillop's view of the Moresby talks was that the Administration had failed to gain a reasonable appreciation of what might be

Baubaguina Village

People of Baubaguina

Women enjoying a chat

Father and son

involved and were floundering around without the expertise to make realistic and sound decisions. Finally, he informed the Administrator that his (McKillop's) objections would be taken on to the Federal Government in an appeal against their stewardship of the public interest, charging the Administration with political dishonesty.

Most appropriate to this situation is an extract from a statement on Australian Policy in Papua and New Guinea, made on 23 August 1960 by the then Minister for Territories, the Honourable Paul Hasluck (now Sir Paul Hasluck, Governor-General of the Commonwealth).

He said, "A people may be able to blunder along without being highly efficient in government but they suffer tragically if there is not fair dealing, probity and regard for the public welfare on the part of those who attain power and a measure of trust among those who are governed."

He also added, "The term 'inhabitant' in the United Nations Charter covers all those who have made their permanent home in the Territory . . . Our policy is to inculcate and uphold respect for each other's rights and allow no one-sided abrogation of those rights. This principle is basic to advancement in civilization . . . We will maintain it."

In fact, there are many, many people in this Territory who firmly believe that if Sir Paul Hasluck had remained Minister, the mess the Administration got itself into would never have occurred, and that the leadership, statesmanship, and probity shown in earlier years has sadly degenerated in the period subsequent to the change in the Ministry.

There was a strange sequel to the meeting of the Bougainville District Advisory Council. During a conversation with Mr Paul Lapun, M.H.A. for South Bougainville, he told me that he had been one of the members at the meeting who had voted, with six other native members, against the land resumption measure.

"After the meeting closed," he said, "I was taken into the district office and told that I had voted wrongly and that I did not understand what the subject was about. I was also told that I must write a letter of apology to the Administrator for having voted against the proposal."

"And did you write that letter?" I asked him.

"No," he replied, "I did not, and I don't intend to. I am here to look after the interests of my people."

The incident was published in subsequent stories I wrote for my paper. For a week there was silence. Then in a special release by the Assistant Administrator, Mr Newman, it stated that Mr

Lapun was not told to write the apology, but only "advised" to do so, a nicety of phrase that does nothing to hide official pressure on those who refuse to be "Yes-men."

At the same time, a public meeting was held in Kieta, attended by about forty people and eighty police, so I was informed, which passed a resolution declaring a vote of no-confidence in the Administration. Afterwards a recording of the meeting was relayed through Radio Bougainville, an Administration station. It gave full feature to a local councillor who had warmly supported the official take-over of land, but mentioned not a word about the vote of no-confidence.

Later, Mr McKillop and I both went and spoke to the officer-in-charge of the station, asking why the recording was censored, particularly as it was made at a public meeting.

We were told that the tape was too long and had to be cut, although just who did the cutting was not explained. When we asked to see the tape we were advised that it had been sent across to headquarters in Port Moresby. So that was that, although one of the Administration's strongest claims is that the people of Bougainville are being kept fully informed through their own radio station.

Although I was most anxious to sound out C.R.A. opinion on the local situation, no opportunity arose for me to interview any of the management people at the Panguna mine site. They were absent from Kieta when I arrived and when they did return, one day before my departure for Rabaul, the senior officials flew direct by helicopter from the Aropa airstrip to Panguna and I had no further time or opportunity to travel back up into the mountains without extending my visit, and facing again the difficulties of air transport back to Rabaul.

I had made one journey to the mining site at the invitation of officials, but I was purely a visitor looking over an industrial undertaking as part of my newspaper duties, and for one full day I received the courtesies and guidance of mine officials who described the project.

The journey forms no part of this particular chapter and can be generally omitted although one tentative question of mine regarding the company's position in the Kieta land dispute was answered by, "We are entirely clear of any disputes in this matter. We have completed our part of the agreement and it is now the Administration's job to handle the land situation."

This, I found, was the prevailing attitude among C.R.A. personnel and, as I was told later, "C.R.A. are bending over backwards to avoid any trouble with the local people," and this was substantiated in many ways.

Fortunately for me, the District Commissioner, Mr Des Ashton, returned from leave before my departure and my interview with him was quickly and easily arranged. Among the questions I had prepared to ask him was one based upon remarks I had heard in Kieta. Allegedly, *he*, the D.C., had known nothing about the Arawa land resumption.

Mr Ashton virtually confirmed this, saying that no mention had been made to him about Arawa before he had gone on leave, and that he had first heard about it while he was in Sydney.

I followed this by asking if it was customary for the central government not to advise the most senior officer in the district on future development plans of this magnitude, and he replied that there had been a number of land propositions put to him, and discussed, but Arawa had not been mentioned.

He told me that the company had put other propositions to the Administration, one of which involved 1,300 acres of Pakia land. This, he said, was unacceptable because it was the most developed area with the heaviest population. The Pakia people, he explained, had already been affected through mining operations in the Panei Valley and were upset at the suggestion of further land acquisition. Consequently the Administration had rejected the proposal.

Of the company's second choice of land I was told that this, too, was considered unsuitable, for it consisted mainly of swamp country which would have involved heavy reclamation costs, although whether this was the actual reason for rejecting the proposal is open to doubt.

A company with assets of $500 million must have been prepared for reclamation costs or they would never have submitted their proposal, and in view of the enormous amount of other ground development work being undertaken, most of it in heavy bush, mountain and timber country, the reclamation of a swamp area should have caused little trouble.

One can only judge the Administration's rejection of this proposal by comparing it with the willingness of the company to accept the area if it were granted. If the company was agreeable, and it must have been, then why did the Administration refuse?

We can only conclude that for some reason of its own the Administration did not consider the company competent enough to know what land was suitable for its own requirements, the implication made to Mr McKillop in Port Moresby, and one that is very hard to accept.

Mr McKillop had told me that when he had first come to Arawa quite a lot of swamp reclamation work was necessary before the plantation could be developed, and Arawa, in comparison with C.R.A., is small.

The fact remains that the company had fully investigated the area at considerable time and expense, and on the grounds of technological competency any sane person would back the company every time.

This is one of many contradictions that run throughout the whole affair.

Referring to compensation for native farmers who will be removed, Mr Ashton said that there were several ideas in view, particularly in resettlement, but none was yet hard and fast.

He thought that the Moroni group, within the actual mining area, would move down from the mountains to join the Pakia people, to whom they were related, and that "several thousands of acres of land have been bought at Mabiri which can be made available as there is little permanent population there."

Mabiri is an almost straight tract of coastal land stretching northwards from Rorovana and ending at Cape Mabiri, in Numa Harbour. Once there had been a proposal for the building of a jet airstrip here which would serve the copper project, but Mr Ashton advised me that this was now "out," and from later reports, it seemed that improvements were to be made to the old Aropa airstrip.

According to information gathered locally there is no shortage of land at Mabiri—a figure of 30,000 to 40,000 acres was given me—and there is the official statement of a small population. Some of the land is "wet," in fact swampy, but if it has been found suitable for a jet airstrip then there must be a fairly large area fit for industrial and urban construction, and again, if they can instal a displaced population there then why could they not instal a township? If Mabiri had been selected there would have been no subsequent Rorovana trouble.

Another argument put up against Mabiri was that it would be too far from the company's operations and this would create other problems. Yet quite a lot of urban residential sites in Australia and other countries are twenty to thirty miles away from the main areas, and Mabiri would not be much farther than the newly proposed site at Kieta.

All discussions revealed that the Administration just did not want to release the Mabiri area, no matter what arguments were put forward or what demands might be made for a full economic

201

survey to be carried out, although it admits to having bought several thousands of acres there from the original native owners, and numbers the displaced people at a few hundreds. Why then, the "several thousands of acres?" Are these to be held in reserve for further overseas capital investment?

What are the company's future land requirements? This, apparently, is still an unanswerable question.

The District Commissioner replied that the company's land needs were only now becoming firm, but could give no specific figures. Already 10,000 acres have been excised under a special mining lease and there are another 1,600 acres in the Arawa area to go. There will be leases for roads, a port site, power units and disposal of tailings, the latter area of unknown size but locally estimated at 4,500 acres, and this is only the beginning.

No wonder there is a fear among the Bougainville people that C.R.A. will eventually become the government. I heard several company employees boast that C.R.A. was *already* the government on Bougainville—"The Administration will do what we tell them from now on," one said. It is this prospect that has given fresh life to the nascent secessionist movement on the island.

The proposed area for dumping tailings, or mullock, from mining operations was pointed out to me from the 3,000-foot ridge that one climbs on the way to Panguna. It lies westwards towards the coast in the direction of Torokina Bay, the country in between being rough and rugged, with precipitous chasms, ridges, and the vast ribs of the mountain chain leading down to swampy lowlands near the coast.

According to the District Commissioner, the dumping will form a pattern of land reclamation which, given time for the poisons to leach out of the soil, could eventually become a grazing area.

It is said that there are few people in the area but what their opinion is has not been recorded.

A point I did raise was the sudden announcement of troop movements through the areas, for the Pacific Islands Regiment were about to show the flag with three civic co-operation teams within a few weeks. From a military source I was told that such troop movements were planned many months in advance and had no relation to the present unrest, but when I asked if it was wise to introduce troops at this time, I was told that soldiers would not be travelling through possible company land, which I understood to mean the affected areas.

At village meetings I subsequently attended, many native leaders declared that the government was sending soldiers against them.

202

It certainly seemed a most inopportune time to show even the minimum signs of military power.

The District Commissioner's awkward position could be appreciated, for he gave me a wide and extremely reasonable account of what was happening from the official viewpoint, but there were many things which conflicted with what Konedobu was saying— and not saying—and the greatest of these was the attitude of the people, which I was to sample very shortly.

The more an outsider peers into this land business the more contradictory it becomes, and there is always that big question— why has the Administration remained so adamant over the Kieta site and refused repeated requests for open conferences, better investigation, and a more reasonable and understanding approach?

One comes to the conclusion that it is not land, or people, or the company's interests that the Administration is concerned about, but that hidden political motives are ruling every decision, for when you take this matter, piece by piece, nothing adds up and you are left with a collection of frayed ends seemingly impossible to splice.

The greater proportion of my available time was spent in travelling to meetings held at various villages and centres, often in the bush and under the shade of trees, and which were attended by groups numbering from fifty up to three hundred people.

Here I could listen, at first hand, to the complaints of these communities over the loss of their land and the destruction of their crops, and here I could question individuals, not only on their own specific complaints, but on their attitudes towards the company and the Administration.

It was surprising how far some of these people had travelled to present their views, for I was briefed regularly by Paul Lapun and others on who were the representatives and the places they came from—some came from many miles away in the foothills and valleys. The word had spread. They flocked in over rough bush tracks and it was easy to see that this was a matter in which all of them felt united, and which all of them were prepared to resist.

Speaker after speaker, at each meeting, stood and declared that his people would resist the taking of their land. "The people of my village have sent me . . ."; "My people have told me that they will fight . . ."; "We will all stand together on this . . . ." This was the general tone of the messages they brought, a story of unity and defiance, and as each one spoke he was cheered and clapped by those around.

I searched for the leader who might have started all this but could find none. It was a spontaneous reaction from them all, and though each group had its own spokesmen, and there was Paul Lapun as their member, not one individual stood out from his people as the man who had inspired this outburst.

Had there been a true leader, with determination and forcefulness, and with breadth of vision to gather the people, violence would have developed long before the actual skirmishing that later happened. But perhaps it is well for the Administration that such a man did not emerge, for blood would surely have been shed.

At every meeting I attended, and on most other trips around the area, the South Bougainville M.H.A., Paul Lapun, was present, and I came away very favourably impressed by the way in which he assisted at the meetings, by his quiet, effective manner, his solid arguments and his well-balanced sense of decorum. No meeting got out of order while Paul was present.

He is not, by any means, a rabble-rouser nor does he seem one to seek notoriety, and, as parliamentary representative of his people, I would rate him as a natural leader and one of the best. The fact that he had taken upon himself the task of patrolling his electorate, night and day, at a time when the true essence of leadership was vitally necessary, speaks well of his sense of responsibility.

It is to his great credit that he did not spare himself; he was on the spot when trouble threatened and, as I well know, he spent many hours of arduous, rough bush-walking to ensure that he could give the utmost assistance to his people in an electorate that was certainly difficult to traverse.

One of my first inquiries had been about the local parliamentary representatives. Bougainville Island has three members, Mr Donatus Mola, North Bougainville; Mr Paul Lapun, South Bougainville; and, Mr Joseph Lue, Bougainville Regional.

At the time of my visit, Mr Mola was in Australia, Mr Lapun was in Bougainville, and Mr Lue, who is also Assistant Minister for Technical Education and Training, was in Port Moresby.

Perhaps Mr Lue could be excused for not visiting his electorate at such a crucial time, and perhaps official duties kept him chained to Port Moresby, but it was quite remarkable that upon the publication of my stories expressing the feelings of his people against the Administration, Mr Lue was one of the first to rush into print in defence of the Administration's actions, charging that I had no understanding of the people.

As a representative of the same people who voted him into office, this seemed quite astounding, especially as I had attempted to report the views then held by his people, and given me by themselves. However, this was his attitude, and it may yet prove to be his cross.

At Kuka village, part of the Arawa area, there were representatives from other near-by villages and a large gathering of farmers who will be directly affected by any resumption.

The meeting, held at night, was very orderly and comparatively quiet with a series of speakers who voiced their fears of a future take-over. It seemed to me, that their immediate concern was the resumption of Arawa Plantation, for although this was not their property, such a move could spell economic disaster.

The majority of the speakers were Kip McKillop's neighbours, people whom he knew personally and whom he had helped over many years so that there had developed between them more of an inter-family relationship, rather than the casual acquaintanceship of neighbours. They regarded themselves as an integral part of Arawa, their future depended largely upon the maintenance of the plantation, their crops were processed at the factory, and their income and whole way of life was closely bound up with the future of Arawa Plantation.

They were argumentative but not hostile. They were fearful because this sudden threat of expropriation was something that none of them fully understood, and they naturally thought that if an area the size of Arawa Plantation, solid and productive, was going to be destroyed, then their own family blocks would go with it.

One speaker put up a very sound argument when he told the meeting that he, with many of his compatriots, had been urged and directed over the years by the Administration to utilize the ground for the growing of cash crops. They had all followed this suggestion, and had been assisted by Mr McKillop. Yet now, the Administration had "turned its talk" and was condemning what it had preached.

"Why does the government do this?" he asked. "Why have I spent all my years growing cocoa because they told me to, and now it is to be destroyed? I am an old man; I cannot go into the bush and start again. I have children. They will never have this land and they will never be able to grow crops as I have done. What are they to do?"

It was a very simple and effective speech. Those in authority, who were responsible for this impasse, should have been there to hear it, for not all the copper in the world could compensate for the shattered lives of this old man and his family.

In and around the area the talk was the same, sadness mixed with fear and ignorance, too, of what it all meant and what might happen later.

It was at Rorovana that I first met the full force of resentment and defiance, a far different attitude from that of the Arawa people who had not been directly affected until then.

Rorovana is a pleasant spot, sheltered in an alcove of the ocean, with wide sandy beaches and coconut groves. From here one can look across the water to Mabiri, a long, low strip with its background of mountains and clouds, and in the brilliant noon sunshine it made an attractive picture.

However, the delightfulness of the surroundings was not reflected in the faces of the people who sat awaiting us, sullen and silent. They gathered around under the shade of a large tree, forming a semi-circle in front of some benches upon which Paul Lapun, the village leaders, and our own party sat.

For a while there was some desultory talk, as if their minds were full but their tongues were tied, until one man stood up and began speaking to Paul. "I was in hospital," he said, "when the first trouble started here and I was brought out by the A.D.C. to come and talk to the people. The government men had come and marked some ground without seeing the people, and when they protested they were told that C.R.A. was getting the land. When the owner asked about his coconuts he was told that everything would be all right.

"Later I came out of hospital, and when I returned I found my own ground had been marked out, and there were pegs in other parts of our land, so I went back to the district office and complained.

"They told me to leave the marks alone and said that if we did not agree to what had been pegged then the whole of our land would be taken."

One of the group interrupted, "That's right. They said, 'You leave those bloody marks alone or we'll take the lot!'."

When he sat down another stood up. "On Monday, the government and a company man came here to mark our land, but we told them to go away and would not let them on the ground. On Wednesday, they came back with police. There were thirty-three policemen and they all had guns, and two surveyors and the government man began marking the ground."

And a third arose. "The company told us that they would put lights in the harbour to mark the passage, and we agreed. But no lights have been put there. Instead their men came to mark our ground, so we chased them away."

By now the talk had become general as each man tried to make himself heard. Paul quietened them and spoke to them, saying

206

that I was there as a newspaperman, and would listen to what they said and print it in the paper.

Then Raphael Bele, their leader, stood up.

It was true what the others had told us, he said. There were thirty-three police with rifles who stood guard while the ground was marked. Nobody asked the people's permission and they just walked in and took control. "They are stealing from us," he exclaimed, "and all the talk they give us is not true. They are going to finish Arawa Plantation, and afterwards they will finish us."

He said that, a few hours before we had arrived, men came there to get ground samples, and they had police with rifles to protect them. Even as he was speaking I saw two armed police come from behind a house at the end of the village, walk slowly along the fringe of timber to meet a surveyor carrying sample bags of dirt, and then, with other police, get into a vehicle on the road and drive off. . . . The villagers sat and watched them in silence.

"They won't speak to us now," Raphael continued. "They walk in and won't show their papers. We are told nothing and we are given no time."

Almost 200 men, women, and children were clustered around. As Raphael sat down, they burst into a babel of shouting and talk. "They can kill us"; "Kill us"; "We will die," came from several throats as men stood and weaved about aimlessly, and for a while there was nothing but one long savage roar from dozens of angry men.

"Do they mean that they will fight the government?" I asked Paul, shouting to make myself heard.

"Yes," he replied. "They will fight anybody who tries to take their land."

When the noise had died down, Paul called one old man over to speak to me. His name was Asina and he was married with four girls and five boys. On his land he told me he had planted 9,000 coconuts and 1,500 cocoa-trees.

"They told me that they would take my land for the company but nobody spoke to me about payment. I asked the district officer but he wouldn't say anything. I will not let them take my land. They can kill me first," he said.

One, named Koba, from Kuka village, the place I had visited the previous night, declared that the people of Kuka would fight too, and that he had been sent to tell this meeting about it.

And there was Auwa, of Kobuan, married with a family, the same as Koba, and he, too, declared the government would not shift him. "They can kill me if they want to," he shouted.

And there were others. They crowded round talking a medley of threats and defiance, with "Kill, kill, kill," being repeated over and over again.

As we were leaving, a man came to me and handed me a letter written in Pidgin. There were three pages from an exercise book. "Put that in the paper," he told me, and said that he would give me more later.

When I read it, I found it to be a statement of most of what had been said at the meeting, an account of the trouble with the surveyors, the police, the attack on the Administration who had told them to plant coconuts and cocoa and now wanted to destroy them, a question about why the government had turned against them, and a challenge. *You come to steal from us. Now come here and fight, because we will fight you. We are declaring war on the government*, it ended.

And as we drove off down the track, Paul Lapun turned to me and said, "These people will fight the government all right. There is going to be a lot of trouble."

In the last few hours of my visit, invitations came to dine at the S.D.A. Mission at Rumba, a few miles inland from Arawa, and to attend a special meeting called by the Nasioi Rural Progress Society, of the Bobo Valley, close by.

The dinner was a social affair with several guests, but conversation inevitably centred on the Arawa acquisition and the disturbed state of mind among the local people.

The Administrator had made an official visit there just previously, and this had given the mission authorities food for thought. The pastor, apparently undisturbed by any previous appearances of high authority, had made inquiries about the coming visit, and had asked if there were any special arrangements to be made.

He was told that this would be a social call, that the Administrator had expressed a wish to see as many people and as much of the area as possible, and that it would be practically a morning-tea affair. But when the Administrator stepped out of his car, one of his first requests had been to make a complete inspection of all station buildings and, there and then, he stepped out for the nearest set of buildings, which happened to be the girls' dormitories.

With no warning of such a change in plans, the pastor was quite unprepared for an official visit embracing the whole station which was then in the process of a morning clean-up. "The girls' rooms were untidy, with clothes lying everywhere and unmade beds, and there had been no time to clean up generally," he said. "There was confusion everywhere; students were running around completely startled to see the Administrator walking around, and the staff were trying to make some attempt at making the place presentable. We had prepared a form of welcome but this sudden decision upset our plans, and the overall disorderliness must have left an impression. It took us completely by surprise."

Their surprise turned to apprehension when, a week later, came the sudden announcement that Arawa Plantation was to be resumed. This, of course, had engendered fears that the mission and the surrounding Bobo Valley native land areas were marked down for future resumption.

Around Kieta there is reasonable speculation that the new Kieta township, once firmly established, will inevitably spread beyond the boundaries of Arawa and its fringes, and that the Bobo Valley will be engulfed. This may not be the Administration's present intention but the situation is developing, in land and social implications, where the Administration will become powerless to put any fence around the boundaries of expansion.

Figures for the potential population of the new town vary from 8,000 to 12,000, and with ancillary services, roads, a port, power installations, and the natural development of mining operations, the town of Kieta may expand more rapidly than Lae has done.

In Lae there is controlled expansion because the prevailing economic factors balance its developmental demands, which still fit into an overall Territory pattern, but at Kieta there will be an over-balance of fast moving, highly organized, heavy industrial growth, foreign to Territory conditions, controlled from overseas sources and forcing its own pace against any standards, to meet its own hidden demands.

District Commissioner Des Ashton told me, "We are going to have a lot of problems," and he wasn't exaggerating. It is doubtful if the Administration realize the problems they are creating. If they do, then they must be viewing them with alarm.

Of the new Kieta population there will be at least 2,000 construction workers, a foreign element, new to the country, skilled to a degree and earning high wages. These undoubtedly will be accommodated on the fringe of the new township—in fact next door to the widespread native farming communities.

The social threat that this holds to the native people is a big one, as anybody who has experienced boom times in a newly developed mining area will know. Infringements of native rights, encroachments on land, prostitution, and the other ills of such an invasion can be predicted, for one cannot imagine 2,000 strong, healthy men, used to big wages, heavy drinking and the delights of the fleshpots, not chasing around after women . . . and the only women available are the native ones. If the men of Bougainville object strongly to the taking of their land, how are they going to react to the taking of their women?

Law and order may prevail, but these will create a surreptitious market, and the ills will spread along other channels.

The social changes that are likely to hit the native people will not necessarily be good ones, and if the natives don't fight against them then they will have to accept whatever comes and let their own way of life be torn to shreds.

The "good, fair price" of $105 an acre for their land does not cover these contingencies, for you can't measure demoralization by dollars.

The following day I walked up into the valley to the Rural Progress Society meeting. It had been widely advertised, and there was an attendance nearing 300, for most of those present were active members of the society, and apart from this, everybody in the region was affected by the latest government moves.

Paul Lapun took over the management of the meeting and handled it well, using quite a lot of persuasion at times to control the more violent moments and to keep the speakers on the track of the subjects to be discussed. Several speakers said that their people feared that when Arawa and some native areas had gone, their own land would come under the hammer. The Administrator's visit to Rumba was taken as a bad indication of future intentions, and it was plain that the word of this had circulated very quickly. Fears for themselves, their wives and children, and their homes, were the dominant topics, and they voiced their alarm at the prospects of social disintegration in phrases that were crude but direct.

"I send my pigs into the bush to eat grass," one little old man exclaimed, "and soon I shall have to go and do the same," and he grovelled on the ground chewing blades of grass while the crowd cheered, applauded, and laughed.

It began to rain, a slow, steady drizzle, but this did not dampen their feelings. Soon a new element came into their talk.

"Give us secession and we will handle the copper company," one man screamed, and his call was taken up by many.

"Stop the company from working, get rid of the government, and then we will be able to run our own affairs and tell the company what to do," shouted another man. The mood of excitement changed suddenly to one of ugliness.

Hands were raised, and there were cries of "Yes. Yes." Paul managed to quieten them down again, but they hadn't finished with the subject. It was taken up again and talked over. Then there was a call for a vote, and a mass of hands went up in support of those who wanted secession. "Let the company stop," they yelled, and it was another ten minutes before reason returned and talk got back to land resumption.

Round about noon the meeting wound up with a vote of no-confidence in the Administration, and threats of fight.

"Do we support the government?" somebody called, and they answered, "No. No," and again hands waved wildly in the air.

We turned to leave as they broke up into small groups, still arguing, still planning, and still voicing menaces.

Back at the hotel that evening I was drinking by myself at the bar when a burly gentleman at the other end called across to me, "I'm a construction worker. We'll bring the $50 million. You can forget the planters and the natives. We're the ones who make the money. Put that in your paper," and sank his head into another foaming glass.

It had started.

A day later I lifted out of Bougainville on a special small plane flight, looking down on a sad and surly island, its beauty enhanced by bright sunshine, its apparent peacefulness a deception, its rural simplicity about to be jolted by bulldozers and gelignite, with touchy Mount Bagana standing ready to blast it with fire and brimstone. We headed straight into an equally black and dangerous tropical storm that blotted out Rabaul, threw us blindly round the sky and bumped us down to coconut-tree level before we eventually crawled down to Lakunai in the growing darkness of a wind-swept night.

There was one other passenger, a woman with an injured leg, and as we climbed shakily out of the plane she murmured, "If there had been a road I would have walked."

It was that kind of a flight.

The troubles and torments of Bougainville are continuing on a wider scale but to a lesser degree; the inflamed threats made under jungle trees and in mountain villages have materialized in skirmishes with police and government officers, in which women as well as men have joined.

Armed police with batons and tear gas have quelled scuffles and removed obstructions; there have been recriminations in the Australian parliament and press; a round-table talk between the Australian Prime Minister, Mr Gorton, and the Bougainville representatives, Paul Lapun and Raphael Bele, and there are legal actions pending against the Administration.

This is a sorry record for an Administration which proclaims the cause of democracy from the housetops, which tries to justify force under the guise of humanitarianism, which panders to excuses for broken promises, and as guardian of the people's interests, stands in surly silence to all public appeals for open dealing.

It is impossible to believe that any modern government, charged with the welfare of an emerging, subjective race, would rebuff all approaches, remain adamant against all suggestions, take refuge behind the dollar sign, cast an implicating slur of incompetence against professional industrialists whom it is trying to woo, and beat its breast over its own infallibility to such an extent. Yet this has happened, and it is continuing; the result of a mentality that existed in 1889, and still persists in 1969, eighty years later.

A persistent by-product of discontent with the Administration is its perverted sense of its own infallibility—it can do no wrong whatever happens, and it will never admit to mistakes—and this adds to the subdued, but steady pressures of official politics which are always operating, though hard to define, and seem to act as an internal government within a government.

One native public servant, in quite a responsible position, told me that he and all his compatriots are fully aware that underground pressures constantly prevent their freedom of expression in matters which vitally affect the people's well-being.

I asked him to be more explicit, but he refused, saying, "You are just as aware of these as I am, and you know I cannot give you names because action in some form will be taken against me if it becomes known. All of us know this happens. The native people talk among themselves and some of the things they say are not very nice."

This is not an isolated example, for as a newspaperman, it is whispered to me continually, by expatriates and native people and mostly from those within the public service.

Numerous officials have told me that they have written books and collected notes which they are hoarding for subsequent publication once they are free of the service. "I have got all this down on paper," is quite a common remark.

Why an all-powerful government agency—the Administration is not a government, it is an agency of the Commonwealth—should adopt such methods of control is beyond comprehension, for it holds a handful of aces and there is little within the Territory which can act independently of the Administration.

It controls the greater proportion of news, through its own newsheets and radio stations; it has a thumb on every activity of the individual native; it is a tribunal for appeals, a prosecutor, a judge;

212

it entirely controls the Territory's finances; it has influential official power over House of Assembly legislation with ten officially appointed members, all senior officials, and a group of Ministers and Assistant Ministers all of whom are expected to support official legislation—and invariably do without question.

If it is thwarted it has a power of veto, as does the Minister and Commonwealth Government; it controls a hierarchy of departmental heads, all expatriates; it superimposes itself upon local government councils and other channels of native endeavour; directs the course of political awareness among the people and employs for itself a highly qualified public relations expert to achieve a better public image of itself and its actions—which is an admission that its public image is not too good.

Threaded throughout the whole community is a network of intelligence people gathering information and reporting, and there is also a dossier of personal files for those individuals who, for any reason, have shown some form of prominence.

The last time I saw mine, on an official desk, there were two files, and each was quite thick, and I have been warned by an official friend to ease up on certain lines of criticism—"it's all put down on the file."

As an interesting aside, I once asked a top businessman in Port Moresby what his opinion was of the effects of a coming national election for the House of Assembly. He replied, "I don't care a damn who they elect. If I want something I drive straight over to Konedobu and tell them." Konedobu is the Administration's headquarters.

One most interesting phenomenon is the recent banning of the Press in the House of Assembly, a motion proposed and moved by an Assistant Minister. All the official members and the ministerial group voted for the ban. Two official members were absent, but this did not alter the intent. Surely one official member wanted a free press, but not one signified it.

It is these characteristics which have contributed to the Bougainville trouble, and will encourage other upsets. They are purely childish symptoms of megalomania—the attitude, "We know what you want, now you do it . . ."—a crooked variety of paternalism that is leading this country and the people into a series of complicated messes.

There has never been a revolt among the people and there has never been justifiable cause for armed police, batons, and tear gas against defenceless men, women, and children.

Once it was a strange sight to see a policeman with a baton, but now you can stand and see riot squads practising their drill openly in public parks to the sounds of bugles synchronizing the men's movements and their own yells, screams and shouts as they swipe, parry and thrust at imaginary opponents, while the native population stands around, astounded.

The last time I saw this sort of thing was in Nazi Germany, at Hamburg, prior to my coming to the Territory, and although, as a child, I was involved in the Irish Rebellion and the subsequent Civil War, I never saw British troops or police, or the "Black and Tans," act in such a manner when the population was subdued and quiet.

The Bougainville upset will be subdued by force if the present negotiations and legal eagles fail, and the efforts of the Moral Re-Armament group, said to be interested, fail to bring peace.

The Arawa settlement is reported to be a down-payment of $400,000, a trust fund of $200,000, and an assessment of produce values over a period of five years for an average which could give Kip McKillop a higher sale price.

There is talk that this principle is to be applied to the native people's land claims, though details are lacking.

A government orchid authority is to evaluate McKillop's private collection, and as this was presumably to be bulldozed into the ground, this is the only kind action in the whole affair, though probably it is of little consolation to the man who devoted a large proportion of his life to the collection.

Yet all this trouble, the bitter hearts, resentment and memories, and the dirty face of the Administration, could have been avoided had some statesmanship and an open approach been shown.

Firstly, there should have been more honest attempts by individuals, organizations, and parliamentary representatives to hold a full-scale investigation of the areas selected for resumption and the alternative sites put forward. The efforts of the Administration to avoid this showed a dishonesty of political purpose.

Secondly, there needed to be an adjustment of benefits whereby the native people—all of them, not just those from Bougainville—could have participated more fully and more directly in the millions of dollars being advertised as coming from this copper project. The most that was held out was an Administration option on 20% equity in a reported fifteen years' time—"if this is to be taken up," to quote the Minister. And that, basically, is no offer at all.

Benefits should have been made available right at the commencement of production, so that they would become tangible assets for the people to enjoy. To say that there will be more hospitals, schools, airfields and roads, is no answer.

214

It is useless, also, to say that this course could not be taken. The Administration is boasting that it will receive $100 million annually through exports, and another $200 to $300 million during the next ten years from revenue, which is an uncomfortable method of solacing dispossessed native landowners who consider themselves fortunate to see $10.

Faced by a crucial national policy decision which will affect the whole of the Territory's population, the course has been one of self-preservation, and in doing so, the government has acquired for itself a time-bomb.

Other mining interests are flocking to the country, all with large grants of prospecting concessions that cover practically the whole Territory. There are bound to be other discoveries of vast mineral deposits so there will be other claims for large areas of native lands, more resistance from the people, and the same response from the Administration. So it looks as if we are now in for a multiplying succession of resumptions, violence, police armed with batons and tear gas.

Bougainville has become a precedent. The Administration has now no option but to continue its original policy.

Once an exploration company invests the required amount of development capital it has a legal right to knock on the official door and demand—not request—the allocation of whatever land it needs, and the government is committed, right up to its ears, to comply.

Nobody disputes the right of industrial development to go ahead, and the native people are all behind it and will co-operate, but there must be fairness in dealing, honesty of purpose, and regard for the people to enjoy social and economic benefits from the wealth of their land—to retain some land rights in fact.

At Bougainville, this has not been done.

A worse spectre is rising, and this among the intellectual and educated classes of native people, the public servants, parliamentarians, professionals, vocal councillors, and determined students. I have been talking to many of them, for they have few land troubles; they are absorbed into our pattern of society, and their old village relationships are fading. Their outlook, consequently, is rather detached from the parochialism of the Bougainville land resumptions but is very much centred on their political future.

They are in doubt, afraid, and disillusioned, and they certainly lack confidence in the government to bring them, as has so often been proclaimed, self-government and ultimate independence. "We can plainly see now why the Minister, Mr Barnes, wanted to halt political and constitutional development for seven years, as he recently stated, for it fits into this pattern of industrial might," one of them told me. "To boost industry for the satisfaction of this Administration means that they must throw overboard all our hopes of becoming an independent nation. That is what we now believe."

They are wise enough to understand that if the government tries, in any way, to foster moves for a future Papua-New Guinea Government, then overseas investment capital would be immediately withdrawn, and they know that the manner in which the Administration has committed itself to the demands of this foreign capital is a kiss of death to their own national hopes.

Their attitude is a very pragmatic one based upon political realism, the substance of which is that they have been promised that political independence from Australia will eventually be theirs.

The ceaseless indoctrination of "when you become independent" has already created within them their own image as a new nation taking their place in the comity of world nations, and they view all Administration and Commonwealth Government political actions in relationship to this one final objective.

The fact that they may not be politically adept, or economically sound, or professionally competent to take over the reins of government are incidental problems in attaining the main goal.

They have been promised national freedom and they expect it.

Now they are beginning to doubt the accepted manner of attaining this prize, and there is a lot of truth in the remark passed to me on one occasion that, "You would never have heard the word 'Secession' if the people's confidence in the Administration had been sustained," for it is a fact that the word was a complete stranger to Territory conversation until a year or so ago.

I have been asked how it is that the Administration could give guarantees and assurances to C.R.A. for many years to come— some say for fifty years—if it is the Administration's intent to bring independence to these people. The only answer that I can find is that the Administration, and the Commonwealth Government, intend to be ruling this country for the next half century, at least.

The fact that whatever assurances have been given will be inherited and assumed by any probable Papua-New Guinea Government is not accepted by thinking native people.

"If we get control of our country, then we will make our own "decisions," they reply, and this is but a reflection of those irate men of Bougainville who cry, "Stop the company, give us independence, and then we will tell the company what to do."

There is a substantial impression that the Westminster system of government which has been loudly and frequently propounded by the Minister, has failed and is of no use to the people. Their minds are now seriously turning towards republicanism, not merely in idle remarks, but in a determined effort to understand its processes and how it differs from the one now being imposed upon them. Study groups are forming, meetings are being held. One I know was attended by a member of parliament, several public servants, a number of college students, and visitors from other places.

I mentioned secession and fragmentation to one of them and he swiftly rejected such ideas. "We want a system of government that will unite us, not split us up. There will be no national unity under the present system of government, so why should we not look for something different?"

One of his arguments was that the Administration plays one group of people against another, the Highlanders against the coastal folk, the New Guineans against the Papuans, the educated against the illiterate, and the people of the islands against the remainder.

"This just will not work," he said. "How are we to obtain unity while this continues? We, ourselves, have buried our old tribal animosities, but official influences and pressures are keeping us divided. This is no way to bring us to political maturity."

Others complain that there is too little progress being made towards encouraging native responsibility in government.

"It is twenty-five years since the war ended, since the time we were promised a 'New Deal' but there are still only one or two of us who are in real positions of authority and responsibility, and they are not at the very top," a student explained to me. "They tell us that we are insufficiently trained, that we are not qualified to assume responsibility, yet most of the children of expatriates, after twenty-five years of upbringing, schooling and training, are in positions of some responsibility. Surely, out of our population of two million, they could have trained a few hundreds, or thousands, by this time so that we could have a select group of trained people who could accept responsible positions in government?"

To many, this continuous blanket overlay of the expatriate is becoming galling. Many feel that despite the great expansion in education and the improvement in social standards, they are facing a dead-end—that whatever high positions they strive to reach, there will always be a white man over the top of them.

As I write, there is protest and a ferment of trouble brewing in Rabaul between those for and against a multi-racial local government, based solely on the fact that they think they should run their own local affairs without the inclusion of Europeans and Asiatics.

The official answer to this has again been plane loads of riot police. Yet it is obvious that suppression by armed force will never eradicate the people's ideas and desires for independence in their own affairs.

They may be a minority, and they may be wrong in acting as they have, but fundamentally it is a visible sign that the people are struggling to express themselves the way they wish, and the Administration has a moral obligation to give consideration to any germ of independence and to guide it in its growth.

That the scheme of a multi-racial council fits into Administration thinking is obvious, and it is equally obvious that any idea of an all-native council running its own affairs does not fit into Administration thinking.

It might be wise to make a closer study of this phenomenon, for minorities have the habit, if they are suppressed, of growing up underground to emerge later as a majority.

First it was Bougainville. Now Rabaul. One may ask, where next?

"We have been told that, when we are ready, we alone can choose the type of government we wish," is the cry of the native leaders. This is the mood they are now in, one demanding independence, and one which will produce problems and headaches unless they are faced, and accepted, as stages of social development.

Settlement terms over the disputed Rorovana land have been announced, and the offer made is quite likely to be acceptable to the people who have stood firm against all previous offers and attempts to take their land.

Once again there has been a readjustment in the area of land claimed. Starting at 600 acres, when the official act of forceful resumption began, the area was reduced to 175 acres. It has now been dropped to 140 acres as the result of a further survey of its requirements by the mining company.

This one factor of land area needed, and its reduction, within a matter of a few weeks, from 600 to 140 acres, reveals the great divergence which must have existed between the Administration's opinion of what the copper company required and C.R.A.'s own professional estimates of its particular needs.

One is inclined to suspect that the Administration, totally unprepared for the resistance which the people put up against acquisition of their land, was using the old and bold method of securing more than the company needed in order to have a reserve of government-owned ground for its own use later on.

218

In April, three months before the land resumption order took effect, the Bougainville District Commissioner, Mr D. Ashton, had told me in Kieta that "the firm requirements of the company's land needs were only then becoming known," a remark that struck me at the time as highlighting the weakness of the Administration's position on local land matters.

It conflicted with the official assertion that the Administration had been explaining the amount of land required to the villagers over the previous two years, a claim that could hardly be substantiated if the actual land needs were still unknown as recently as a few months before.

At that time there were three very obvious facts: that the Administration had flatly rejected two areas of land investigated by the company and considered by C.R.A. to suit their requirements; that the Government were all out to bulldoze the Arawa land resumption through, irrespective of what opposition it met; and that the Administration's own land acquisition programme bore no relation to the copper company's needs, and it was very doubtful if an official programme actually existed.

Now, the Assistant Administrator for Economic Affairs, Mr A. J. P. Newman, has announced the terms of the new offer. These included, $7,000 as an annual rent; $30,000 compensation for land damage; shares to the value of $7,000 in the company and a lease for forty-two years, with an option of renewal for a further period with similar financial benefits should the offer be taken up. There are other conditions covering land improvement on unused areas.

This has been announced officially as a company offer and the remarkable difference between the Administration offer of $105 an acre, with certain limited compensation features, and the per acre valuation of $1,000 on company figures, is astounding.

Actually the whole deal for the native landholders will bring them almost (an estimated) half-a-million dollars over the period, and they will still retain possession of their land.

The Administration offer would have brought only about $25,000 with no immediate participation in copper mining benefits and with every possibility of disputes over land tenure.

The most important aspect of this deal is that the Administration has openly renounced its own land-policy laws because circumstances, and the government's own untenable position, have permitted direct land dealing between a private, non-official party and native landowners, contrary to the law which gives the Administration complete omnipotence over all land transactions.

This is a precedent of tremendous national importance, for the native people of the Territory and to the future of all economic, industrial, and agricultural development, for it acknowledges that native landowners can deal directly with prospective lessees. Furthermore, the law, which provides heavy fines, with possible imprisonment, and the ejection of an occupier for such direct negotiating, can be legally challenged as unconstitutional on the basis of the Administration's about-face.

This is a complete reversal of official land policy. The manner of its implementation is virtually an admittal that past official actions in land transactions have not been for the benefit of the native people. No other conclusion can be entertained.

It is obvious that company pressure and urgency dictated that the Rorovana land dispute should be taken out of official hands, that time and the unfavourable political situation did not permit further procrastination and displays of force, and that the methods being used were antique and entirely out of focus with the prevailing circumstances.

The consequence is that the Administration was put into a situation where it could do nothing but repudiate its own methods and attitudes, and in doing so, threw its own land laws into the wastepaper basket.

Immediately ahead lies a still greater repercussion.

With the new Rorovana conditions being so beneficial to native landholders, no future government offers in land transactions that do not give the same proportion of benefits will be accepted by other landowners.

Right on the government's doorstep is its intention to resume another 640 acres of native land at Arawa, adjacent to the already negotiated Arawa plantation site. This is not to be a time-lease but a complete, outright resumption in which the people will lose their land for ever, and from my own observations and discussions with the Arawa people, they will fight more determinedly than their neighbours have done.

Once again, it looks as if the copper company will have to take over direct negotiations while the Administration falls into line, for this involves the future new Kieta townsite, and with the plantation site having gone under the hammer, the acquisition of the adjoining native properties are vitally necessary.

The Arawa people now understand that their land is worth $1,000 an acre, and this they will demand, and as the word spreads through the Territory, all other landholders will respond the same way.

The determined, but token stand, made by the Rorovana people must ultimately change the whole face and attitude of official administration in this country. If the Commonwealth Government is wise, it will take immediate constitutional moves to find out where, and why, this Administration has failed, and carry out a full-scale, public investigation on future government policies in relation to the early advancement of the people towards a more responsible position of independence, with a progressive programme leading to national independence in the form they wish. This means "target dates" and not a series of blind, amorphous promises, committing no-one to anything and getting the people nowhere.

Whatever new changes may occur, the people's land will remain the basis of their social, economic, and political advancement, and this concept must be accepted by authority or it surely will be faced by an upsurge of internal revolt by the people within the foreseeable future.

The class distinctions which now exist, and are a cornerstone of Administration public service policy, have developed from the government's blind faith in its own omnipotence, the complete lack of elasticity of thought and understanding, and its overwhelming determination always to rule the roost, even when circumstances and conditions indicate otherwise.

Antagonism of people's attitude at its ineptness of action may have carried the Administration beyond the point where it can recover its lost prestige, for the ferment of unrest is brewing much faster than is officially admitted, and there are fair indications that the emergence of a true, native, national leadership, uninfluenced by present Administration policies, is not too far away.

The Bougainville incident has given a tremendous impetus to this new movement and has proved conclusively that the Administration can no longer blindly ignore the voice and desires of the people for economic and political betterment.

It has taken an important private industrial concern of international standing to bring this fact into the open, and the people are fully aware that the company has won. And in a sense, *they* have won also.

The people have made their challenge and have succeeded. Only the futility of outraged pride could maintain that "next time they will do as they're told."

journey into the future | 8

CRYSTAL BALL GAZING may be an abstract science but it forms no part of national development in an undeveloped country and among an underprivileged people. However, it is natural to speculate upon the future, for the future, in this primitive land, often looms more importantly in people's minds than the present, and there have been promises, and plans, and projects, all of which look to the years to come and carry such a substantial amount of incredibility and hope that even a degree of fulfilment might become possible.

The biggest and most important promise of all has been that of independence. It seems to have generated an attitude of mind which must be very noticeable to strangers.

An A.B.C. newsman visiting here recently spoke to me about it. "It is amazing how the word 'independence' is in everybody's mind up here," he remarked, an impression which is quite prevalent among newcomers.

There is a very good reason for this because the idea was released to an uncomprehending and startled native population whose knowledge of independence was confined to the limited boundaries of their own subsistence standards. Since then it has become a fixation, for it has been pumped into their minds, at times without rhyme or reason, and is now accepted as something that will be handed to them like their weekly wages, a reward for certain tasks performed, irrespective of whether the reward is something that they are totally incapable of handling.

In one way it has been a national disgrace, much in the nature of a vast confidence trick upon an unsophisticated people who believe, or did at one time, that everything the government says is above question.

222

Since the early burst of enthusiasm it has been steadily played down by the official sector and now the term has degenerated into a means of urging self-help by the people. "Help build a road, you will need it when independence comes," is typical of its present import.

Now we are vaguely assured that independence must come, a statement that cannot be contradicted, and that the people of the Territory will themselves say when they are ready for it.

This last condition, too, skates on very thin ice, for there has now emerged a sector of native thinking which is quite capable of understanding the magnetism of independence, the rewards that are offering for those in the box seat, and the far horizons which it will embrace. It requires only one group with understanding and prestige to demand self-government and independence to put the Commonwealth Government and the Administration in a spot. It will mean that the promises will either have to be honoured, and the white officials hand over their powers, or the government will have to sidetrack the demand in order to maintain its holding on the people and the country.

At present the country is run by a system of bilateral administration, one way being the almost desperate search for large overseas finance as investment and the other an attempt to maintain development within the country and among the people, from the Territory's own financial resources.

A close study of the two roads show that they are somewhat incompatible, for if international finance and investment take over, as is indicated, then national independence flies out of the window for many, many decades, and if the ace cards of self-government and independence are flushed from the sleeve too often, then foreign money will hesitate to plunge in too heavily.

One could hardly expect that a combine worth $100 million would be prepared to allow an unsophisticated native government to take full charge of its investments, a fact of which the government must be fully aware, and it is fully prepared to let any independence issue degenerate into a hoarsely whispered hope.

This makes the official campaign to bring self-government and eventual independence a subject worth investigating.

What does it intend to introduce? A real one hundred per cent stand for a proper, self-governing national entity, or an ersatz window-dressed variety produced by a selective method through the House of Assembly?

If it is the former, then the already top-heavy loading of the expatriate public service will have to cease and eventually be

223

disbanded. If it is the latter then the people who are now mainly providers of labour, and hewers of wood and drawers of water, will be likely to remain that way. There are many people of high accomplishments who consider that it is the second method that will prevail.

The general trend of government policies indicates that the Commonwealth Government has little intention of getting out of the Territory. Strengthened military forces, improved status and conditions for police, the tightening of law regulations, the almost complete abandonment of full-scale political education, the maze-like complexities of administration, the retention of land governing rights and of timber rights are only some of the indications that the Australian Government is here to stay.

Another sign is the fact that guarantees of security for large overseas interests covering twenty-five or more years ahead could not have been made unless the Commonwealth's intention was to remain in command. Assurances of this nature are not made haphazardly.

That there is an imbalance of development, particularly as it affects the internal development of native economy and society, is illustrated by the growing awareness of the native people. Until a few years ago nobody ever heard the word "secession." Today the word is common, for the thoughts of the people react sharply if there is the slightest hope for their improvement. Secession has been held up to them as one remedy for national neglect and they are prepared to go for it.

To the native mind it appears inconsistent that the Administration can laud the vision of national independence through training and at the same time condemn secessionist movements by denigrating the ability of the people to learn how to govern. "If we are told that we are being prepared to take over the government of our country, then why does the same government say that it is impossible for us to prepare ourselves for secession?" one native leader asked me. Beyond the statement of the claims of those who wish to secede there has never been an open investigation into the reasons that would clear up the causes for such demands.

The leaders of the movement declare that their people have been and are still being neglected in their social and economic development and that their contribution to the national economy is far away and beyond that of the benefits they receive.

That is straight talking, but there has never been a straight official answer in reply. Injunctions that the people could not manage to run their own government are evading the main point. What are the real reasons for this bitterness towards the Administration and the fact that the people feel impelled to take action?

One must treat official announcements with reserve, particularly as there has already been a public notice that the Administration is seeking a public relations officer in order that the government's actions may be publicised in a good light.

I once overheard an American tourist remark, "This country must be a very profitable institution. All the government literature speaks only of the advances being made. If that's so, why do they want to borrow money from the States?"

This practice of always being right, of always being the best, and of using self-praise to the utmost can generate some dangerous thinking.

Secession, like independence, is not likely to score any successes while the main road of future policy heads towards the consolidation of big business and bureaucracy, and this has put the future of the country in the doubtful position of being viewed from two separate and unrelated angles. Is it to become an independent country run by its own people, or a business and government satellite of Australia and overseas interests?

Officially, the two are related but the point of juncture is so minute as to be almost undiscernible. They are related only where the continuation of small-scale cash-earning farmers and providers of labour and materials are of use to big business. Beyond that there are two separate social systems. An infinitesimal section of native people will make the higher grades, mainly through their own exertions, but this will have no bearing on the general outcome.

As John Kaputin writes regarding the new five-years plan, "The expatriates have the apple, we are left with the core."

The infusion of foreign capital carries a number of implications, one of which is that the government may have abandoned the idea of developing the country into any form of a viable economy.

That primary industries covering the needs of the people could be developed within the Territory has been the subject for argument over many years, but little has been done to implement such a proposition. Rice, sugar, and foodcrops, naturally grown and processed, have always been subjected to Australian business interests, and the inclination of the government is clearly to fully support this position. It will not interfere by encouraging to a positive degree the establishment of similar home industries.

Socially and economically the bad effects fall upon the people, for workers are not being trained to manage their own industries, the natural increase of internal wealth is stifled, standards of living

225

remain low, and the people remain, as they always have been, underprivileged and dejected.

The accent of promotion and social betterment is upon the armed forces and the police, where recruits can rise to commissioned ranks and become proficient in the trades, they can enjoy good housing, better food, and a number of other privileges.

In the Administration, promotion to higher, more responsible positions seems limited to the Health Department and, to a degree, the Education Department, but in both of these the social benefits fall short of what expatriates enjoy, while conditions of living, for some local officers, are deplorable.

Land Ordinances, in New Guinea since 1922, and in Papua since 1888, are still in existence and have become powerful implements of the government's policy. It can refuse, it can favour, and what is worse, it can make a profit on native land and forests. Land and timber must be some of the more productive sources of government income, for they are purchased at a stipulated official price, tendered at a stipulated official rent, and re-assessed periodically by government officers. The actual seller and the purchaser have nothing to say in the deal, and in the case of timber, which is purchased selectively by government officers, a small proportion of the sale price is paid to the owners with the balance going into Government Bonds, with interest accruing over long periods.

That these out-of-date laws, which once gave full protection to native owners, are restrictive upon the native people is well known, but while they secure government income it is doubtful if they will be relaxed. There is an urgent need for land reform so that share farming between an outside investor and the owner of the land can be effected by direct negotiation, without government participation except in cases under dispute. Another method would be to allow short-term leases between the two parties. As it now stands, land once sold by a native owner to the government is lost forever. If it is abandoned by the leaseholder, then it reverts to the government and may stay idle for decades if no other tenderers appear.

Under the present system it is a long-term government investment, bought originally at minimum rates, and remaining the property of the government for ever, to be leased and re-leased whenever it is considered desirable. There is no substance in the argument that only a small percentage of the whole area of the country has been taken over, nor can the protection of native owners be claimed as paramount as this amounts to an anomaly. Native people can now purchase trucks, cars, farm vehicles, houses, or businesses; they can run plantations, apply for tenders, hold bank accounts, vote at elections, and pass Bills through parliament, but they are not considered either capable or fit people to sell one acre of their land or one solitary tree to outside interests.

A district type of judicial committee could easily be established to deal with disputes or doubtful cases, with sufficient power to withhold sale if it were against the interest of the owner. Limited areas that would not affect the owner's land holdings should be handled directly between the two interested parties, while for areas covering plantation estates, or other large sections, a combined committee of official and private persons, at which the owner and applicant were represented, is all that would be required. The same should apply to timber sales.

It is of no benefit for the present day urbanized native man to sell his land or timber for the comparatively small payment received, when he can go to work and earn, within a few weeks or months, the same amount of money and still possess his land and timber.

There is a noticeable inclination among the more understanding of native people to refuse further land sales and it is based mainly upon the fact that they are the ones who eventually come out the poorer, in money and in property.

The gradual change in national policy must inevitably reflect later upon the form of government. At present there is a tendency towards specialization in personnel. Standards of public service duties are being raised, and for local officers it is essential now that they continue their studies to further their positions. All this is constitutionally good within the public service, but it will take time before the local officers reach standards that are acceptable in the higher positions of government, but this, like all other factors, is governed by limitations.

Were the progress of the local public service being compensated by a balancing reduction of expatriate officers, the expense factor of government personnel, in salaries, housing and benefits, would level out and possibly show a downward trend. However, this is not happening, for the expatriate service is growing, and the wages-bill for its maintenance is increasing. Roughly speaking, the expatriate service now numbers about 6,000 and the local service around 15,000, and according to the new five-year plan announced recently, the expatriate service is to increase, with a call for more and more specialist officers.

That there must be an eventual limit to this is obvious, for the cost factor alone will call a halt sometime. We have a ratio of over one public servant for every hundred of our population, which includes the very primitive people who know nothing of government. It would not be surprising if, in five years or so, this Administration as we now know it were absorbed into the Commonwealth Government and the country left with a local public service controlled by specially seconded officers from Canberra. The occasion would call for a new form of government, a self-governing body elected through the House of Assembly and directed by Australian public servants serving terms on overseas duty. Not only is this an obvious way to reduce an expensive service, but it would also settle a lot of domestic differences between the Territory's expatriate service and the Commonwealth, as well as stabilizing the two-structure salary scales dispute which is still a matter of importance.

Politically a lot of Canberra's problems could be solved in this way. The Territory would be nominally self-governing, overseas criticism would be subdued, the call for target dates would become redundant, and there would still remain a tight Commonwealth control over the Territory, its people, and the economy.

The developing political climate within the country, through the elections of 1972, could well bring in a situation where some such readjustment would become necessary. Possibly, by then, there will be two parliamentary houses, an upper and a lower, the former a functional institution constituted by representatives of all groups, both native and expatriate.

In addition, the rising tide of demand for a positive approach to self-government will have to be met, and as I said before, the situation will have to be met squarely, for it cannot be avoided.

To do so would be to bring an upsurge of nationalism which, though dormant at present, can be seen in the expressed desires of the peoples' leaders and requires only loud and frequent repetition to stimulate a wave of national feeling.

If it is ignored there could be the danger of political upheaval and the demise of political freedom, and as history shows, these invariably lead to other national disorders.

I am inclined to have faith in the West Irian refugees' warning that outside danger threatens this Territory, for when they spoke with me it was to give me a concise understanding of what they knew, without elaboration and without any obvious benefit accruing to themselves.

In fact, if danger does eventuate, then these refugees will be "the buffer," as they described themselves, for they will go down first and face extermination, so that whatever happens afterwards, as far as this country is concerned, would not interest them.

The warning was not given for the purpose of securing Australian

228

or other aid for their own cause, for they are well aware that such aid would not be forthcoming and that no minority group's struggles would justify the use of another country's armed forces. Judging by these facts alone, I believe that their words were sincere and with the pattern of Indonesia's turbulent history over the last few years to guide us, the probability exists that sometime in the future Papua-New Guinea may have to face a threat of annexation. The forces which are likely to be aimed against us carry an entirely different conception of development and independence.

I have been chasing information on this matter ever since I was a guest of the refugees, where I first heard it mentioned and I have yet to find a person with sufficient knowledge who will conclusively deny the possibility as it exists.

It is true that I have heard two different versions of future possibilities, one of armed assault and the other of political infiltration, and both seem quite likely to fulfil an aggressor's purpose. The information given to me, which was proved from official Indonesian documents, shows that Communism in Indonesia is not by any means a dead force. "It will not be Russian Communism," one informant told me, "but the Chinese variety, for the Chinese influence is growing and is again mounting as a threat to the Indonesian Government. This political movement will encourage and foster ideas of political aggrandisement and the prospect of securing the whole island of New Guinea, east and west, as one country is very alluring, even to some elements loyal to the government of Indonesia."

This person discounted the possibility of armed attack or invasion. "That would be very risky," he explained. "Far more effective would be an intensely directed campaign of infiltration at ground level, and this is the likeliest possibility."

The overall plan, as far as this man knew, was an extensive one. First, Papua-New Guinea, as East Irian. Then Australia as South Irian, and finally, New Zealand as South-east Irian.

"All this has been said before so it is no secret," he said, "but people are inclined to forget with the passing changes in the political climate. First, you must realize, that time is of no account. The movement may work insidiously for years until it feels confident that it cannot be beaten, but the threat is there, and it is a positive one."

We discussed this at some length. "The main difference between Western democracy and Asiatic Communism, in this country, is that the former is weighted with theoretical idealism while the latter is interpreted in terms of practical idealism," he continued. "For

229

example, Asiatic Communism will go to the villages and live with the people. It will work the soil and produce crops of food which the villagers can eat. It can exist at all levels, subsistence or otherwise. It will be political only when it has produced a practical result that will substantiate its ideals.

"On the other hand, your western government is filled with plans and projects, some of which never mature. Your white Australian official will be shocked if he is told to live with villagers at subsistence levels for months, or perhaps years. He wants his good house, his refrigeration, his car, his club, his privileges and prestige, and his real association with the native people comes only through his office staff, his household servants, or an occasional official visit to a native meeting.

"Your official never becomes one with the people he governs, whereas the Asiatic does and makes this his first duty."

And when you consider it, this is pretty true and is happening and has happened in other places and among other people.

Furthermore, after spending over thirty years with these native people, I am still of the opinion that they are ripe for Asiatic Communism if it really pressed its beliefs amongst them.

The understanding that Western democracy has given them is very weak, lying like a thin veneer over desires which they still interpret in black-man fashion, desires that lie submerged awaiting another black man's thoughts to crystallize them into positive action.

There were examples of this during the Japanese occupation. If Japanese militarism had not set out to subjugate the population, it might have left a much more uncomfortable residue of disaffection today.

Communism is far more subtle. It will not browbeat a subjective race when it is trying to win its confidence. It works from within, at one with the peasants, in the garden, around the fire at night, in the village tasks, absorbing the people's beliefs, directing their thoughts without despising their ideas, and showing, by long and practical example, that something can be attained through personal effort and communal co-operation.

Their method is not a half-hour's talk by an agricultural officer, or an exhortation to lawfulness by a district official, or promises of better times ahead from a visiting dignitary, or the accomplishment of a new highway or a new wharf that none of them can use and few can understand the purpose of.

Annexation could happen here very easily, and with a land frontier of 350 miles, plus seaward approaches, there is easy access generally. Troops, guns, and planes are not the answer to this threat. This is a problem for the future and may be with us even now. To stop it will require a positive approach towards the conjunction of the need for the advancement of the people with the influx of large amounts of overseas capital, so that the mass of uneducated and under-privileged men and women may participate in the material advantages of progress.

It is not sufficient to allocate funds only where there is a certainty that profits will be returned, for there are some dividends which are not to be reckoned like the material ones, in dollars and cents; these human dividends are just as important, perhaps more so, especially if their neglect stores up trouble for the future.

index

Aidia village 47, 50–6
Aïrd Hills 2, 59
Aitape 70, 73, 77–80, 85, 127
Alexishafen 176
Ali Island 84–5
Andersen, Skipper 1
Aramia 19
Arawa Plantation 191–3, 195–209,
    210, 214, 220
Ashton, Des 200, 201, 209, 219
Australasian Petroleum Company
    26

Baimuru sawmill 1
Baubaguina village 22, 30, 47
Barikewa 59
Beharell, Jim 110
Bele, Raphael 207, 211
Bougainville 190, 213–5, 216, 218,
    221
Brown, Bill 95
Buguru ceremony 5, 19, 44
Bulolo 163, 166

cacao 163
Campbell, Gordon 128
Cape Blackwood 2
cargo cultism 174–80
Chalmers, Dr 29, 30, 31

Chawner, Dr Bill 87
Chimbu District 162
Christie, Bill 122
Christie, George 96–8, 102
coffee 163
Conzinc Riotinto of Australia 190,
    192, 194, 199, 202, 206, 216, 218
copra 37–8, 84, 163
Copra Marketing Board 38
crocodile shooting 19

Daru 91, 124
Delta Division 4
Dom, Father 82–3
Dopima Number One village 29
Dopima village 24, 26, 37
dubu houses 12–13, 43–4, 63
Dubumubu village 47

Eastern Highlands 162
Ely, Dick 89

Finisterre Ranges 163
Fly River 91, 94, 117

Goaribari Island 4, 24, 49
Goaribaries 11, 16, 107

Gogol River 168, 169
Goodwin, Kevin 79
Goroka 163
Gouri village 47
Great Papuan Plateau 20
Guise, John 181

Hanuabada 76
Hasluck, Sir Paul 198
Hawa'a dance 5, 19, 35, 44
Highlanders 164–6
Holland, Cyril 192
Hombrom Bluff 60

initiation customs 13
Iungazim 108–9

John Mac 21, 22
Jouwe, Nicolas 139

Kabu ceremony 187–9
Kainantu 167
Kamea village 47
Kassam Pass 167
Kerewa village 16, 38
Kieta 191, 194, 199, 201, 209
Kikori 4, 12, 18, 20, 56, 58, 61
Kikori delta 1
Kikori River 20
Kiunga 88, 95–6, 118
Kivau, chief 35
Kiwai 31
Konedobu 213
Kuka 205, 207
Kuru 1
Kuru village 59

Lae 162, 166, 168, 209
Laloki 60
land purchases 74–6
Lapun, Paul 198–9, 203–4, 206–7,
    208, 210, 211

Lawrence, Professor Peter 175,
    180
Leo, Father 83–4
Leonard Murray Mountains 20
Lue Joseph 204

Mabiri 201
McKillop, R. (Kip) 191–2, 194–8,
    200, 205, 214
Madang 133, 160, 162, 166, 168,
    169–70, 171, 172–3, 180, 181
Madiri 89–90
mangrove bark industry 59
Manus Island 149, 160, 161
Markham Valley 163, 166, 167–8
Mati lime kiln 58–9
Middletown 59
Mola, Donatus 204
Morobe 162
Mount Bosavi 25
Mount Hagen 162, 166, 167, 168

Nasioi Rural Progress Society 208,
    209
New Guinea Planters' Association
    192, 196
Newman, A. J. P. 219
Nomad 108

Omati River 49

Panguna mine 194
Papuan Chief 1
Pes 83
Poe, John 181
Port Moresby 46, 47, 58, 162,
    196–7, 199
Port Romilly 62
Purari 65
Purari Delta 2, 61
puri-puri (sorcerers) 7
pyrethrum 163

Rabaul 191, 217–18
Ramu road 168
Ramu Valley 163, 168, 171
Rentoul River 108
Risk Point 25
Road Belong Cargo 175
Rorovana 201, 206, 218, 220–1
rubber 57, 60
Rumba 208

Saidor 181, 182
Sekotchiau 128, 129
Senior, John 21, 59
Sepik 133
Siau Local Government Council
70, 73
Sor 182
Southern Highlands 162
Stanley, G. A. V. 2
Sukarnapura 125, 133, 138, 140,
147, 155, 160
Suki people 90

tea industry 163
Tetley, Keith 21, 22, 111
timber industry 126–7, 163
Tomkins, Rev. Oliver 29, 31
Tugeri people 90–1

Tumleo 82

Ukaravi 62
United Political Society 192–3
Upper Strickland River 19, 87,
102, 103, 108
Usino 168

Vanimo 70, 73, 81, 125–8, 134,
147, 151, 158, 159, 161
village constable 6

Wau 166
Wawoi 19
West Irian refugees 133, 137–49,
154–8, 160, 228
West Sepik District 70, 126
Western Highlands 162
Wewak 70, 127, 160, 161
widows' dubus 14
Williams, F. E. 65
Wutung 148, 158

Yabalol 182
Yali movement 180–9
Yali Singina 180–9
Yakoi 84